Around The Coast In A Campervan

Jon Gunter

Copyright © 2016 Jon Gunter

All rights reserved worldwide.

No part of this publication may be reproduced or transmitted in any form or by any means, electronic or mechanical, including photocopying, recording, or any information storage and retrieval system without prior written permission of the Author. Your support of author's rights is appreciated.

All images, including the front and back covers, copyright © 2012 Jon Gunter

ISBN-13: 978-1530754120
ISBN-10: 1530754127

For everyone that kept me company from afar.

Preparation

The Plan	5
The Van	8
Being Realistic	12
To Blog, Or Not To Blog	14
Useful Stuff	16

The Blog

Trial Run - The Evening	23
Trial Run - The Morning	26
One More Sleep	28
Portishead to Blue Anchor	30
Dunster to Woolacombe	33
Woolacombe and Mortehoe	36
Croyde Bay to Hartland	39
Hartland and Mouthmill	42
Bude to St Teath	44
Port Isaac to Porthcothan	46
Bedruthen Steps to St Ives	48
St Ives	51
Sennen Cove to Penzance	53
Marazion to The Lizard	56
The Lizard to Come-To-Good	59
St Mawes to Pentewan	61
The Eden Project	64
Charlestown to Penhale	67
Seaton to Kingsbridge	70
East Prawle to Goodrington	73
Paignton to Dawlish Warren	76
Starcross to Seaton	79

Lyme Regis to Chickerell	81
Portland and Weymouth	84
Osmington Mills to Lulworth Cove	86
Kimmeridge Bay to Hengistbury Head	89
Highcliffe Castle to Warsash	92
Hill Head to Southsea	95
Southsea and Hayling Island	97
Southsea, Portsmouth and Gosport	99
Bosham to Shoreham-by-Sea	102
Hove to Norman's Bay	105
Bexhill to Folkestone	108
Capel-le-Ferne to Sandwich	111
Pegwell to Westgate on Sea	114
Reculver to Rochester	116
Gravesend to Burnham-on-Crouch	119
Bradwell Waterside to Tollesbury	122
West Mersea to Clacton-on-Sea	125
Frinton-on-Sea to Mistley	127
Shotley Gate to Felixstowe	129
Woodbridge to Snape	132
Aldeburgh to Walberswick	135
Southwold to Lowestoft	138
Norwich	140
Still Norwich	143
Gorleston-on-Sea to Horsey	145
Waxham to Overstrand	149
Cromer, West Runton and Sheringham	153
Weybourne to Wells-next-the-Sea	157
Wells-next-the-Sea to Hunstanton	160
Hunstanton	163

Heacham to Sandringham	165
Castle Rising to Freiston Shore	168
Wainfleet All Saints to Gibraltar Point	171
Skegness	174
Ingoldmells to Mablethorpe	176
Mablethorpe	178
Mablethorpe to Cleethorpes	180
Grimsby to Barrow Haven	182
Hull to Spurn Head	184
Withernsea to Hornsea	186
Bridlington to Reighton Gap	188
Filey to Scarborough	191
Scarborough (campsite)	193
Scarborough	195
Cloughton Wyke to Robin Hood's Bay	198
Whitby to Runswick Bay	201
Staithes to Redcar	205
Middlesbrough	207
Seaton Sands to Hartlepool	209
Horden Beach to Whitley Bay	212
Whitley Bay and St Mary's Island	215
Collywell Bay to Alnmouth	217
Alnwick to Beadnell Bay	220
Seahouses to Lindisfarne	223
Beadnell Bay to Berwick-upon-Tweed	227
Eyemouth to Dunbar	230
Belhaven to Edinburgh	233
Edinburgh	236
Queensferry to Lower Largo	239
Earlsferry to St Andrews	241

St Andrews to Monifieth	245
Carnoustie to Inverbervie	248
Kinneff to Walker Park	250
Aberdeen to Rattray Head	253
Cairnbulg Point to Findochty	256
Portessie to Nairn	259
Fort George to Rosemarkie	262
Cromarty to Dalchalm	264
Helmsdale to Hill o' Many Stanes	267
Cairn o' Get to Dunnet Bay	269
Dunnet Head and The Orkney Islands	272
Gills to Thurso	275
Sandside Bay to Durness	278
Cape Wrath and Balnakiel	281
Kinlochbervie to Clachtoll	285
Achmelvich to Ullapool	288
Corrieshalloch Gorge to Poolewe	291
Gairloch to Lower Diabaig	294
Shieldaig to Lochcarron	298
Stromemore to Loch Greshornish	302
Uig to Old Man of Storr	305
Stein to Neist Point	310
Struan to Arisaig	313
Glenuig to Strontian	316
Lochaline to Fort William	319
Ben Nevis	322
South Ballachulish to Oban	325
Oban, Mull, Staffa and Iona	328
Clachan to Lochgilphead	332
Ardrishaig to Carradale Bay	334

Grogport to Clachan	337
Cairndow to Toward	340
Strone to Helensburgh	343
Luss	346
Dumbarton to Prestwick	348
Ayr	351
Dunure to Stranraer	354
Corsewall Point to New England Bay	358
Sandhead to Graplin	361
Kirkcudbright to Powfoot	364
Annan to Allonby	367
Keswick	371
Lake Windermere and Haverthwaite	373
Helm Crag and Easdale Tarn	375
Maryport to St Bees	378
Braystones to South End	381
Vickerstown to Grange-over-Sands	385
Sandside to Fleetwood	388
Cleveleys to Crosby	391
Liverpool	395
Port Sunlight to Thurstaston	397
Parkgate to Rhos-on-Sea	401
Penrhyn Bay to Bangor	405
Beaumaris to Trearddur	408
Borthwen Bay to Caernarfon	411
Llanberis and Betwys-y-Coed	415
Dinas Dinlle to Abersoch	418
Llanbedrog to Harlech	422
Llandanwg to Borth	426
Clarach Bay to New Quay	430

Cwmtydu to Penbryn	433
Tresaith to Newport	436
Cwm-yr-Eglwys to St Justinian	439
Caerfai Bay to Little Haven	443
St Brides Haven to Angle	448
Freshwater West to Tenby	451
Saundersfoot to Llanelli	454
Pen-clawdd to Threecliff Bay	457
Caswell Bay to Dunraven Bay	460
Monknash to Cardiff	463
Peterstone Wentlooge to Severn Beach	467

Home Again

Back To The Real(ish) World	473
The Emotional Farewell	476

Around The Coast In A Campervan

Preparation

What I was going to do, why I was going to do it, and how I went about (vaguely) planning how to do it.

The Plan

I honestly don't remember the exact point in time that I decided to do it, or the thought process that led to the decision. But I'm pretty sure I remember when the seed was planted.

On the 23rd January 2007 I returned to Bristol after three months of travelling around the world. When I got home that evening, to the house where I lived with friends, some 'friends of friends' had been invited over and were showing their photos of a recent surfing holiday in the northwest of Scotland. I admit I felt that my thunder had been stolen a little, but I love to hear people talk about places that they've visited. They spoke about how they had driven up to Scotland in their VW campervan and were able to surf from deserted beaches. Now I'm not a surfer, and I don't even swim very well, but the thought of parking a campervan overnight behind my own private Scottish beach left an indelible imprint on my subconscious.

Maybe that seed grew over time, or maybe it sprouted all of a sudden, I don't recall, but roughly half way through 2010 I decided that I really ought to take some time off work, buy myself a campervan and drive it around the coast of mainland Great Britain.

My approach to going travelling for any longer than a week is as follows: I'll tell a few friends and family what I'm planning to do. They'll smile and nod and assume I'm joking. I'll tell a few more family and friends what I'm planning to do. I'll tell a few random people, that I've never met before, what I'm planning to do. I'll tell a bunch more friends what I'm planning to do. Eventually I'll reach a critical mass, whereby I've told so many people what I'm planning to do that I'll feel like a fool if I don't go off and actually do what I'm planning to do. I find that the threat of embarrassment helps me to overcome the apathy of never getting around to doing what I'm planning to do.

Embarrassment and fear. I'm not an overly self-confident person, I'm not someone that could leave my fairly comfortable life behind and spend the rest of my days moving from place to place, from country to country, living each day as it came, at the whim of fate. Much as I would like to. There will always, for me, be a certain amount of fear of the unknown, of the 'what if's. But, the fear of growing old without having done what I was planning to do eventually outweighs the fear of actually doing it. I'd rather not look back on my life and think "why didn't I do that when I had the chance?".

The critical mass of 'people told' was achieved before the end of 2010. I had told most of my friends, and several strangers (generally at weddings), so I informed my employers that I was going to take some time off, whether they liked it or not. It had been a fairly stressful year, work wise, and there was more to come in 2011, so at that point I needed something to look forward to. But I wasn't going to rush into things, I felt committed to the project that I was working on at the time, which had several more months left to run, and I wanted another year's salary behind me. I also wanted plenty of time to decide on which campervan to buy, and maybe to fully convince myself that I was really going to do it. So I decided that I would work until the end of 2011 and aim to start the trip in March 2012.

It certainly helped to have something to look forward to, even if it seemed like an awfully long time away. Some dark days at work were just that little bit brighter in the knowledge that it would all come to an end. My employers were good to me, I had assumed that I would need to resign but they offered me a sabbatical. A 12 month sabbatical in fact, which was more than I could have hoped for and which I gleefully accepted.

By the end of 2011 my plan had progressed. I was going

to buy a campervan and drive it around the coast of mainland Great Britain, and I was going to do it anti-clockwise! Don't ask me why, it just seemed like the right direction to do it in. I figured it would take me around six months, I thought I might nip over to France on the way, to visit the Normandy Beaches, and if I got around in good time I would head around the coast of Ireland too.

The Van

I wanted to give myself plenty of time to find the right campervan, so I started looking mid way through 2011.

Everybody knows the iconic VW Campervan, the epitome of cool camping, ideal for trendy beach parties or a weekend away with your surfboard. But did I want to live in one for several months, and most likely have to learn how to maintain and repair these notoriously unreliable machines for the sake of looking good? No, I can't say that I did, but what would that leave me with? Well, quite a lot of choice as it happened, I honestly had no idea how many different makes and models were available until I started to look around.

I had assumed that all campervans and motorhomes were purpose built, like the VWs. But I soon came to realise that many of them were converted from base vehicles such as Fiat Ducatos, Ford Transits, Renault Trafics etc, by various companies such as Auto Sleeper, Swift, Adria and Timberland, who fitted them out with beds, cupboards, cookers, sinks, toilets and all sorts of other essential and luxury fittings, in a range of different layouts. There were panel vans of various sizes, with fixed roofs, rising roofs and high-tops, which were basically conversions within the original shell of the base vehicle. There were coachbuilts, where the original shell had been replaced with a larger custom built shell, characterised by an extension over the cab to provide sleeping or storage space. Or there was the larger A-class, where only the chassis of the base vehicle remained, but these were much larger than I required. The layouts varied considerably, some had a sofa bed along one side of the van, some had a fixed bed, some had rear lounges with seats around a table that had to be removed to make up the bed. Some had toilets and showers, sometimes at the rear of the van, often on one side of the van.

One of the first vans that I actually saw was a Timberland Freedom, a panel van conversion based on a Fiat Ducato. The layout of the van appealed to me, it felt quite open and airy. Across the back of the van was a toilet and washbasin on one side and a wardrobe on the other side, between which was a gap that could be closed off from the main compartment and used as a shower cubicle, and also provided access centrally through the rear doors. The main compartment had a sofa bed opposite the sliding side door, with a sink on one side and a good size oven and four burner hob on the other side. The central corridor meant that there was some visibility out of the back whilst driving, and the position of the oven and hob meant that you could cook while standing in the main compartment, near the side door, rather than tucked away in a side corridor at the rear of the van, as was the case in some other models. If I had known then what I know now, I would probably have bought it, but I had only just started looking at that point, so I didn't really know any better.

I have to admit that I wasn't looking forward to driving a large van, I had never driven anything larger than a car before and didn't even like driving hire cars rather than my own car. So for a while I agonised over whether I should go for one of the smaller models, that weren't as long and would be easier to fit into parking spaces, but eventually I persuaded myself to man up and not worry about it, there was no point buying something smaller and finding that it didn't give me enough room to live in a certain degree of comfort, or enough cupboard space to fit everything that I wanted to take with me.

A friend of mine, Cheryl, was an experienced campervanner, so I went to spend an evening with her to take a look at her van. It was a really useful exercise to spend time talking to someone that had been there and done that, and to get a good long look at a van and see how all of its fixtures and fittings worked. I came away armed with various useful tips, and with plenty to think about.

I continued to look around, now and again, for the rest of 2011, but nothing that I saw matched up to the Timberland Freedom. A few models came close but the Freedom just, well, felt right. I hadn't seen any more of them in person, but I had noted a small number of them on the internet, dotted around the country. I had considered a custom conversion, where certain companies will assist you in buying a suitable base vehicle and then convert it to your specification, which can be a cheaper alternative to buying one 'off the shelf', but it was an option that I never fully explored.

The end of 2011 came around and I parted company with my job for a year, replacing it with a feeling of relief and freedom that is hard to describe but thoroughly recommended! Yet I still had the small matter of a van to procure, and I now had no excuse for not dedicating myself to the task. I was spending the Christmas period at my sister's in Coventry when I sat down and searched the internet for Timberland Freedoms. There weren't many of them around but there was one in Nottingham, so I gave them a call to make sure they still had it and set off the following morning.

I arrived at the dealers and asked to take a look at the Freedom, which they left me to view at my leisure. Everything looked good, it was in excellent condition and once again it just felt like the right choice, my memory of the van that I had viewed six months ago, just for once, had not let me down. Without even asking, the dealer knocked a few thousand off the sale price, then mentioned that he thought the van had a DVD player and flat screen TV, which he went to look for in the office. When he came back and confirmed this to be true, I pretty much made my mind up there and then. He was happy to hold onto the van until

I needed it in mid February, and would start a six month warranty from that point, so I put pen to paper and bought myself a campervan.

It had suddenly all become very real.

Being Realistic

Roughly two weeks before I set off, I sat down and had a proper look at a map of Britain. It suddenly dawned on me that maybe the trip was on a somewhat larger scale than I had imagined. Looking at a single page picture of Britain was all very well, but when I looked at a scale that showed individual towns and villages and started following the line of the coast, I soon realised how much ground I had to cover.

It was at that point that I decided that I probably wouldn't bother nipping across the English Channel to take a look at the Normandy Beaches, and that it was unlikely that I would travel the coast of Ireland too.

Not only did I want to see as much of the British mainline coast as possible, I also wanted to learn new skills. I wanted to learn all about photography and how to write iPhone applications. I wanted to read lots of books and research any burning questions that popped into my head. I imagined myself spending my days sat in beachside cafes, sipping exotically named coffees while using my laptop to satisfy my thirst for knowledge. Basically I wanted to do all those things that I don't find (or make) the time to do in my everyday life. The reality turned out to be somewhat different, partly because it wasn't always possible to fit all of those things into the daily travelling, sightseeing and blogging, and partly because I'm not as dynamic as I sometimes like to think I am!

On the positive side, my gut feeling to travel around the coast anti-clockwise was looking like a good one. It meant that I would be travelling through the narrow lanes of Cornwall during the off season, so although the weather may not be as good as during the summer it would be a much quieter place, with less traffic on the roads and no crowds of people in the more popular areas. Starting from my hometown of Bristol at the beginning of March meant that I would most likely be in Scotland during late spring and summer, so there was a chance that I might get the occasional day without any rain (I know, that's a very stereotypical view of Scottish weather).

It was around this time, in mid February, that I returned to my sister's in Coventry. Her partner, Steve, gave me a lift to the dealers in Nottingham and I drove away in my very own campervan. I immediately realised that I wasn't going to be going anywhere fast, and that I would have to get used to giving myself plenty of time to pull out at junctions or to attempt to overtake anything, but then it wasn't as if I'd ever be in much of a hurry. The motorway journey was easy enough, but having to reverse down a narrow lane behind my sister's house to park up for the night gave me some early jangling of the nerves. The following day I drove it back to Bristol and thankfully found a place to park it not too far from the house.

The next two weeks were spent running around like a madman, rummaging through my belongings for - or buying - all of the things that I was to take with me. I basically needed everything that I needed in everyday life, things for wearing, cooking, eating, cleaning, washing, sleeping and entertaining myself. The van was to be my home; my kitchen, dining room, living room, bathroom and bedroom. I eventually decided that taking my rollerblades was one step too far, but they were pretty much the only things that I couldn't fit in.

To Blog, Or Not To Blog

Blogging is a double edged sword, in my experience. People blog for various reasons; because they have important things to say, because they think they have important things to say, because it's a source of income, for example.

For the most part I see it as a way of keeping my family and friends informed of where I am and what I'm doing, through narrative and photos. It's also a way of keeping in touch with those people and feeling that no matter how far away you are from home, you're never really that far from the people that mean something to you. Having a message board on your blog allows people to leave comments and take the Mickey out of you, just as they would in person.

The downside is the time and commitment. It can be a time consuming process, documenting your life, and once you've started you may feel obliged to continue to the bitter end, no matter how much you would rather be doing something else, or how hard it is to think of something interesting (or not) to say about what you did that day. I find that my life can be taken over by a travel blog, I spend each day thinking about what I'll write about that evening, and my decisions on what to do in places are often influenced by whether the blog would benefit from it.

It's also easy to obsess over who's reading your blog, or perhaps more accurately, who isn't reading it. Nobody is obliged to read your blog, certainly not on a daily basis. Some friends and family may read it daily, some may look at it now and again, some may never read it. There's no point in worrying about whether somebody has or hasn't read it, or being upset because nobody has posted a comment on your message board recently, people have their own lives to lead. You may be off enjoying yourself on an adventure, but most other people are living their usual hectic lives.

For good or for bad, I always had it at the back of my mind that I would turn the blog into this book. I'll let you decide whether that was a good thing or not.

Useful Stuff

Having a lot of time to think about the trip allowed me to research various things, both through the internet and through talking to experienced campervanners, like Cheryl. As a result I ended up buying a number of books, joining a number of organisations, and picking up a number of hints and tips, all of which would (hopefully) help to make the trip a more enjoyable experience.

Books:
- Motorhomes: The Complete Guide, by David and Fiona Batten-Hill - A guide to choosing, buying, understanding and enjoying the various different types of motorhomes/campervans.
- The Motorcaravan Manual (Haynes), by John Wickersham - A guide to choosing, using, and most importantly maintaining and customising a motorhome/campervan.
- The Most Amazing Places on Britain's Coast, by Reader's Digest - A guide to over 1,000 beautiful and unusual places along the coastline of England, Scotland and Wales. How handy is that?!
- Secret Beaches: Southwest, by Rob Smith - A guide to visiting 50 of the most secluded beaches on the southwest coast of England. Secret Beaches: Wales is also now available.

Organisations:
- The Camping and Caravanning Club (www.campingandcaravanningclub.co.uk) - Joining the Camping and Caravanning Club gives you information about more than 4,000 UK campsites and 1,500 member-only sites, from large caravan parks to small

'five van' sites that accommodate a maximum of five caravans or campervans, plus over 100 Club Sites and around 20 Camping in the Forest sites. The web site provides a wealth of information and services to members, including online booking of the Club Sites.
- The Caravan Club (www.caravanclub.co.uk) - As with the Camping and Caravanning Club, joining the Caravan Club gives you access to a further 2,500 member-only sites and over 200 Club Sites, with similar information and services via the web site.
- Wild Camping (www.wildcamping.co.uk) - A web site that gives you access to a whole community of people that have been there and done that when it comes to campervans and motorhomes. Blogs and forums provide all sorts of information, either in general or as answers to other member's questions. For a small fee you can become a full member, which among other things allows you to download a set of 'point of interest' files that can be used with Google Earth and various SatNav systems to show you car parks, lay-bys and pubs where you can 'wild camp', or in other words park your campervan or motorhome overnight for free, without fear of being moved on by the Police or other authorities.
- The National Trust (www.nationaltrust.org.uk) - Joining the National Trust gives you free or discounted entry to over 300 historic houses, gardens, mills, forests, woods, fens, beaches, islands, archaeological remains, nature reserves, villages, pubs and car parks, as well as areas of coastline, farmland and moorland, all over the UK.
- English Heritage (www.english-heritage.org.uk) - Joining English Heritage gives you free or discounted entry to over 400 castles, stately homes, gardens,

monuments, ruins and other historic sites, as well as over 100 associated attractions.

Hints and tips:
- Rubber mats or foam lining - You're going to become annoyed fairly quickly if the contents of your cupboards and shelves regularly and audibly shift around while you're driving. Rubber mats can be used to line the shelves and drawers to provide some friction to prevent things from slipping around. Alternatively, layers of upholstery foam, which can be custom cut to size or bought in large sheets of varying thicknesses. Layers of the foam can be built up and holes can be cut to fit certain objects, such as glasses or mugs.
- Rubber bands - One use for a rubber band is to place it around the end of the electric hookup cable that connects to the van, and over the plastic flap that protects the hookup point, thereby preventing the flap from noisily flapping around in the wind.
- Hose attachments - If you're intending to use a hosepipe to fill your freshwater tank, it's worth getting hold of a selection of attachments for the different taps that you'll come across. Some taps will have a screw thread on them, generally one of two different diameters, for which you can use a single attachment that caters for both diameters, and for most other taps you can use an attachment that has a rubber grommet to fit over the tap and a steel band around it to tighten it. These attachments will all connect to a standard garden hose connector on the hosepipe. You can buy them cheaply from garden centres, hardware stores or from many of the Club Sites.
- Washing up bowl - If you'd prefer to wash up your cooking gear in the camp site utility rooms, rather than

in the van, be sure to take a washing up bowl for carrying everything there and back.
- Cash for pitches - Make sure that you've always got enough cash on you to pay for the next campsite, many of them don't accept cards and may not be anywhere near a cash point.
- Coins for car parks - Make sure that you've always got plenty of coins for the inevitable occasions when you'll have to pay to park somewhere.
- 'Pitch in use' sign - It's a good idea to have a sign that you can place on your pitch while you take the van elsewhere, to prevent somebody else from thinking the pitch is empty and taking it for themselves. You can make your own sign, with some string to hang it or a pole to plant it, or you can buy one from camping shops or many of the Club Sites.

The Blog

So this is what happened, as it happened, in the form of a daily blog that I wrote every evening and published whenever I had a decent internet connection. I've added addendums to a few of the entries, based on things that I discovered after I had returned home.

The route that I followed and all of the 12,500 holiday snaps that I took can be viewed online at:

jongunter.co.uk/uk_coast

(I suppose I should probably add a disclaimer, just in case the website is no longer available because somebody has deleted the internet, or it's been overrun by intelligent space lizards, or I've forgotten to pay my web hosting bill - in order of the most to least likely)

Trial Run - The Evening
Thursday, 1st March

Rather than head off into the sunset, only to have to come home the next day because I'd forgotten my underwear, or had filled the van with petrol instead of diesel, it made sense to go somewhere local for a trial night. This would give me a chance to test all of the different features of the van, make a list of anything I'd forgotten to pack, and maybe learn a few things along the way.

And I'm glad that I did!

I was a mere one mile away from home when I took a ninety degree turn to the left and heard an almighty crash from behind me. I glanced over my shoulder and saw the drawer containing the china plates and bowls lying on the floor, with at least one breakage. Ah well, I'd have to rethink that one then, either with something to prevent the weight of the china from throwing the drawer open, or I'd have to give up on the china and resort to plastic plates.

After pulling into a lay-by outside the Bath Chew Valley Caravan Park, in Bishop Sutton, and hastily shoving the drawer back into place (one broken bowl, 80p from Ikea, could have been worse), I checked in at reception and was shown to my pitch. The place had been almost full when I booked it a few days ago, so I had a full service pitch rather than just an electrical hookup, which basically meant I had my own fresh water tap and waste water drain.

I stepped from the driver's seat into the back of the van to survey my kingdom, turned back around and hit my head against the over cab locker. No major damage, could have been worse.

Okay, so, time to figure out my arrival checklist. I had switched on the fridge before leaving home; check. I uncoiled the hookup cable and plugged it into the van first, as per the instructions, then into the socket on the pitch. Nothing went bang or caught fire, the trip test on the fuse box worked, and the control panel showed a charging current; check. Note to self, 25 metres of cable is going to be a pain in the butt to wind up again, consider some kind of cable spool.

I turned the gas on at the tank and tested the hob. No explosions, just blue flamey goodness; check. Next for the water. I'd not really given a lot of thought to filling the water tank or emptying the waste water tank, other than getting a couple of water carriers that could be rolled up, but it struck me that it might be useful to get a hose to get water directly from the tap to the tank, and maybe a second to get the waste water to the drain on the odd occasion that I get a full service pitch again. At about that time I got a phone call from Cheryl, my campervan mentor, who I had just texted to say I'd arrived, and asked her what she did about water. She uses a hose and a watering can. I filled one of my 10 litre water carriers from the tap, took the filler cap off the water tank and, uhhh, realised that the nozzle on the water carrier wasn't long enough to direct the water into the tank. Note to self, get a hose and a watering can.

While my brain pondered this minor setback I filled the toilet flush tank from the water carrier, put some toilet blue into the removable toilet waste cassette tank, and added some water from the tap. Fortunately, I had a 2 litre bottle of water in the fridge, which would fit into the water tank filler cap, so after nine refills I had about 20 litres in the water tank. I switched on the water pump, opened the taps, and after a few seconds of air and bubbly rumblings I had fresh flowing water; check. Next I just needed to get it heated, so I switched on the water heater and ran some more water through the taps, until the control panel started beeping to tell me I didn't have much water left. Humph.

Ten more refills of the water bottle later and all appeared well, with hot water on tap; check. By this time it was dark so I decided to shut all the blinds and start cooking, which I did once I'd remembered where I'd put everything and had all the necessary pots, pans and utensils to hand. After a while I realised that the steam from the rice was condensing on the locker doors, so I opened up the sunroof. Next I had to silence the fire alarm, which went off in protest at my wok. Note to self, cook earlier in the evening with the side door open.

Assuming I would make it through the night without food poisoning, I decided to consider the cooking to be a minor success; check. But I was very aware of not making too much mess, and of not putting anything nasty down the sink plughole, which would presumably just live in the waste water tank and eventually grow large enough to burst out of the tank and attack me during the night. So I washed up a few things as I went but took the pots and pans to the park utility room.

All that remained was to write my first blog entry; check. And to see whether I could get any sleep.

Trial Run - The Morning
Friday, 2nd March

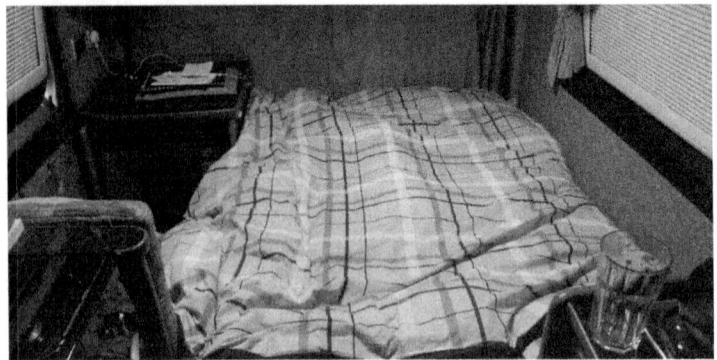

Well it took me ages to get to sleep, but it was pretty darn snug and comfy, if a little harder than a normal mattress. It was a bit chilly when I woke up in the morning, so I put the heater on for 10 minutes and tucked myself back under the duvet.

After a very nice shower (not in the van), it took me five minutes or so to fold up the duvet and sheet in the confined space and stuff everything into the over cab locker, before cooking myself a bacon sandwich and washing it down with a cold glass of orange juice. I'd like to think I'll be having a bacon sandwich every morning, but life just isn't that perfect.

I spent a while going through my departure checklist, switching things off, unplugging the hookup cable (I just know that one day I'll drive off and drag the campsite along behind me), stowing everything and closing all the lockers and drawers, before heading back home again.

All in all, a successful and very useful trial run, I've got a list of kinks to iron out and I'll probably give myself an extra day to get myself ready to head off for real, but I'm now officially excited.

By the way, if you're looking for a caravan park in the South West/Bristol region, Bath Chew Valley is excellent, the facilities are very good and the staff are friendly and informative, as long as you promise to check the van before you leave to make sure you don't have one of their cats on board. I fear I've started out at the upper end of the scale.

One More Sleep

Tuesday, 6th March

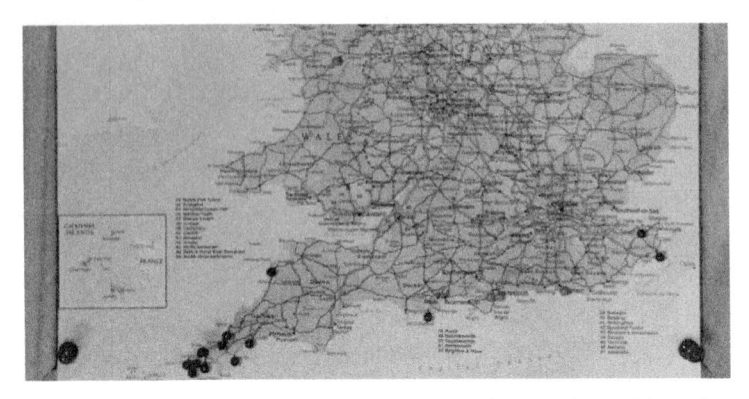

That's it, everything's ready, I can't think of anything else I need to do before I set off. No doubt that will change when I'm 10 miles down the road.

The broken bowl has been replaced, the heavier plates have been moved out of the drawer into a side pocket, I have a washing up bowl for carrying stuff to the campsite utility rooms, a hose for fresh water and a hose for waste water (I'm hoping not to get them mixed up), and an assortment of different tap attachments. Pretty much every square inch of space in the van has had something wedged into it, sometimes two things.

All being well I'll be spending tomorrow night in a field overlooking the sea, between Watchet and Minehead. I may well spend two nights there and have a relaxing day in between, it's been a bit full-on getting everything ready over the past two weeks. From there on I'll take it all as it comes. I've got a lot of ground to cover if I'm going to get all the way around the coast in the next six months or so. But I'm not laying down any rules about anything, I'll stick to the coast where I can but come inland if I need to or feel like it, I'll linger in some places and pass quickly through others, and I'll blog when I can but not religiously (although I may not be able to help myself).

The glorious weather of the last few days looks to be giving way to rain tomorrow. It's all in the timing.

Portishead to Blue Anchor
Wednesday, 7th March

Well that was a pretty miserable start to the day, with the rain falling and the wind blowing as I made a few trips to the van (parked up the road) to load my remaining gear, until a space became available in front of the house. But as I secured the bike to the back (while also breaking and, hopefully, fixing the bike lock) the sun shone briefly through the clouds and some seagulls argued overhead, which I took to be a good sign.

At 10:13am, all out of goodbyes, I set off.

The 'Bristol Riviera' is not exactly the jewel in the British coastline, and it's an area I was already familiar with, but I thought it would be rude if I did not start off at pretty much the closest point to home, Portishead, and work my way through Clevedon and Weston-super-Mare to Burnham-on-Sea. When I reached Portishead the rain had cleared up and the clouds had broken, so I wandered along the seafront (or Severn Estuaryfront), past an artificial lake and a lido, to a small lighthouse on Battery Point. As I walked along the seafront at Clevedon, past a pier towards a boating lake, the rain came back in again, horizontally, but it had disappeared for the day by the time I got to Weston. Only the wind remained pretty constant.

I'd been to Burnham-on-Sea before, but never taken the time to walk along the beach to the lighthouse, which you can rent for special occasions, apparently. It was further than it looked from the promenade, and was also quite a long way from any water at low tide, but it was an interesting landmark.

From Burnham I started the final and longest leg of the day towards Blue Anchor, which would be my stop for the first night. The roads had been pretty easy up until then and I hadn't needed to worry about the width of the van, but as I drove into one of the narrower lanes a car came from the other direction with amber flashing top lights and stopped in the middle of the road, while the driver spoke to someone on the phone. He didn't pay me any attention, or offer any suggestion as to why he had stopped, and eventually pulled away again, so I did the same, just as a house came around the corner on the back of a lorry. My brain had seen this coming, it just failed to communicate the information to the rest of me. Fortunately I was just beyond an entrance way so I reversed up and let him pass. Some of the later lanes were pretty narrow too, although luckily I didn't meet anyone coming the other way, but it's only a matter of time.

The road to Blue Anchor took me through Watchet, so I stopped for a quick look at the harbour, from where I'd been sea fishing before. I only caught conger eels that day and couldn't see much for the fog. Today the harbour hadn't seen much sea, given the almost complete lack of any water in it at that time of day. A statue of the Ancient Mariner stood above the harbour. He appeared to have shot a swan with a crossbow and tied himself to it, for some reason currently unknown to me. I guess I shall just have to read 'The Rime of the Ancient Mariner' sometime soon.

A few miles later I was driving down fairly steeply into Blue Anchor, about three miles short of Minehead. It's a quiet little place, mostly made up of caravan parks, with its own railway station and a pebble beach. I parked up in the touring field of the Hoburne holiday park, only separated from the sea by a road and a grassy bank. I think I may be in for a windy night, but all in all it's not particularly noisy in the van at the moment and it only rocks around occasionally when the wind catches it.

Phew, day one completed, with no embarrassing mishaps as yet. The thing I've been dreading most is not making it through the first day, for whatever reason. Who knows, I may not make it through the second day, but who cares, I'm already living the dream!

Addendum: Having said that I was already familiar with the 'Bristol Riviera', I had no idea until recently that Portishead had a marina! So on a sunny October morning I went to take a look. The marina was originally a deep-water dock that was built to serve ships too large to reach Bristol harbour. It was also the site of two coal fed power stations through the mid twentieth century. The whole area has been transformed into an attractive marina, bustling with yachts and surrounded by houses, restaurants and waterfront apartments, several blocks of which were still under development. It just goes to show that you don't always realise what you have on your own doorstep.

Dunster to Woolacombe
Thursday, 8th March

There once was a young man named Jon
(I'm not sure I can get away with young any longer, but it scans better)
With a campervan one inch too long
(that's 2.54cm in new money)
While reversing one day
(8th March)
A small dog in the way
(one of those tiny ones that live in handbags)
<the last line of this limerick has been removed to protect the sensitive and avoid a law suit>

Nahhh, I'm kidding.

There was a chilly but blue start to the day today. I'd decided to move on, rather than spend a day at Blue Anchor, so after looking into possible places to stay tonight I got going the short distance to Dunster Castle. Having driven past a car park as I entered Dunster, and not noticing the glaringly obvious car park sign as I drove past the castle, the road through Dunster got narrower before I just about managed to squeeze into another car park and turn around, once again passing the castle car park and paying to park in the first car park. As I walked up to the castle I finally noticed the free car park for National Trust members. Doh! The castle didn't open for the season until Saturday. Doh! Still, nice little place though.

Just down the road from Dunster was Minehead, which I stopped in just long enough to take a photo and nearly get stuck in a car park covered in sand drifts with a stupidly tight angled exit.

I negotiated a one in four winding rise up Porlock Hill, drove a winding but delightful road across the top of Exmoor, into North Devon, and descended the winding Countisbury Hill down into Lynmouth for my next stop. Lynmouth was a lovely place to spend some time, down by its pebbly beach and harbour (once again, absent any water), or you could take a funicular railway up a steep hill to Lynton. As I'm supposed to be getting fit during this trip I walked up a path that criss crossed several bridges over the railway track, and rewarded myself with lunch in the Cliff Top 'Cafaurant' at the top.

After lunch I walked back down to the harbour and set off towards Ilfracombe. I'd intended to stop in Watermouth, but due to limited parking options and turning points I drove straight through it. Instead I came across Hele Bay just beyond it, a tiny little place with a beach overlooked by static caravans.

When I reached Ilfracombe I parked in the town and walked down to the harbour, before climbing Capstone Hill, from where I could look down to the 'distinctive' Landmark Theatre, which kind of looked like a power plant to me. A statue on the hill was dedicated to a Russian girl who fell to her death from nearby Hillsborough.

From Ilfracombe I continued on to the Golden Coast Holiday Village, just short of Woolacombe, home for tonight. Now, to be honest with you, the Golden Coast is my idea of a holiday nightmare. It's geared up for families, with various kid's activities, a games arcade, a night club and cabaret (shudder), but this early in the season it's cheap, quiet, has a decent shop, and the sports bar is showing the Manchester United match tonight, so it'll do nicely. Plus I have a full service pitch and have successfully used my fresh water hose! I might even give the waste water hose a go tomorrow.

There are a couple of speakers in the 'living' area of the van, which didn't appear to be hooked up to anything as they don't work when you use the DVD player, but today I realised they're wired to the car stereo. So I'm sat in the van writing this, with the side door open, listening to Dummy by Portishead, which is not only significant because it was my first port of call yesterday, but also because I blogged about listening to it a few years ago while sat on a coach from Picton to Kaikoura on South Island New Zealand. Good times.

I think the fridge is on too high, the Sprite has turned to Slush Puppy.

Woolacombe and Mortehoe
Friday, 9ᵗʰ March

I'm developing a new technique, which I like to call the 'cheek hold'. My extensive research of two camping and caravanning sites has shown me that 100% of the camping and caravanning sites on the British Mainland have the kind of shower that's activated by pushing a spring loaded button. When the spring returns the button to its resting position the water is cut off. The length of time between pushing the button and the water cutting off again, or 'water time' as I like to call it, can range from sub-second to a respectable 15 to 20 seconds before you have to depress the button again. Not ideal when you need both hands free to wash yourself.

So, the 'cheek hold' involves facing away from the button, selecting a butt cheek, and using it to apply pressure to the button. Eh voilà, continual running water. Now this may sound simple, but there are many factors to consider, such as 'cheek fatigue', which can occur if the same cheek is used for too long a period or over too many consecutive days. Depending on your height you may need to stand on tippy toes or crouch down, which requires good core stability and stamina in the leg muscles. I'm considering creating an exercise DVD once my journal on the technique has been fully researched and published.

I decided to leave the van where it was today and take my legs for a spin, even though it was due to be overcast all day. After a breakfast of toast with three fruits marmalade (available from www.tregunter-online.co.uk, purveyors of exceptionally good preserves) I donned my walking boots, packed some sandwiches in my rucksack along with some homemade chocolate cookies (thanks Mum) and some homemade hazelnut and chocolate marble cake (thanks Mum), bought a bottle of Sprite (in liquid form) from the shop and set off along the mile and a half road into Woolacombe.

Woolacombe Beach was a vast expanse of sand, almost entirely deserted today but for a handful of people and a single keen surfer going through his warm-up routine. Heading north, the northern edge of the beach pretty much merged into Barricane Beach, Combesgate Beach and Grunta Beach (no relation), before I left the sand behind and passed Windy Cove as I turned to the west on my way to the headland of Morte Point. Coming back east again I rose and fell with the coast until I came to Rockham Beach. I have a book called 'Secret Beaches' by Rob Smith, which describes 50 secluded beaches and hidden coves on the Southwest coast. I'd already missed three of them between Lynmouth and here, and would no doubt miss more of them, but Rockham Beach was the first I'd made the effort to see.

Rather than carry on to a flight of steps that led down to the beach, as described in the book, I scrambled down the cliff at the southern edge of the beach, slipping and falling on my backside at one point. This end of the beach was a forest of rocks, all projecting from the beach at an angle, as if straining to reach the warmth of the hidden sun. I started picking my way between the rocks to reach the sandy part of the beach, often having to turn back as I found my path blocked by a rock pool with steep sides, or rocks that were too jagged or slippery. When I finally reached the sand I found myself on my own private beach, which I claimed in the name of me and sat down on the steps for some lunch. The sandwiches had been squashed beyond all recognition and the cookies and cake had merged into a mass of chocolate and hazelnut cookie marble cake. Still tasted nice though.

Continuing along the coast path I had a quick look at Bull Point lighthouse before turning back on myself and heading inland to the sleepy village of Mortehoe, where the book recommended 'The Ship Aground' pub. I fully intended to spend some time there reading another book, so I ordered myself a pint of Doom Bar and settled myself in next to some locals and a dog, who fairly promptly got up and left, as did the barman who had served me. After browsing t'interweb for a while on the free WiFi I was just about to open my book when a couple came in and were turned away by the barmaid, "sorry, we're just closing". Well that was a quick pint then, and before I knew it I was back outside and walking the two and a half miles back to the Golden Coast Holiday Village, passing several other caravan parks and holiday villages along the way, some of them not opening until mid March or April.

Exhausted by my efforts, I crashed out on the sofa and watched an episode of Frozen Planet. I am in awe of this programme, there's so much that I didn't know about the Arctic and Antarctic, it makes me sit there with my mouth open in wonder. It's a beautiful and complex planet that we live on, it would be a shame not to get out there and see some of it.

Croyde Bay to Hartland
Saturday, 10th March

Where did the world go?!

I woke up and got underway in thick fog this morning, which made the short journey from Woolacombe to Croyde Bay fairly interesting, if not exactly scenic. Having ended up the wrong side of the bay to the National Trust car park, I paid an exorbitant £3 for what turned out to be half an hour's parking, and the attendant asked me to move my van up to the end of the parking rows. Maybe he was being optimistic, or maybe it was soon to fill up with surfers. There were a handful of surfers already in the water, covered almost entirely in their wetsuits, socks and balaclavas.

Moving on, I stopped briefly in Appledore to survey the foggy waterfront, paying a far more acceptable 30p for parking, before continuing on to Westward Ho! for a longer stop (£1.20, in case you were wondering). Westward Ho! had a long beach, barely visible when I arrived, that curved around the base of a links golf course back towards Appledore. The seafront was a mix of static caravans, colourful beach huts and modern apartment buildings, with a few arcades and fish and chip shops thrown in. Westward

Ho! is also quite a long walk from Clovelly, which some friends and I found out while staying there a few years ago (you've never heard so much moaning as when we realised it was further than we thought). After wandering around for a while the fog lifted a little and patches of blue sky appeared, only to disappear again later in the day.

After reading my book for a while over a coffee I moved on to Clovelly, which is quite a long walk from Westward Ho!. Incidentally, Westward Ho! was named after a book written by Charles Kingsley while staying in Clovelly. I think it was about the inappropriate use of exclamation marks, or maybe he attempted to walk there and realised how far it was. Clovelly was a little village set around a steep narrow cobbled street leading down to a quay that dated back to the 14th century. The street was too steep for cars and for centuries donkeys were the main form of transport. These days they're excused heavy duties and live in a stable at the top of the village, replaced by sledges used for carrying goods. The village is private, owned by a single family, but you're more than welcome to visit, you just have to pay to enter it as a result of the transformation of Clovelly from a bustling fishing port to a tourist attraction. Having been an area that has witnessed many shipwrecks, Clovelly has had its own lifeboat station since 1870. A long beach, covered in large pebbles, ran off into the distance, with a waterfall cascading down to it a hundred yards from the quay.

Once I'd puffed my way back up the narrow street I set off to find my stop for the night, Cheristow Lavender Farm, just beyond the village of Hartland. I am the only resident here tonight, so I have a field to myself with just sheep for company. I'm currently writing this in the Lavender Tea Rooms, situated within the working farm. Oddly enough it smells of lavender, which appears to be growing in rows outside the window. The tea rooms closed a little while ago but the owner told me to stay here as long as I like, as it's also their home. She's also given me access to their WiFi and just invited me to have homemade pizza with them, yay!

The forecast suggests more fog and cloud over the next few days, but I'm hoping to do some more walking tomorrow and find another 'secret beach'.

Hartland and Mouthmill
Sunday, 11th March

Another foggy start this morning, as expected, although it had lifted a little by the time I started walking from Lavender Farm. I didn't have enough cash on me to pay for a second night so I took a mile and a half detour into Hartland village and had to pay to withdraw some money from a Link machine (I cannot express how much I hate having to pay for the privilege of withdrawing my own money!).

From Hartland I walked west through Stoke, made up of a few houses and a church that loomed out of the increasing fog, and on to Hartland Quay. After a quick look at the quay I joined the coast path running north along the grassy tops of the cliffs. There was a gentle breeze and a hint of sun behind me, but only about a hundred metres visibility. I could only hear the sea far below, but before long the path descended and I could see the waves. The path continued to rise and fall far too frequently for my liking. Every descent brought the promise of the sight of a beach or cove, but also the despair of having to climb back up the other side.

Eventually I came to Hartland Point, the most

northwesterly part of the Hartland coastline. Apparently there was a lighthouse down there, but I couldn't see it for the fog. There was blue sky poking through the clouds to the east so I decided to have lunch (more ham sandwiches and hazelnut and chocolate cookie marble cake) and wait to see what happened. Sure enough, the fog started to drift further away from the cliffs and a lighthouse appeared.

I continued around the coast to the east, but with everything now visible on what was becoming a very pleasant day. The path also stayed fairly level and I passed high above Shipload Bay and Beckland Bay before Mouthmill Beach, another 'secret beach', came into view. I'd been on the go for nearly five hours by then and the coastal sign posts suggested I was still two miles away from the beach, but I wanted to get down there and take a closer look at the unique rock formation at the far end.

The coast path dropped down into a wood with a stream running through it, but inevitably I had to climb back out of it again and continue along the top of the cliffs until it finally descended into another wood and out onto the beach. The tide was on its way in so I didn't have much time to step across the rocks onto the last remaining patch of sand, but it was well worth the effort with the sun starting to get lower in the sky.

After climbing back out of the forest and finding a car park at Brownsham I set off along the three miles of road back to Lavender Farm, getting back just before 5:00pm with sore feet and desperate for a cold drink. I think I might feel this one in the morning.

Bude to St Teath
Monday, 12th March

It was a shame to be leaving Hartland, a quiet and beautiful area, and Cheristow Lavender Farm, where Michelle and Eric were brilliant and welcomed me into their home. They were already well on their way to becoming self sufficient and will hopefully soon have their own wind turbine and source of water. Anyone that knows me knows that I'm not particularly sociable with people that I don't know, but now and again I get to meet genuinely decent people. If you're ever near Hartland, or particularly around Clovelly, I recommend taking the time to drop into Cheristow Lavender Tea Rooms.

I seem to be destined to spend the rest of my life in fog, like some half human, half clammy-skinned mist monster. I've barely been out of it today. From Hartland I rejoined the A39 and crossed from Devon into Cornwall, where the A39 became the Atlantic Highway. I dropped into Bude to take a quick look at the canal before following the coastal road to Widemouth Bay, which is where widemouth frogs tend to live due to the lack of crocodiles. If you haven't heard the joke about the widemouth frog you won't have a clue what I'm on about.

From Widemouth Bay I continued to Boscastle, which you may remember suffered from terrible flooding in 2004. I decided to park up the van and catch a bus for the 10 minute journey to Tintagel, from where I could walk back along the coast to Boscastle.

Tintagel was a bit of a strange place on account of it being the birthplace of King Arthur and the site of his castle. There were shops, pubs and caves named after Arthur, Merlin and other characters of Arthurian legend. I had some lunch before following the signs to Tintagel Castle, but never once actually saw it. It may have been hidden in the fog, or I may not have gone far enough out of the village, but from the point that I hit the coastline I turned right towards Boscastle.

There was another 'secret beach' along the route, Benoath Cove, but I kind of stumbled upon it from high above, barely visible through the fog, rather than finding the path down to it. Further along I came to Rocky Valley, aptly named with a stream riding several small waterfalls through the rocks down to the sea. After about three miles of hearing but not seeing the sea, the path descended to Boscombe Quay, where the river ran out to meet the sea.

Collecting the van again I made my way towards tonight's stop, inland and just outside St Teath. The roads were thick with fog until I suddenly burst out into bright sunshine amidst a small wind turbine farm, before dropping back down into the fog and reaching Rosebud Farm, where the owner saw me coming and guided me in. I had a long chat with him about various places to visit in Cornwall and he described the glorious views of Bodmin Moor that I would have been able to see from my parking space on a clear day.

Once again I have a campsite to myself, with just rabbits for company this time.

Port Isaac to Porthcothan
Tuesday, 13th March

Oh come on, this is getting ridiculous! Visibility on the roads was about 50 metres as I made my way to Port Isaac. I parked just outside the village in a rough and ready car park that I understand has been built with campervans in mind, due to the increased interest in Port Isaac generated by Doc Martin; part time physician, part time boot maker.

I wandered around and watched a few fishermen going about their business, then walked a short distance around the corner to Port Gaverne, before setting off to Polzeath. The surf season hasn't got underway yet, but Polzeath will be ready when it does, with surf shops and advertising hoardings aplenty to entice the would-be surfer or paddle boarder. Just around the corner from Polzeath were New Polzeath and Hayle Bay, quieter and devoid of surf paraphernalia.

Onwards to Padstow, or Padstein as it's become known since Rick Stein has opened up a restaurant, cafe, deli or fish and chip shop in every other building. It was quite a nice place though, with boats in the harbour and a fair amount of people milling around, probably the busiest place I'd been to so far, but not a patch on how it will be in the high season. I caught the ferry over to Rock, expecting to see at least half a dozen of the Royal Family roaming around, but strangely there were none, nor many commoners either.

Back in Padstow I settled down outside a cafe for a while to think about where I was going to stay for the night, before driving the 15 minutes to Old MacDonald's Farm (seriously) just outside Porthcothan. Old MacDonald wasn't home, but somebody else staying there (oh yeah, there are actually a few people staying at this one) told me to just pick a pitch and pay later.

I've had a few mishaps with some camera equipment this last week. While climbing up and down the cliffs between Hartland Quay and Hartland Point I got to the very top of one of the rises and realised the lens cap was no longer on the lens. After cursing myself I tramped all the way back down to the bottom, found the lens cap lying on the path and puffed my way back up again. When I got to the campsite today, intending to go for a walk, I realised I'd lost the memory card, so I got back in the van and headed back to the cafe in Padstow, where I'd had it in my pocket, and found it lying on the seat. Stupid, but lucky, so far.

On the way back again I parked up in Porthcothan itself. Porthcothan Bay was immense. It wasn't particularly wide, but it went out a lonnng way before it met the sea. I set off on foot to walk back along the coast towards Padstow, but only as far as Constantine Bay. Along the way, thankfully with very little up and down this time, I passed Minnows Islands, Fox Cove, Pepper Cove, Warren Cove and Treyarnon Bay. Fox Cove was another 'secret beach', and once again I viewed it from above with no obvious route down to it.

When I got back to the van I drove the short distance back to Old MacDonald's Farm and found someone to pay for the pitch, shortly before he drove off. I hope he worked there.

Bedruthen Steps to St Ives
Wednesday, 14th March

Want to guess what the weather was like this morning? If you guessed fog, you were wrong, it was clear!

I wanted to tread some more coastline this morning so I set off on foot early, along the roads in the other direction to yesterday, towards Bedruthen Steps. The tide was nearly in (I was beginning to think the moon had gone on strike and stopped orbiting) so there were no beaches to be seen, and a flight of 142 steep steps led me down to the water. The Bedruthen Steps were a typically craggy Cornish sight, with jagged rocks jutting out of the sea.

On the way there and back I passed another 'secret beach', Diggory's Island Sand, with a route down to the submerged sand described as 'precarious'. At 8:30 in the morning, everything seems precarious to me. Rob Smith and I clearly don't share the same views on everything, he states "Don't forget your swimming things. No matter how low the water temperature is, you're going to want to jump in and splash around". No Rob, I'm not, and I suspect you haven't been here in your Speedos on a chilly March morning.

I followed the coastline back to Porthcothan Bay, a

fraction of the size it was yesterday afternoon, passing Porth Mear and a little sandy cove on the way, and stomped back to the van. I've been going a week now, which has gone fairly quickly, but it's still hard to comprehend that I could have another five months or so ahead of me. Part of me cannot believe that it will take that long to drive around the entire coast, but another part of me has studied a map and seen how many places there are to see along the way. Anyway, I've been driving and walking almost continuously for seven days and I fancied a day off, so I decided to cover a bit of ground today and find somewhere nice to stop for the next two nights.

I set off in the van for Newquay, intending to stop at Watergate Bay, and also liked the look of Mawgan Porth when I approached it, but both were entered and exited via steep roads with hairpin bends at the bottom, and I blinked and missed the car parks at both. Instead I stopped at Porth, just short of Newquay, and walked a little way along the coast until I could see some of Newquay Bay. I didn't particularly want to head into Newquay itself, so I skirted around the town centre to get to Fistral Beach, one of the most well known British surfing beaches.

From Newquay I carried on to Perranporth, a beautiful large beach on a now sunny day, albeit a little windy at times, before moving on to St Agnes. If someone hadn't recommended St Agnes to me I would have sailed through it without a thought, as the small main road didn't give much hint of the sea just half a mile away. And I'm glad I stopped, what a lovely little place. The local RNLI crew were driving their little tractor and rib around in circles on the beach. I got talking to one of them, who turned out to be responsible for 35 RNLI stations in the Southwest and explained that they had just taken delivery of the specialist amphibious tractor to replace their old agricultural tractor. He suggested taking a look at the lifeboat station on the

Lizard if I wanted to see the contrast between a small station like St Agnes and one of the largest, newest stations.

Next stop was Portreath, which also turned out to be a really nice place, with a decent size beach and a multi sectioned harbour. I think I'll come back to this area sometime in the future, Perranporth, St Agnes and Portreath all warrant some more time spent in my opinion. But today I was carrying on to my stop for my day off tomorrow, St Ives. My route took me around the back of St Ives, rather than along the waterfront, which keeps most of it nice and fresh for tomorrow, but my pitch is overlooking the sea, beach and town. It's the kind of pitch I've been looking forward to, perfect for a couple of nights.

I've just been 'next door' with the neighbours. When I arrived, Dave asked me if I needed a hand with anything, and later on he and his wife Jill, both of them originally from Bristol, now living in Chard, gave me a glass of wine to go with my meal. We've been sat in their van for an hour and a half talking about travelling and campervans. They've campervanned for years, but have recently retired and intend to make the most of their new found freedom.

St Ives
Thursday, 15th March

I made a lazy start to this morning, I didn't rush to get up before wandering down the hill into the centre of St Ives. It's a great place, comprising of several beaches and a harbour set around a town that's a rabbit warren of narrow cobbled streets. The sea was clear and blue, shame it was cloudy today otherwise it would have been near perfect.

I took a stroll around the harbour, keeping an eye out for pasty shops, through the backstreets to Porthgwidden Beach, around a headland called The Island, with a little chapel perched on the highest point, to Porthmeor Beach. Overlooking Porthmeor was Tate St Ives, built there largely to showcase local artists, and the only one of the Tate buildings to be purpose built. It was an interesting building, and the current exhibition wasn't bad, but overall I'm not a fan of modern art, I prefer art that clearly represents something and shows a degree of talent, rather than piling a load of bricks in an empty room and offering no explanation as to why, for example.

I headed back to the harbour area and selected a pasty shop to sample a real Cornish pasty. And very nice it was too. To wash it down I sat in The Sloop Inn for a while with a pint of Doom Bar and my book. Fortunately this time the pub stayed open and I was able to leave at my leisure.

To wash down the pint I thought it only right that I should have a real Cornish ice cream. And very nice it was too (chocolate waffle cone, two scoops, mint choc chip and rum & raisin, in case you were wondering). I figured I wasn't really going to spend the whole day lazing around, so I set off to see some of the other beaches, heading southeast from the harbour, first to Porthminster Beach, then to Carbis Bay, then up a hill and over a small headland to what I think counted as the far end of Hayle Beach, but if not it was certainly the same body of sand. This was another long beach, that ran as far as Gwithian, but to get from one end to the other I would have had to have walked some way inland to negotiate an estuary. I called it a day there and stopped at Lelant to get the train back to St Ives. There was a little note against the timetable to say that the train stopped on request. I don't think I've ever had to flag down a train before.

I've just finished off the day with grilled sea bass and chips. And very nice it was too!

Sennen Cove to Penzance
Friday, 16th March

I set out this morning with the aim of moving from the west coast to the south coast, so from St Ives I followed the coastal road through Zennor and Porthmeor, past the Geevor Tin Mine and through St Just on my way to Sennen Cove. Stopping at the cove gave me about a mile to walk along the coast to Land's End, the most westerly point of mainland England, as well as a more scenic and cheaper car park.

Land's End was not the most attractive place, the main group of buildings was a little tacky, as was the signpost next to which you could pay a bored photographer to take a photo of you (no, I didn't), but the single building that actually marked the most westerly point, 'The First & Last House', was a bit more endearing. From there I looked out to nothing but sea and the Longships Lighthouse.

From Sennen Cove I headed to a place that I was particularly looking forward to visiting, Porthcurno, a beautiful little place with a lot to offer. As I walked down to the beach at Porthcurno I passed a small, insignificant looking hut. It was in fact the point at which 14 undersea telegraph cables from around the British Empire came ashore. I had hoped to learn more, but the Telegraph Museum a couple of hundred yards inland was only open on Sundays and Mondays at this time of year.

On the right hand side of the sandy beach was a stone staircase that wound its way up to the truly remarkable open air Minack Theatre. The theatre was planned, financed and built by Rowena Wade, from 1931 until she died in 1983. Since the first performance of 'The Tempest' in 1932 the Minack has played host to many Shakespeare and other plays, and to many well known stars in the making. It was an awe inspiring place, to see what could be achieved through one woman's passion and dedication, and it must be a magical experience to watch a play there on a warm summer night, overlooking the sea and Porthcurno beach.

With no plays to be seen today I continued on my way. I've been getting a bit more adventurous with the van recently, not being too bothered about where I attempt to take it, as the B roads are mostly double track, or have passing points where they become single track, and the roads in general are very quiet at the moment, so even the smaller roads leading off of the B roads aren't too bad. So without checking ahead I decided to head into Mousehole, but as I got further into the little village the road got narrower and narrower and I just managed to squeeze around a couple of bends. Not knowing what lay ahead, or whether I could turn around at the bottom, I beat a hasty retreat and turned around while I still could. In hindsight, after looking at a more detailed satellite image, I'd have been fine, a little further and I'd have reached a car park by the harbour. Oh well.

Instead I made my way to Penzance and parked up for the night at a small family run caravan park just on the outskirts. The owner had clearly been drinking, but seemed a nice enough chap, and his wife appeared sober and gave me a cup of tea and showed me around. I walked to the seafront to have a look around. There wasn't a hell of a lot to see from what I could tell, but the most impressive sight was that of St Michael's Mount, a small island with a medieval castle perched atop it, across the bay at Marazion.

Marazion to The Lizard
Saturday, 17th March

The tide has turned against me.

I mean literally, not metaphorically. When I got to Marazion the causeway that ran out to St Michael's Mount was submerged. I watched the ferry sail across from the Island and drive itself up onto the beach. I asked one of the crew if it was possible to get onto the island, but the ferry only takes passengers when the castle is open and the tide wouldn't be out again until late afternoon.

So I moved on to find another 'secret beach', parking in a little car park at the end of a very narrow and pot-holey lane. Rinsey Beach was a stones throw from the car park and was overlooked by one of the many disused Cornish tin mine stacks. It seems that every beach, no matter how remote or secluded, has a certain amount of litter on it. I would like to think that it has all been washed ashore rather than left behind by people, but I'm not sure that's much better, to be honest.

From Rinsey I took a short trip to Porthleven. As I left the van on the road running down to the harbour it started to rain, so I took an unscheduled coffee stop in a cafe and ice cream parlour called Nauti But Ice. Making use of their

WiFi, I checked the weather forecast, which has been changing by the hour recently, but the latest outlook was sunshine for the rest of today and the next couple of days. Porthleven was quite nice, with a multi sectioned harbour with a clock tower at one side of it and a long beach while the tide was out. Coastal defences have become more apparent on the south coast, with the odd WWII gun emplacement dotted around, or in the case of Porthleven a couple of canons on either side of the harbour.

By the time I'd driven to Mullion Cove it was raining again, but just a short shower. I had a quick look at the small sheltered harbour before getting going again to Lizard village, from where I intended to take a nine mile walk around the bottom of the peninsula. Walking east I came to the coast at Church Cove, where a couple of houses balanced at the top of a steep slipway. Shortly after sitting down to eat my lunch a little black dog came to join me. It soon became apparent that he was after my chicken sandwiches, and he did his best to liberate them from me, the little bugger, before his owner called him away.

Not far from Church Cove was the newly refitted Lizard Lifeboat Station, looking very new and modern nestled under the cliff. I carried on around Bass Point and came to the second 'secret beach' of the day, Housel Cove, set beneath the Housel Bay Hotel, but there was barely a beach to be seen today. Carrying on again I walked past the Lizard Lighthouse before coming to a small collection of buildings, including a cafe and gift shop, at Lizard Point, the most southerly point in mainland Britain, and site of the previous Lizard Lifeboat Station.

Continuing along the coast brought me to the third and final 'secret beach', Pentreath Beach. Apparently it's a favourite amongst in-the-know local surfers, due to its Atlantic powered waves and lack of submerged offshore rocks, but again there was little to see today. A number of

Shetland Ponies were grazing the coastal slopes in designated areas. They paid me enough attention to ascertain that I didn't have any food, before ignoring me and returning to cutting the grass.

At the far end of Pentreath Beach was 'Lion Rock', a rock that looks like, well, a lion, if that's what you're told it looks like. A little further around the coast from Lion Rock was Kynance Cove, with a collection of large rocks and isles that would no doubt form an interesting beach to wander around had the tide been out. It was still a nice place to spend some time though, a cafe and grassy terrace overlooked the beach and provided an ideal place to sit at a bench and sample some more Cornish ice cream. Cornish cream and strawberries this time, with big lumps of Cornish clotted cream in it. Yum.

Once I'd walked across the fields back to Lizard village I drove a short distance up the A3083 to my stop for the night, Little Trethvas Farm, owned by a little old lady with no teeth, which made her a little hard to understand. Once again I have my own personal campsite. There's a football lying in the centre of the next field over from mine, which I couldn't resist ambling over to and giving a quick flick up in the air, for no apparent reason.

I've just stepped out of the van into complete and utter darkness, I mean proper country darkness. If I'd backed away a few metres and spun around I may not have found the van again. But the sky is pretty clear and the major constellations are all on show. I think I'll use the toilet in the van tonight!

The Lizard to Come-To-Good
Sunday, 18th March

It was a nice sunny start to the day this morning, by the time I got to Coverack on the southeast coast of the Lizard peninsula the beach looked beautiful with the early morning sun reflecting off the sea. As I walked down the steps to the beach I said hello to a woman sitting on the steps reading a paper, with her little terrier dog. After standing in the sun on the beach for a while, looking out at the large tankers that are common in the deep waters off the Lizard, I walked back to the steps and asked her if this was her favourite spot. About half an hour later I bid her farewell, having learnt quite a lot about Dicken, 65, and her dog Bogbrush. I fully expect to see her on the news sometime in the future when she carries out her threat of walking from Coverack to London to take the Government to task, collecting other disillusioned pensioners along the way. I think I convinced her to take in as much of the coast as possible and go via Brighton.

From Coverack I headed to the north of the Lizard, to Helford, having briefly stopped at Goonhilly to take a look at the large satellite dishes. As I understand it BT have closed the visitor centre indefinitely, clearly there's something suspicious going on. I suspect they've been using the dishes recently to suck data through my iPhone, as my data usage has strangely gone from 30% to 100% of my monthly allowance in the last few days, which may make my blog updates a little sporadic for the next couple of weeks.

Helford presented me with a bit of a change of scenery for a walk along the Helford Estuary towards the mouth of the Helford River, which marks the northern edge of the Lizard peninsula. Both shores offered a number of little beaches and the south shore took me through wooded hillsides, dropping down to each beach along the way. As I approached the mouth of the river I could see Falmouth and a lighthouse on St Anthony's Head to the north.

I think I need to take a few days off the walking, my legs scream at me whenever I have to climb a hill. The way I see it, I'll either push through it and become a hardened walker, or my legs will simply fall off. There are documented cases, it happened to Bear Grylls once while he was trekking through the Hindu Kush, but being the survival mentalist that he is he just stitched them back on with some dental floss and a needle that he whittled from a yak's wishbone. I bet you didn't even know that yaks had wishbones.

Walking back along the same route I returned to the van and drove along the back roads, through places like Gweek and Brill, to Falmouth, where I parked up on the street and wandered into the windy harbour area. Falmouth was one of the larger towns I had passed through so far, with several large naval support vessels moored in the docks and home to the National Maritime Museum. I ate my lunch while watching a group of people in kayaks playing some kind of handball game, then settled myself in a cafe for a while to use their WiFi.

I've stopped for the night on a farm in Come-To-Good, with sheep and geese for company. I got my first wave from a passing campervanner today. I feel like I belong.

St Mawes to Pentewan
Monday, 19th March

What a perfect start to the day. The sun was shining and after just over a mile I pretty much drove straight onto the King Harry Ferry for the five minute crossing of the River Fal. Twenty minutes later I was in the quiet harbour of St Mawes, looking out over Falmouth Bay. St Mawes Castle sat above the village and looked across to Pendennis Castle on the Falmouth side. I could see across to St Anthony Head, which was where I headed next, having to go back on myself to work my way around the Percuil River.

Within sight of the St Anthony Head Lighthouse was Molunan, another 'secret beach', split into three sections by rocky outcrops. I walked around to the main section of the beach and spent about half an hour talking to a couple with a bonkers 11 year old dog. They had recently sold their split screen VW camper, but had spent many years driving campervans around all over the place, including taking their six kids out to France for a week and staying for nine. I felt a little over-equipped as they told me how they used to take a metal barbecue with them and use it to cook everything, including making coffee.

Heading north back up the peninsula, I left the large

tankers behind me. There was something about them that appealed to me that I can't really explain, maybe it was seeing the huge vessels so close to the tranquil coast of Cornwall, or maybe because they offered an ever changing view. They also reminded me of Vancouver, one of my favourite places.

I stopped briefly at Portscatho before continuing east around the coast to Caerhays and Porthluney Cove. The very picturesque Caerhays Castle was set in grounds just behind the beach. Moving on through the coastal roads I had a quick look at Gorran Haven before turning north again towards Mevagissey. I'd been warned about getting my van wedged solid if I approached Mevagissey from the south, so I skirted around it past the Lost Gardens of Heligan to come in from the north and park in a large car park before the streets got too narrow.

Mevagissey appeared to me to be one of those proper Cornish fishing villages, with a harbour rammed full of fishing boats and a little lighthouse at the end of the harbour breakwater, more often than not with a few shady looking guys ignoring the signs and fishing off the end of it, no doubt. There were several ice cream parlours and pasty shops, with roughly half of them open, so I figured I would have another pasty to compare to the one in St Ives. I think St Ives shaded it for taste, but Mevagissey won it for size. A couple of seagulls stood by my feet and begged for scraps, but to no avail.

Moving a short distance north brought me to Pentewan, where I stopped to take a look at the beach. I passed a pub that looked incredibly familiar, and I could picture myself and some friends sitting on the benches that ran along the outside wall, but I can't for the life of me remember going there before. Maybe it was a sign, as I realised the pub had WiFi so I sat on one of the benches and uploaded yesterday's blog. I had found a caravan site just north of St

Austell, where I intended to stay tonight, but the beach at Pentewan had a caravan park behind it, with four or five campervans dotted about facing the sea, which looked too good an opportunity to miss. So I drove the van around to the entrance and parked myself amongst the other vans.

Tonight I cooked my dinner with a view of the sea and a smile on my face.

The Eden Project
Tuesday, 20th March

Bit of a lazy day today, my housemates were coming to meet me at Pentewan this afternoon, so I decided I would go and see the Eden Project in the morning, not far from St Austell. The Eden Project was set in an old china clay pit that had been converted into multiple levels of gardens, with sculptures, educational exhibits and two massive biomes that housed plants from tropical and Mediterranean regions, plus various other buildings including a visitor centre and a stage used for outdoor concerts.

When I got there I was directed into a car park that had very little room in it and no turning space at the end. While I was struggling to reverse the van into a parking space between two cars, so that I could turn around, one of the attendants came and apologised for not realising how big my van was and told me I could park in one of the other car parks with more room, which I did once I had managed to turn around without scraping any other cars.

Personally I think the Eden Project is brilliant. I like the way it has been sculpted into the landscape, the buildings were interesting, particularly the biomes, like something out of a sci-fi film, and there was so much there to see, even for someone like myself that isn't particularly interested in plants. The whole place seemed to be full of little innovations and there was a lot of educational material for kids, or even adults that wished to learn something new. I particularly liked the main restaurant/bakery, which was an open area where you could watch the chefs prepare the food. You could take what you liked, and when you'd finished eating you would go to one of the pay points and tell the cashier what you'd had.

By 1:00pm I was back at the caravan site at Pentewan to meet up with Trev, Jules and Defor dog, who gave me a "where the hell have you been, my tummy doesn't rub itself!" look. I mean Defor, obviously, not Trev. After a cup of tea in the van (Jules had given me my whistling kettle and wanted to see it in action) and a photo shoot of me and the van for my mum's benefit, we went the short distance to the Ship Inn for lunch. I'd been stealing their WiFi by sitting outside the pub with my laptop, which I felt bad about, so I was glad we were going to spend some money there.

Once we'd all finished a fine meal of beef stew with dumplings and a pint of Tribute, Jules drove us to Mevagissey to have a lazy wander around, while Defor barked at anything and anyone in earshot. All too soon it was time to go and they dropped me at the caravan site before they headed back to Tintagel where they were staying for the week. But they left me with my post (I've won £25 on the Premium Bonds!) and a Red Cross parcel of chocolate, jelly babies, dib dabs, sherbet dips and an assortment of other travel sweets, plus a big bottle of scrumpy cider!

I'm currently sat writing this in the caravan site laundrette, where the machines are programmed to take as much of your money as possible while cleaning your clothes as little as possible. Oh for crying out loud, I've just taken everything out of the drier, with one sock missing, and found it stuck to the drum of the washer. It's just going to have to dry in its own time.

Tomorrow morning I'll probably go and sit outside the Ship Inn with my laptop to steal their WiFi again.

Charlestown to Penhale
Wednesday, 21st March

I skirted around St Austell this morning to my first stop at Charlestown, another one of those places that you could easily pass by if you weren't looking for it. As I drove down the wide main road into Charlestown I wondered if my eyes were deceiving me as I saw what looked like the masts of several tall ships. But that's exactly what you'll often find in the small harbour. As it turns out, two of the three ships hailed from Bristol. As I looked at the narrow harbour entrance beyond I couldn't help but wonder how they manage to get the ships in and out without damaging them.

Leaving Charlestown I moved just around the corner to Carlyon Bay, a beach in disrepair that was waiting on a stalled development of beachside properties that had met with a certain amount of resistance from the locals. The beach itself was unusual in that most of the sand was actually a grey mineral quartz that originated as waste from tin and china clay works at Carclaze and other areas, which washed downstream and formed the beach over approximately a 100 year period. With this waste no longer being disposed of in the stream, I wondered whether the properties will be developed at the same time as the beach gradually washes away.

Just beyond Carlyon Bay was Par Sands, which in all honesty didn't offer much to see, but the car park had more pot holes per square metre than possibly any other in the UK. So after bouncing my way in and out of it again I headed for the northern edge of Fowey, from where I took the Bodinnick Car Ferry across the River Fowey and drove around the headland opposite Fowey, to Polruan, which not only offered a great view across to the colourful houses of Fowey, stacked above each other on the hillside, but also had a small passenger ferry running over to it. Which I hopped on.

Another son of Bristol, the Matthew, was at anchor in the River Fowey, away from its usual mooring next to the SS Great Britain in Bristol docks. It will be there for a while before joining many other ships in London for the Queen's Jubilee. The Matthew is a replica of the ship that John Cabot sailed to Newfoundland, thereby discovering America before Christopher Columbus, and has made the same voyage itself.

Walking through the narrow streets of Fowey I first headed south to the beach at Readymoney, before returning to Fowey in search of a Cornish cream tea. The pubs and restaurants on and around the quay didn't seem to offer them, but I almost stumbled upon a charming little place called Pinky Murphy's Cafe on one of the streets away from the waterfront. I was only given one scone, but enough clotted cream and strawberry jam for two scones, which I took as a challenge. A good base of clotted cream provides ample stability for a large dollop of strawberry jam. And my word was it nice!

Feeling a little sick, I took the ferry back across to Polruan, staggered up the steep hill back to the car park and set off again for Polperro. When I arrived at a car park in Polperro I found that the minimum charge was £4 for three hours, which is outrageous if you ask me, I only needed about 30 minutes, tops. I refused to pay and set off again, but was annoyed that I hadn't been able to stop, so a little further up the road I turned around and came back, intending to have a quick look around without paying. But as I walked away from the van a car park attendant was making his rounds, so I sneaked back to the van and set off again. Still smarting about the whole thing I pulled into a lay-by a little way up the road and walked back down the hill. I'm glad I stopped, but even more glad that I didn't pay £4 for the privilege.

Onwards again, having sweated my way back up the hill, towards Looe, where the parking was a much more reasonable 60p for one hour. I may sound a little obsessed by parking fees, but when you're stopping at several places each day the charges can soon mount up, and currently one of the most rewarding aspects of my days is when I find a free car park, or one that hasn't started its charging season yet. I had a quick look around from a bridge across the River Looe, which split Looe into two parts, imaginatively named East Looe and West Looe.

Fifteen minutes later I arrived at Penhale Farm, a small caravan site, deserted apart from a couple of geese that really don't like me, with views out to sea towards Rame Head at the far east of Cornwall.

Seaton to Kingsbridge

Thursday, 22nd March

I made two early stops in quick succession this morning. Firstly Seaton, followed by neighbouring Downderry, before passing through Portwrinkle and dropping down onto a magnificent coastal road that ran along the side of the cliffs with a view of the beach below. From Sharrow Point I could see the fourteenth century St Michael's Chapel on Rame Head, as well as several lifeguard huts along the beach.

By the time I reached Rame Head I had driven down several lanes so narrow that branches were brushing both sides of the van. I really wouldn't fancy driving around some of these lanes during the busy months, but at this time of year the chances of meeting another vehicle in the worst spots are fairly slim. I walked to the chapel from a car park next to a coastguard station. On a clear day you would see Cornwall unfolding before you to the west and a little of Devon to the east. In front of the chapel ruins were the remains of two gun emplacements. Two entirely different kinds of faith sitting beside each other.

From Rame Head I moved north to Cremyll, from where I could see out across The Sound and over to Plymouth.

You could catch a ferry to Plymouth from Cremyll, but only on foot. Rather than having to go some considerable distance to skirt around the Lynher River of St Germans to cross into Devon over the Tamar Bridge from Saltash, I instead opted for the shorter route around St John's Lake to Torpoint, from where I caught the Torpoint Ferry into Plymouth. The Torpoint Ferry was the largest ferry I'd caught so far, but a bargain at only £1.50. And with that, I left Cornwall and re-entered Devon, this time on its south coast.

Cornwall is a magical place, you could live an entire lifetime there and not see everything it has to offer. You could walk the entire coastline, but unless you saw each and every beach, path and headland at high tide and low tide, in every season, you wouldn't see the hidden coves and beaches, or the way the light plays at different times of the day, or the many colours of the changing seasons. It's been a good time of year to visit, nice and quiet, and the weather has been good to me, but even that has denied me the drama of heavy waves under an angry sky, crashing against a secluded cove. It won't be the last time I'll visit Cornwall though, of that I'm sure.

Plymouth was an entirely different beast, all of a sudden there were big roads, cars everywhere, and more people than I'd seen for the previous two weeks. I headed straight for the Hoe, under a fairly dreary sky, and had a look at the various monuments and the obligatory big wheel that seems to have become common place in many cities. I then wandered into town to find a bank to pay in my Premium Bond winnings and get some lunch.

Fed and watered, and with a couple of extra nights' pitch money in my bank account, it was time to explore South Devon. I decided not to take a detour to Newton Ferrers and Noss Mayo as I'd been there fairly recently, but I can thoroughly recommend the area for a weekend away, and the Ship Inn at Noss Mayo is a very nice place to spend some time. Try the steak.

Instead I continued along the A379 until I could join a B road down to Bigbury-on-Sea. The final approach to the sea revealed something that I wasn't really expecting. Dead ahead was Burgh Island, attached to the mainland by a spit of sand with the sea on one side and the mouth of the River Avon on the other. At high tide the sand is covered but the island and its handful of buildings, including an Art Deco hotel, can still be reached by a 'sea tractor', with a carriage raised high above its wheels.

To get from Bigbury-on-Sea to Salcombe I had to come back inland to get across the River Avon. I set my SatNav and surveyed the chosen route, as usual, but didn't really look at it closely and assumed it would take me back up the B road. Instead it took me down to the banks of the River Avon, onto a road that was not only supposedly out of bounds for the weight of my van, but also subject to being covered by the tide. Luckily the tide was out and I didn't end up crashing through any weak spots in the road.

Salcombe wasn't much better, a diversion took me through narrow streets to what at first appeared to be a dead end, but turned out to be the entrance to a small car park, from where I had a quick wander around while the sky decided whether it was going to rain or not. Which it did shortly after I arrived at Parklands, just outside Kingsbridge, my stop for the night amidst several caravans.

East Prawle to Goodrington
Friday, 23rd March

It was time for another walk and some more 'secret beaches', which naturally meant the fog had returned this morning. But by the time I'd parked up by a village green in East Prawle, at the most southerly tip of Devon, the fog had gone and it was looking like a nice day.

The walk took me first to Moor Sands, the second beach I'd come across with a fixed rope to help get down and back up the lower section of the path. From there I could see back to the chapel on Rame Head. I then doubled back on myself to pass Macely Beach and Elender Cove before rounding Prawle Head and passing a coastguard station on my way past Sharpers Head to Horseley Cove. I could see another layer of fog lying on top of the hills, but the cove was warm and sunny.

Back in East Prawle I had a quick look around the village. The Piglet Cafe and the Pigs Nose Inn both overlooked the village green. I'm not entirely sure where the porcine fascination comes from. Apparently the Pigs Nose has played host to The Yardbirds, The Animals and, bizarrely, Curiosity Killed the Cat in recent years. Hiding behind the telephone box was what appeared to be one of Banksy's rats.

Leaving the village, I drove through the country lanes, into the fog that I'd seen from the cove, and on to Torcross, which lay on Slapton Sands, a long shingle beach in Start Bay. On the other side of the road to the beach, barely visible in the fog, was Slapton Ley, a shallow freshwater lake and nature reserve popular amongst bird watchers. During the run up to D-Day in WWII, Torcross, Slapton and many other areas of South Hams were taken over by the US Army to prepare and train for the Allied invasion, with Slapton Sands considered to be very similar to Utah, one of the five Normandy beaches. The preparations were not without casualties, particularly as live ammunition was used in the later stages, but the biggest tragedy occurred in the early hours of 28th April 1944, during a full scale rehearsal called Operation Tiger. Nine German E-Boats patrolling the channel came across a convoy of ships taking part in the exercise and torpedoed four of them, sinking two. A Sherman tank, lost during the practice landings but later recovered from the sea bed, stands at Torcross as a memorial to the 749 US servicemen that lost their lives that night.

I found another memorial a few minutes further along Slapton Sands, dedicated by the US Army to the people of South Hams, who left their homes and their land to allow the preparations to take place. Moving on from Slapton Sands, I climbed high above the sea before dropping down into Blackpool Sands and emerging into bright sunshine again. A beautiful beach with a cafe gave me a perfect place to stop for lunch and compare a Devon cream tea to its Cornish cousin. Cornwall won, by a long shot. To be fair, Pinky Murphy's Cafe won over The Venus Cafe, who provided two scones but let themselves down with small tubs of cream and strawberry jam, rather than a big dish overflowing with cream and a far superior jam. I would say that I felt equally sick afterwards, though.

From Blackpool Sands I made my way to a pretty busy Dartmouth, where I stopped briefly before catching the higher ferry across the River Dart and continuing on to Brixham, where I parked up and went for a walk around the harbour. At least I assumed I was in Brixham, the harbour was covered in thick fog and I couldn't see from one side to the other. I did spot a replica of Sir Francis Drake's ship however, the Golden Hind, sitting on the sand in the inner harbour. Walking to the end of a pretty lengthy breakwater, where several people were fishing by a little lighthouse, the fog drifted around, opening and closing pockets of visibility on the seaward side and eventually clearing enough to be able to see most of the harbour and the colourful houses above it.

Once I'd purchased some groceries (including chocolate, I ran out last night), I returned to the van and made my way to Beverley Park caravan site in Goodrington, just short of Paignton, and settled in for the evening.

Paignton to Dawlish Warren
Saturday, 24th March

I got going a little earlier than usual this morning. I didn't have particularly far to go but I was going to meet some friends for the afternoon. I had a look at a couple of the beaches in Goodrington before moving down the main road to Paignton, stopping at a couple of places along the seafront to see the pier and some of the colourful beach huts.

Just north of Paignton was Torquay, with wide promenades and palm trees. I parked the van on the seafront and walked around to a harbour, packed with yachts. It was already a nice clear day and I could see back down the coast to Paignton and Goodrington. On the way out of Torquay I came off the main road and headed to Anstey's Cove. Walking down to the cove, the first thing that I saw was a pointed rock sticking up into the air, like a tooth. The next thing that I saw was a bunch of guys in wetsuits, lifejackets and helmets, 'tombstoning' from another rock into the water.

Moving on to Babbacombe, I stopped to take a look at the beach from high above, and a cliff railway that saves the legs of many holidaymakers. The road north from

Babbacombe wound high above the sea in places. I'd intended to take a look at Watcombe Beach and Maidencombe, but I didn't like the look of the road down to Watcombe Beach and I came across a van blocking my way down to Maidencombe, so instead I carried on and stopped at Shaldon, on the banks of the River Teign, looking across to Teignmouth. The mouth of the Teign was wide and fast flowing, but a spit of sand on the Teignmouth side jutted out most of the way across it.

Crossing the River Teign by bridge, I found that Teignmouth was absolutely heaving with cars, as everyone came out to make the most of the good weather. I was lucky to find a parking space and walked back along the seafront towards the river, along the dark red sand, while kids on scooters and skateboards terrorised the elderly along the promenade.

My next stop was Dawlish, where Dawlish Water flowed over a series of small weirs through the pretty, ornamental gardens, called The Lawn, and black swans are often seen. A railway ran right along and above the beach, with a raised station at the end of the gardens and an underpass providing access to the beach. Just north of Dawlish was Dawlish Warren, where I checked into the Peppermint Holiday Park, another sprawling mini village of static caravans and pitches, still quiet but with quite a few campervans around.

Once I'd settled in I was joined by Rick and Juanita, who had come down from Exeter to meet me and take a walk around the mile and a half spit of sand that juts out into the Exe estuary. Dawlish Warren is a popular holiday resort, and it was pretty obvious to see. The Peppermint Holiday Park was just one of many, and the entrance to the sand spit was a narrow tunnel under the railway that emerged into a funfair. If you can fight the urge to turn around and run away at the sight of the funfair, you're rewarded by a very scenic walk around an area that includes a sandy beach, dunes, mudflats and salt marshes, part of a National Nature Reserve, as well as a golf course. After walking around the whole area, much of it looking across to Exmouth, we sat down for a drink outside the Boathouse Tavern, thankful that it wasn't the middle of summer and full of families and kids.

Starcross to Seaton
Sunday, 25th March

I stopped briefly in Starcross, climbing the stairs to a bridge over a railway track, from where I could hear and just about see a power boat race on the other side of the estuary, before making my way around the estuary, past Exeter, and down to Exmouth and the beginning of the Jurassic Coast.

Exmouth was a pretty pleasant place to be on a sunny Sunday morning, where a sandy beach and promenade continued for quite some distance. People were milling around and several runners were preparing for the Sport Relief Mile taking place later in the morning. Groups of colourful beach huts looked out over one section of the beach.

Equally pleasant was Budleigh Salterton. Red sandstone cliffs rose to the western end of the town and a memorial to those lost during WWII sat on the highest point of a road overlooking the beach, which was home to a collection of small boats and white beach huts.

Sidmouth continued the theme of red sandstone cliffs, but was a much larger and busier town than Budleigh Salterton. The beach was pretty much in two sections, joined by a walkway that hugged a section of the cliff that has had hundreds of names and messages scratched into it, some of which must have taken a fair amount of time to complete. I spent an hour wandering around and making myself some lunch in the van, before spending another hour in a cafe.

I love Beer... but I prefer cider.

Now let's be straight about one thing, I didn't want to make some second rate pun about Beer, but if I hadn't you'd have made up one of your own. You're probably making one up anyway. But Beer was indeed a lovely place and had a little bit of everything. Beach huts sat at the base of the white chalk cliffs that surrounded the pebble beach, which sloped in several shelves down to the sea. Fishing boats, bringing back the day's punters, were winched slowly up to the top of the shelves, watched by people from their deck chairs, eating ice creams and drinking tea from several cafes. At the eastern end of the beach I could look around the corner to Seaton and beyond. I bought myself an ice cream (single scoop, mint choc chip, regular kind of cone) and sat under an umbrella outside a cafe for a while, before dozing off on the beach to the sound of the sea. It was the first time I'd really sat outside in one place for any length of time.

Less attractive was Seaton. It wasn't a bad place by any means, but the beach with a road and shops running behind it just didn't have the same kind of charm as its neighbours. But it was still home to a group of youngsters (well, younger than me) sitting on the beach, playing instruments as the sun started heading for the horizon.

Tonight I am making a detour inland, I'll be spending the evening and having a meal with Dave and Jill, who I met in St Ives, at their home in Chard. They've offered me a bed for the night, or an electric hookup on their drive. I just might take the bed, for old times' sake.

Lyme Regis to Chickerell
Monday, 26th March

I didn't sleep much last night, maybe it was the cup of coffee I had before turning in, or maybe I felt bad about sleeping in a bed, indoors, while my trusty van fended for itself on the drive. But then again, it was pretty cold this morning, with a frost on the ground, so it may not have been such a bad idea after all. I said goodbye to Dave and Jill, thanked them for their hospitality and wished them well for their upcoming five week trip to France in their van, before I set off back towards the coast and into Dorset.

Lyme Regis was gorgeous this morning, sunny and quiet. The beach had been pisted, with the same corduroy effect that you get on ski slopes first thing in the day. I almost felt bad about walking on it. The centre piece of Lyme Regis was The Cobb, a sturdy 183m long stone breakwater that snaked its way around the harbour, the top of which sloped towards the sea as if trying to shrug off anything that attempted to cross it. It was a bacon butty and cup of tea kind of morning, and who was I to argue.

My main aim today was to climb Golden Cap, a sandstone peak that rose to 189m above the sea. I had intended to climb it from Seatown, nestled below it to the east, but when I arrived in Charmouth I figured I had plenty of time to walk the five or six mile return route from the west, possibly dropping down to Seatown too. It wasn't a direct climb from Charmouth, I first climbed a lower peak and dropped down again before climbing Golden Cap. On a warm day, with clouds of midges flying around, it was hard work, but well worth the view and the warm breeze at the top while eating some sandwiches. I abandoned the idea of walking down to Seatown and having to climb back up again, my legs have not yet become the hardened steel pistons that I'm hoping for.

When I got back to the van I drove around to Seatown, parked up and walked east again for another mile or so up to Thorncombe Beacon, which was pretty easy in comparison. From there I could see to West Bay and beyond to Chesil Beach and, far off in the haze, the Isle of Portland.

Back in the van again I dropped into West Bay, also with a steep cliff rising from the beach to the east, but I avoided the temptation to climb that one. By then it was getting on in the afternoon and I'd had no phone signal for most of the day, so I hadn't yet found anywhere to stay. So I got on my way towards a touring site called Bagwell Farm, that Dave and Jill had recommended, a little short of Weymouth, but I first wanted to set foot on the western end of Chesil Beach.

I got my chance at Cogden, where I finally found a National Trust car park that I could use for free. I started off down to the beach, realised I hadn't put my National Trust sticker in the window, returned to the van and set off for the beach again. Sod's law says that if I hadn't put the sticker up I'd have been fined for not paying and displaying, no matter how unlikely that may have been.

Chesil Beach was an impressive sight, it ran for some 17 miles or so and in places rose to about 12m. Roughly half of the beach was backed by a lagoon called The Fleet, which turned it into a long slender strip with water either side. At Cogden the beach was made up of small pebbles, which get larger as you travel east.

I made one last quick stop at the side of the road just as I came over a rise before Abbotsbury, from where I could see Chesil Beach, The Fleet and Portland stretching out before me, but also a building that caught my attention, standing tall and large alone on a hilltop.

When I got to Bagwell Farm I was given a pitch high up at the back of the site, overlooking The Fleet and Chesil Beach. I was thinking to myself today that the only thing I miss at the moment is not being able to have a nice soak in a bath, rather than a shower. Well they only flippin' well have some baths! I may indulge myself tomorrow as I'll be spending two nights here.

Portland and Weymouth

Tuesday, 27th March

I had a bit of a lie in this morning as my mum was coming down from Bristol to see me, arriving at about 10:30am. I locked up the van and she drove us towards the village of Fleet to see if we could get a good view of The Fleet and Chesil Beach, but we just ended up in the car park of a hotel, looking over a wall, so we turned around and headed for Portland, stopping at a car park on a thin strip of land that connected the mainland to Portland and the end of Chesil Beach.

Once there we walked up to the top of the mound of pebbles running along the centre of the beach. There were several guys fishing from the beach, one of whom got caught out as one wave came in much further than the previous waves, up to his ankles. The sea was throwing itself against the beach before rushing out again, creating quite a strong undertow and spinning the pebbles around. On the other side of the road was the massive Portland Harbour, protected by long breakwaters just visible in the haze. The harbour is popular amongst wind and kite surfers, several of which were setting up their kites and testing the waters. Weymouth and Portland are home to various sailing and surfing academies and schools, and will be home to the Olympic sailing events this year.

Moving on we drove onto Portland and up to a viewpoint at the high northern end, where we could see down to the harbour and look along the length of Chesil Beach and The Fleet, or at least as far as the haze would allow, before continuing south along the length of Portland to Portland Bill at the lower southern tip. On the way we passed several quarries from which Portland stone is still produced. If you want to see Portland stone, take a look at St Paul's Cathedral or Buckingham Palace. A large red and white lighthouse stood proud over the flat landscape. We stopped for lunch in a restaurant, where I was nearly tempted by a Dorset cream tea, but I'll maybe leave that for another day.

After lunch we left Portland and parked on the seafront in Weymouth. Weymouth to me is one of those typical seaside resort towns, with a long promenade backed by hotels and guest houses, many of them dating back to the late eighteenth, early nineteenth century. The beach was a wide one, part pebbles part sand. Walking along the beach, past the Weymouth Pavilion, we continued on to a stretch of docks, crammed with yachts and smaller boats.

On the way back along the promenade to the car, a powered paraglider buzzed the beach a couple of times, winding up several dogs that set off in pursuit. We drove back to Bagwell Farm for a cup of tea before my mum set off on the journey back to Bristol.

Osmington Mills to Lulworth Cove
Wednesday, 28th March

Well that was a damn near perfect day.

The glorious weather looked set to continue as I headed for the coast east of Weymouth at Osmington Mills. The Smugglers Inn looked very inviting, apparently having stood there since the thirteenth century, and the coastline offered clear views across to Weymouth, Portland Harbour and Portland. I walked about a mile and a half to Ringstead, emerging from the trees at a little green with a couple of whitewashed houses behind it, and dropped down onto a pebble beach. Behind the beach was Burning Cliff. In the 1820s the oil rich shale in the cliff caught fire and burned for several years.

After walking back to the van I drove 15 minutes to my stop for the night, even though it was only just midday. One of the main things that made this trip seem like a good idea to me was the thought of spending some time at Durdle Door. I knew there was a campsite just above it and having looked it up a couple of days ago I parked up on a strip of grass at the front of the site, just behind a public car park, overlooking the sea.

While I made myself some lunch I was serenaded by the

staccato sound of machine gun fire from the nearby Royal Armoured Corp tank and gunnery range, and the sight of smoke rising above it. I changed into my walking trousers and favourite walking hat (don't tell my other hats) and set off down the path to Durdle Door.

Durdle Door is an outcrop of limestone with a huge archway carved out of it by the sea. You'll have no doubt seen photos of it, even if you don't realise it. The archway was in the right hand section of a hammerhead formation that jutted out into the sea. On either side were shingle coves. On the horizon was Weymouth and Portland.

From Durdle Door I walked a short distance west up the side of a steep cliff, from where I could look down on Durdle Door to the east and Butter Rock and Bat's Head to the west, the former a chalk sea stack, the latter a chalk outcrop with a small hole through its base. Walking back down again I followed the steps that led down to the two coves, one either side of the archway. After a quick look around I walked a further distance west, up and over another cliff, to Lulworth Cove.

Lulworth Cove was an almost perfect oval shaped cove, surrounded by chalk cliffs apart from the opening to the sea. The many layers in the rock could be seen twisting over at angles on either side of the cove entrance. I climbed a set of steps up and over the back of the cove, following a fence that marked the western edge of the firing range, with red flags flying to show that the range was in use. I was hoping to catch sight of a tank on manoeuvres, given the mix of machine gun fire and shelling that was taking place, but I could only see more smoke in the distance.

Walking back to the van I formulated a plan for the evening. After a quick shower I put on my 'chilled' playlist, had a cup of tea and cooked some dinner, took a walk up to a mound that overlooks Lulworth Cove and the campsite, then made a start on today's blog entry. Just before 7:30pm, as the sun was getting low, I packed my laptop, camera and head torch into my rucksack, grabbed my tripod and walked back down to Durdle Door, where a few groups of people were still sitting on the beach, some of them with barbecues.

I took a few photos and settled down on a rock to continue writing the blog as it gradually got darker. Eventually I set up the tripod and took some more photos. Each time I looked up another few stars had winked into view. With barely any light left I started up the steps and took a few more photos half way up as the remaining people on the beach climbed past me. Packing up for the last time I put my head torch on and hoped I could find the correct path back to the campsite. Head torches are all very nice, but they do tend to encourage every midge in a 10 mile radius to fly into your face, so I switched it off again and followed the silhouettes of the people in front of me until I came up to the lights of the campsite, just before 9:00pm.

A most satisfying day. The coastline around Durdle Door and Lulworth Cove is beautiful, especially on a day like today, and Durdle Door itself holds a fascination for me that I can't really explain. Sitting on the beach while the sun went down fulfilled a long time ambition, even if the sun goes down in the wrong spot for a decent photo.

Kimmeridge Bay to Hengistbury Head
Thursday, 29th March

I had hoped to go to Tyneham and walk to Warbarrow Bay first thing this morning, but with the firing range in use, and both of them situated within the range, that wasn't going to be possible. The village of Tyneham was evacuated in 1943 when the range was first opened, and has been deserted ever since. It was a shame not to be able to drive through the range too, as now and again you can see the burnt out shells of tanks used for target practice.

Instead I skirted around the range to Kimmeridge Bay. There was a £5 toll to get to Kimmeridge but there was nobody manning the booth. Up on the crumbling cliff on one side of the bay was a 'nodding donkey' that pumps out roughly one million gallons of oil a year. Above the other side of the bay was Clavell Tower, built between 1830 and 1831 by the Rev John Clavell as an observatory and folly. Between 2005 and 2008 the tower was dismantled and rebuilt further back from the cliff's edge, to prevent it falling victim to erosion.

Next I headed back inland towards the village of Corfe. The first thing that entered my mind as Corfe Castle came into view was 'wow!'. The castle was a ruin, but it sat atop a hill overlooking the village and made quite an impression. Finally getting to make some real use of my National Trust membership, I parked and entered the castle for free and had a quick look around before it was swamped by several school classes. Just at the base of the castle was a garden terrace belonging to the National Trust Tea Room, an ideal place for the third round of my county cream tea tasting, this time representing Dorset, but unfortunately not included in my National Trust membership. One scone on this occasion, with the cream and strawberry jam again served in little pots, but this time the pots were for presentation purposes and had been filled with fresh cream and jam. Not bad at all, better than the Venus Cafe in Devon but not as good as Pinky Murphy's in Cornwall. I didn't feel quite so sick this time, but I didn't finish all of the jam either

Back on the road again I stopped in Swanage briefly, and again at Studland Bay, before taking a car ferry from Studland across the mouth of Poole Harbour to Sandbanks, a small peninsula southeast of Poole with the fourth highest valued land, by area, in the world. I don't believe they have a caravan site on Sandbanks, and I doubt I could afford to stay there if they did. I drove a little way in towards Poole, parked at Whitecliff Harbourside Park and walked along the shore around to a quay and back.

Heading east again I stopped in Bournemouth and walked down to the pier before continuing on to another pier at Boscombe, then stopped briefly on the cliffs at Southbourne, from where I could look along the entire stretch of sand that ran from Sandbanks in the west, through Bournemouth and Boscombe to Hengistbury Head in the east. When I reached a car park at the western end of Hengistbury Head I found it was the first car park I had come across with a height restriction, preventing me from entering. So, muttering injustices to myself, I parked on the road in a spot limited to one hour, knowing full well I'd be gone for longer.

Hengistbury Head, south of Christchurch Harbour, was another place that I wanted to spend a bit of time, so I walked along a beach below Warren Hill to a dog leg turn at the end that brought me onto Mudeford Sandbank, a strip of dunes that almost encloses Christchurch Harbour. The sandbank was home to several hundred brightly coloured beach huts, nearly all of a different design. At the end of the sandbank was a narrow entrance to the harbour, known as the Run, across which was Mudeford Quay and Mudeford itself. I managed to buy an ice lolly just before a cafe on the sandbank closed and walked back to the van along the top of Warren Hill, which provided great views of the sandbank, the harbour, Mudeford, Hengistbury Head, and east to the Isle of Wight.

Tonight I'm staying on a small site outside Christchurch, in the grounds of Oak Cottage. It's one of the many 'five van' sites that cater for no more than five caravans or motorhomes, often with limited facilities. I don't have this one to myself this time, only one of the pitches is empty. The resident sheepdog appeared in my doorway while I was eating my dinner. I tried to strike up a conversation with him but he growled at me, so I pulled the door shut and have no intention of wandering around outside in the dark tonight.

Highcliffe Castle to Warsash
Friday, 30th March

My first stop this morning, and my last in Dorset, was at Highcliffe Castle, built in the 1830s by Lord Stuart de Rothesay, whoever he was. Just behind the castle were steps leading down to a pleasant sandy beach with views of Mudeford Sandbank and Hengistbury Head.

I drove on, into Hampshire, stopping briefly on the cliffs at Barton on Sea and Milford on Sea before reaching Keyhaven, a quiet inlet with a sailing club and marshes that formed part of the Lymington-Keyhaven Nature Reserve. A ferry ran from Keyhaven to Hurst Castle, built by Henry VIII, which sat at the end of a spit that could also be reached by a two mile stretch of causeway that started near Milford.

Driving through the New Forest beyond Lymington to Calshot on a nice day like today was a very pleasant experience, a long wide road ran through open heathland inhabited by dozens of ponies, roaming around and grazing. I also passed a couple of cows by the side of the road and came across a little green full of donkeys in the pretty little village of Beaulieu. Calshot Spit was a bit of a strange place, it lay on the corner of Southampton Water and the Solent and was home to Calshot Castle, also built by Henry VIII.

It played a major role in the development of flying boats, with the Royal Flying Corp establishing Calshot Naval Air Station there in 1913, and some of the vast hangers still remained, although today they were mostly home to an activity centre that catered for water sports, climbing, snowboarding and track cycling. The tall tower of Fawley Power Station overlooked the area.

Heading north along the western side of Southampton Water, I stopped in Southampton to take a look at the waterfront, with large ships and a cruise liner on show, before heading south down the eastern side to Netley and the Royal Queen Victoria Country Park. The country park covered over 200 acres overlooking Southampton Water and was once home to a huge military hospital opened in 1856 by Queen Victoria to care for casualties of the Crimean War. All that remained of the hospital today was the chapel. It was a nice place to stroll or cycle around on a sunny day.

A nice place for longer walks was Hamble-le-Rice. A narrow high street opened out onto a view of the River Hamble that was packed full of little boats and yachts, with about five marinas in the area. You could walk quite a long way up the River Hamble before crossing it and walking back down the other side through a nature reserve to Warsash. I took the shorter route and caught a little pink Hamble-Warsash ferry across, which wound its way through the many moored craft. Warsash offered more of the same as Hamble, as well as being home to Warsash Maritime Academy and a lifeboat training facility. Walking back to the ferry, the skipper saw me coming and shouted to me to ask whether I wanted to cross, to which I shouted 'yes' and then felt obliged to run the 100 yards or so, although he would have waited for me.

Back on the Hamble side I sat in a cafe overlooking the river and started on today's blog entry. From here I'll be heading inland to stay with some friends in Winchester tonight, before heading to Fareham tomorrow evening to see another friend and spending Saturday and Sunday night with some more friends in Southsea. So basically a weekend off.

Hill Head to Southsea
Saturday, 31ˢᵗ March

I had a bit of a lie in today in Winchester, in a real bed again, at Karen and Martin's. We went out for pizza last night with another friend, Lisa, who came over to meet us this morning before we all set off towards the coast at Hill Head. From there we took a walk inland to Titchfield along the edge of the Titchfield Haven National Nature Reserve. We had a leisurely lunch in Titchfield before walking back again and having a look around the nature reserve visitor centre. All too soon we had to head back to Winchester again.

Once I'd said my goodbyes I took a quick stop at Sainsbury's to top up on chocolate and fuel. There was no sign of panic buying there (fuel, not chocolate), but I still passed several garages with no fuel left. A recent threat of a strike by fuel tanker drivers has been handled in a typically shambolic fashion by both the Government and the general public. I had decided to take most of the day off from driving, which meant I had to drive pretty much the same route that Martin had driven us today, to get to Fareham where I was dropping in on another friend, Don, and his wife Tracey, for a very nice meal and a chance to catch up and talk at length about travelling.

    I left Fareham fairly late in the evening and made my way to Southsea, where I was going to spend a couple of nights with David and Caroline and their kids, Joe and Amy.

Southsea and Hayling Island
Sunday, 1st April

Caroline was taking Amy to a Brownies get together today, so David, Joe and I got on our bikes for a cycle ride, the first time I'd taken the bike off the back of the van. I was relieved to find that the bike lock that I had appeared to have broken when I hastily loaded the bike nearly a month ago seemed to be working okay and unlocked with no problems.

We cycled the short distance from the house to the Southsea waterfront and joined a cycle lane running along the side of the promenade towards Eastney, until we ran out of land at the Hayling Island Ferry. We got lucky with the timing as the ferry only ran once an hour but turned up within about five minutes. Once on Hayling Island we continued on the bikes until we got to a funfair just behind the beach, purely for Joe's benefit, obviously.

As we walked into the funfair towards some kind of super-spinny-death-contraption, someone's shoe detached itself from the whirling mass of screaming bodies and arced across the sky, landing next to an unsuspecting woman. Apparently David and Joe had been on that one before and both felt sick afterwards, so we kept on walking to the dodgems. Joe and I also had a go on the hardly-spinning-at-all-atron, which was somewhat disappointing. Moving into an arcade, we won a few rounds on the horses and Joe found three two pence pieces in the tray of one of the two-pence-pieces-hanging-precariously machines. He proceeded to convert them into a handful of two pence pieces, then eventually into no two pence pieces, but collected two toys along the way that had dropped with the coins. A good day's gambling in anyone's book.

On the way back we stopped at a pub restaurant just by the ferry, for a Sunday roast and a sickly sweet pudding, timing it just right to cycle straight onto the ferry and back home again. It had been good to get out on the bike so I jumped at the offer of spending an extra night tomorrow and decided I would spend another day in the saddle, as it were.

Southsea, Portsmouth and Gosport
Monday, 2nd April

I had big plans for today, forgetting that yesterday's bike ride was one of only a handful in the last 20 years or so. I intended to catch the ferry across to Gosport and cycle to Lee-on-the-Solent, then come back again and catch the ferry over to Hayling Island and cycle the full length of the island before returning to Southsea. So I set off for the seafront and turned right towards Portsmouth.

The first things I noticed as I looked out to the Solent were several large tankers lying at anchor and the Palmerston Forts. The circular Spitbank, St Helens, Horse Sand and No Mans Land Forts were built in the late eighteen hundreds to defend the Portsmouth dockyard from French invasion. Three of the forts now belong to Clarenco (whose Executive Chairman was the founder of Dreams, for all your bed and mattress needs), a company that specialises in unusual and unique luxury hotels and venues. You can hire one of them for around £7,000 a night, rooms only, no breakfast.

I made my way along the Southsea seafront, past Southsea Castle, wide expanses of green parkland and the Naval Memorial, towards the Spinnaker Tower, towering high above Gunwharf Quays. The tower was intended to open for the Millennium, but due to delays and funding requests it wasn't completed until 2005. Personally I think it was well worth the wait.

Not far beyond Gunwharf Quays was the Gosport Ferry, which I caught over to Gosport on the other side of the mouth of Portsmouth Harbour. Not long after setting off on the bike again I realised that there was no way I was going to get to Lee-on-the-Solent and the far end of Hayling Island, I didn't have enough time to fit everything in and I doubt my legs would have coped with it. So instead I did a short circuit of part of Gosport, passing the Royal Navy Submarine Museum along the way, and caught the ferry back across to Portsmouth.

A stone's throw from the ferry was the Historic Dockyard, home to HMS Victory, HMS Warrior, the Mary Rose and various museums, attractions and exhibitions. I'd been there earlier in the year with David and the kids and my year long ticket entitled me to free re-entry to HMS Warrior and a harbour tour that I hadn't yet used. I'd used up my one time tour of HMS Victory, but I can thoroughly recommend it as an interesting and informative tour. I spent a bit of time on the Warrior, a ship launched in 1860 to counter French developments in naval shipbuilding, and the largest, fastest, most powerful ship in the world at the time. The Warrior led various lives after 22 years of active service, including depot ship, floating workshop and oil jetty, until in 1979 she was towed to Hartlepool to be restored to her original condition. She's a fascinating ship, a real fighting ship loaded with canons, muskets and swords.

After having some lunch in Gunwharf Quays I made use of my harbour tour ticket, an hour long tour of Portsmouth Harbour that picked up and set down at both the Historic Dockyard and Gunwharf Quays. I had no idea how many naval ships were currently at anchor in the harbour, including two aircraft carriers (Ark Royal and Illustrious) and several destroyers (Manchester, Liverpool, Bristol, Gloucester, York, Dauntless and Diamond) and frigates (Lancaster and Kent), among others. Many of the ships had been decommissioned due to cutbacks and were waiting to be scrapped. The harbour tour gave an excellent view of Portsmouth and Gosport, plus Portchester Castle, which together with Southsea is an area of the coast that I particularly like, and it nearly always seems to be sunny whenever I go there.

Rather than heading straight back to the house I cycled back along the seafront to the Hayling Island ferry, but didn't intend to cross this time, and had just missed it anyway, before arriving at the house just after Caroline, Joe and Amy had got home. I settled down in a nice hot bath and dozed off for a while before joining Joe and Amy at the dining room table for some homework (blog writing). When David got back from a day of travelling for work (I recognise the word 'work', I just don't remember what it means) we all sat down for an evening meal.

Bosham to Shoreham-by-Sea
Tuesday, 3rd April

It was time to get back on the road this morning, so I said my farewells, loaded the bike back onto the van and got underway. Before long I'd passed into West Sussex and also passed the 1,000 mile mark before making my first stop of the day at Bosham (pronounced 'Bozzam'), a small village sitting on the edge of Bosham Channel. Apart from being a picturesque little place with plenty of swans and a working quay, Bosham was also home to the Saxon Holy Trinity Church, which features in the Bayeux Tapestry, no less, and is the burial place of King Canute's daughter, who drowned in Bosham Creek in 1020 at the tender age of eight.

From Bosham I headed to West Wittering, but with an estate that controlled access to the beach and a parking charge that I deemed not worthy, I continued on to East Wittering instead. The pebble beach had a little hut above it selling fresh fish and had plenty of the wooden groynes that have become a familiar sight along this stretch of coast. To the west I could just make out the Spinnaker Tower at Portsmouth.

Next I made my way to East Beach at Selsey, with a large car park and green parkland behind a sea wall and a lifeboat station to the south, where you could also apparently buy fresh fish and shellfish, before coming back on myself and heading around to Bognor Regis.

Bognor was another seaside resort with a pier and a promenade, backed by fish and chip shops, but no real charm to it. I walked one street back to the high street to get some lunch before setting off again, past Butlins (shudder). I was aiming for Middleton-on-Sea but passed through it without spotting any obvious signs to a beach or seafront and instead ended up in Elmer, where I parked and followed a short footpath to find a stretch of beach with a series of crescent shaped rocky breakwaters.

Onwards again to Littlehampton, where I pulled into a car park and was about to get out of the van when a gentleman tapped on the window and warned me that the height barrier at the entrance to the car park had only just been removed to let a van in that was unloading at the nearby cafe, so was likely to be closed again when the van left. I thanked him and moved on, not wishing to be stuck for the rest of the day, and ended up parking on a street for free. Littlehampton was quite nice, the beach was backed by a large area of parkland and playgrounds and there were various artistic pieces lining the promenade, such as a continuous bench that rose and fell and wrapped around itself at various points, and an unusual roof on the aforementioned cafe.

From Littlehampton I drove through Rustington, Ferring and Goring-by-Sea before coming back to a beach at Worthing and eventually reaching a palm tree lined promenade and pier and continuing on to South Lancing. I had my first case today of phoning a caravan site that was fully booked, although I've found a small site almost next door to it that isn't busy. It will be interesting to see if I'm able to find places without too many problems over the Easter weekend and the rest of the school holidays.

The site in Lancing is about three miles away from another friend, Tim, in Shoreham-by-Sea, so I got the bike out and cycled over to see him, his girlfriend Eddie and their cat Sable for the evening and a very nice meal out. It's been a sociable stretch of coast over the last five days, but tomorrow I'll be back to taking each day as it comes with no particular stopping points other than wherever I end up at the end of each day.

It was starting to spot with rain as I cycled back to the van, and it's just started coming down heavily. I understand there's snow up north, hopefully it will stay up there.

Hove to Norman's Bay
Wednesday, 4th April

Despite a bit of rain here and there, all while I was in the van, it was largely another warm and sunny day today. I started off in East Sussex with a quick stop in Hove to take a look at the promenade, with wide areas of green running behind it with play areas, a skate park and a small lake for waterskiing and wake boarding using an overhead track system. Next I parked up on the seafront at Brighton, grumbled about the massive £6 for two hours of parking, but grudgingly paid it as I wanted to spend a couple of hours there.

Brighton is perhaps the king of seaside resorts, it had a massive pier, the remains of another pier, a long beach backed by cafes below a promenade and road that ran in front of large buildings and grand hotels. It has a grandeur and relaxed nature about it, and no small amount of 'odd' people. Within five minutes of arriving, a guy passed me blaring rock music from a boombox and declaring loudly something about 1966 and the king of rock and roll (before my time). Brighton also sports all of the modern attractions such as shopping malls, and a large choice of restaurants and nightlife, plus the more unusual, such as the Royal

Pavilion, an Indian style palace built for the Prince Regent in the early nineteenth century.

Once I'd had my money's worth of parking, I drove out of Brighton and up onto white chalk cliffs through Rottingdean and Saltdean, stopping in Peacehaven to take a look back towards Brighton and get some groceries, before continuing through Newhaven, from where you could catch a ferry to Dieppe.

It had started to rain in Newhaven and got heavier in Seaford, but there was more blue sky behind the grey clouds, so I stopped and made some lunch while they passed over and the sun returned. Standing on a pebble beach at Seaford I got a good view of the white cliffs either side of me, but not as good a view as from Seaford Head. Parking in a car park just outside a nature reserve, I walked into the reserve towards a beach at Cuckmere Haven, with the Seven Sisters spread out in front of me, white chalk cliffs that rose and fell between Cuckmere Haven and Birling Gap. There were actually eight peaks, supposedly, but I guess Eight Sisters wouldn't have sounded as good.

Returning to the van, I drove around to Birling Gap, stopping briefly before spending a little longer at Beachy Head, where I walked along the top of the cliffs with nothing but my own common sense to stop me from falling to the beach below (I don't like to rely on my common sense at the best of times). A lighthouse stood on top of the cliffs and a second, red and white lighthouse at the base of the cliffs. I didn't really get a sense of how high up I was when I was stood near the edge, but my slightly wobbly legs made up for my lack of common sense and told me not to get close enough to find out. Several paragliders were preparing to fly off the cliffs, from an area from where I could just about make out a power station at Dungeness.

As I rejoined the main roads I dropped down into Eastbourne, where you could spend as little as 20p for 15 minutes parking, most commendable. Eastbourne was a little like a small version of Brighton, with a pier, promenade, large buildings etc, and was also quite a nice place to be.

I carried on past Pevensey Bay to my stop for the night at Norman's Bay. After calling them earlier in the day I was expecting a grass pitch with no hookup, as they were quite busy, but they managed to find me a spot where I could plug in, although I had to wait a while because they were getting used to a new computer system. For the first time since I left home I've booked a pitch a day in advance, with places getting busy for the Easter weekend, so I've got a fair bit of ground to cover tomorrow to get to Folkestone.

I've just had the worst shower in the history of mankind, with practically no water pressure, I'd have been better off if I'd just poured a glass of lukewarm water over myself.

Bexhill to Folkestone
Thursday, 5th April

There was no sign of the sun today, just cloud and a biting wind at times. Maybe it doesn't spend much time in the southeast, it was probably having a cream tea in Cornwall.

My first stop this morning was at Bexhill. There wasn't much to see there, with the main focal point behind a shingle beach being the De La Warr Pavilion, built in 1935 and restored in 2005 as an arts venue. Apparently Bexhill was the first place in Britain to allow mixed bathing on the beach, in 1901. I would imagine it was warmer and sunnier than today. I was glad to get back in the comparative warmth of the van.

Next I stopped at St Leonards and walked a mile or so along the seafront to Hastings. Another long beach, promenade and pier, although this time the pier was home to the burnt out remains of some buildings. In 1066 William the Conqueror (nee 'of Normandy') crossed the channel with a bunch of his Saxon mates on a stag weekend. They landed at Pevensey and made their way to Hastings pier where William, off his face on mead, became furious with the pathetic attempts of the grabby-crane machine to lock its pincers around a stuffed Bart Simpson doll. In a pique of rage he torched the amusements barn, called the owner a 'poo poo head' and called him out for a fight. The next morning, slightly hungover, they met on the field of battle, six miles inland from Hastings, at a place conveniently called Battle. And the rest, as they say, is history, apart from the whole episode being called the Battle of Hastings, rather than the Battle of Battle, a masterstroke by the Hastings Tourist Board.

If Hastings had a saving grace, it was the old town, with its narrow lanes, timbered houses, funicular railway running up to East Hill, and the Stade. The Stade was the harbour area, where fishing boats were winched onto the shingle beach and all the buildings were painted black. Many of them were tall sheds known as 'net shops' that were originally used for drying nets but are now used for storage. The buildings looked like they came from a Tim Burton film.

From Hastings I came inland for a while, passing through Winchelsea and Rye before returning to the coast at Camber, in Rye Bay. A sandy beach was backed by cafes and sand dunes, and for some reason had a Sussex Police office in the car park. I didn't hang around long enough to find out why. Instead I drove through marshland into Kent, through Lydd and onto a windy shingle promontory at Dungeness.

Dungeness was a strange place. The wide expanse of flat nothingness was home to random buildings and ramshackle huts, two lighthouses, one of them decommissioned, and was at one end of the Romney, Hythe and Dymchurch Railway, with its miniature steam trains. Oh yeah, and a power station, which you couldn't exactly miss. The whole area seemed the most unlikely place for anyone to actually live, and yet it had at least one pub and a 'mystical gift shop' for all your mystical gift needs. I felt compelled to have tea and cake at the railway cafe.

As I headed north up the coast a short distance, through Lydd-on-Sea, Greatstone-on-Sea and Littleton-on-Sea, I passed back into traditional civilisation, with rows of houses behind a beach. Lydd-on-Sea seemed very popular with kite surfers. Further north again, Dymchurch sat behind the Dymchurch Wall, more than 2m below high tide level. A Martello Tower, one of many small defensive forts built around the British Empire in the nineteenth century, poked its head above the wall, looking out to a guy standing on a surf board with a single long paddle to propel himself along.

After a quick stop at Sandgate I took a diversion to the Kent Battle of Britain Museum, which was closed, rather disappointingly, so I headed to Folkestone harbour to take a look around. A disused railway track ran across a bridge that split the harbour into two, and small fishing boats were lined up on the mud. Outside of the harbour, overlooking a sandy beach, was a bronze statue of a naked woman looking out to sea, as if she would rather sit naked and cold on a rock than turn her gaze on Folkestone. Having been there, I empathise with her.

On the other side of a headland that overlooked the harbour, topped by another Martello Tower, was my campsite for the night, accessed by a crumbling pot holed track, but with views over the sea and a beach just below it.

Capel-le-Ferne to Sandwich
Friday, 6th April

Well I didn't expect to see the sun this morning, but there it was, with a few wispy clouds for company, as I treated myself to scotch pancakes and bacon with maple syrup.

Just outside Folkestone, at the entrance to Capel-le-Ferne, was the Battle of Britain Memorial. In the summer and autumn of 1940 the skies over this area were the scene of countless dogfights as the Luftwaffe sought to gain air superiority over the RAF. Had the Luftwaffe succeeded, Adolf Hitler would most certainly have launched Operation Sealion, the invasion of Great Britain. The memorial laid on the top of the cliff was in the shape of a huge propeller, with blades 37m long. In the centre of the propeller was a statue of a pilot gazing into the sky. Behind the memorial were a replica Spitfire and Hurricane and a wall engraved with the names of the aircrew involved in the battle, including that of my great uncle, who lost his life flying a Hurricane. From the cliff top in front of the memorial I could look down to last night's campsite and over Folkestone to Dungeness.

Just before entering Dover I turned back on myself on the A20 to take a look at Samphire Hoe. A traffic light controlled the flow of traffic through a single lane tunnel that passed through a cliff. The Hoe was a long promenade, roughly halfway between Folkestone and Dover, created from the chalk spoil dug out of the Channel Tunnel. An 'artistic' blue tower, inspired by lighthouses and the huts for hanging nets, looked out across the Channel to France, visible on a clear day like today. Within it I found a large bumblebee tirelessly trying to fly through the glass. I left the door behind it open in the hope that it might take a pause for breath sometime and look over its shoulder.

I have to say I quite liked the beach and harbour area of Dover, and I really wasn't expecting to. The promenade had obviously had a bit of a makeover in recent years and the sunshine certainly helped. I can't speak for the rest of the town, mind you. Regardless of the town itself, I couldn't help but be impressed by the magnificent Dover Castle that sat high above it. I already knew there was a castle there, but I had no idea how large or intact it was. I made my way up to a car park and joined the Bank Holiday crowds within the castle walls. The queue for the secret wartime tunnels was an hour long, so I gave that a miss and just wandered around the grounds. The castle had been built up since the late eleven hundreds through numerous wars and perceived threats. Some of the tunnels were used to plan the Dunkirk evacuations. Also within the walls was the Anglo-Saxon church of St Mary-in-Castro. The castle walls offered commanding views of several large cross-channel ferries in the harbour, winding queues of lorries waiting to board them, and a sideways glance at the White Cliffs of Dover.

After spending a while at the castle and making some lunch in the car park, I set off again, stopped briefly not far away at a National Trust sight overlooking the harbour, and continued through St Margaret's at Cliffe and into Kingsdown, where I parked on a street and wandered through the village down to a shingle beach. The beach ran continuously past Walmer, where it was backed by long greens and fishing boats were winched onto its banks, and onto Deal and beyond.

Deal seemed to be an example of not particularly ambitious-ness. The pier was quite narrow with not much at the end of it, and a castle not far from the pier was tiny compared to its neighbour at Dover. It did however have a statue at the entrance to the pier of a man in a bathtub wrestling a fish (no, me neither), more fishing boats winched onto the beach, and the Timeball Tower, a time keeping mechanism used by sailors to check their chronometers.

Leaving the sea behind I headed to Sandwich, probably most famous these days for its golf courses. Sandwich is the northern most of the Cinque Ports (Hastings, New Romney, Hythe, Dover and Sandwich) originally formed for military and trade purposes, but today is nearly two miles inland, reached by a five mile channel of the River Stour. I didn't stop for long before moving on to secure a place to stay for the next two nights.

I've got a little ahead of myself today, I'm staying beyond some of the places I'm intending to visit, but I knew that I could get a couple of nights at Two Chimneys Camping and Caravan Park near Birchington, albeit for an extortionate price as everyone flocks to these kinds of places for the Bank Holiday weekend. Tomorrow I can take things a little easier and return to where I left off today.

Pegwell to Westgate on Sea
Saturday, 7ᵗʰ April

I was in no hurry to get going this morning, so I was still in the campsite when some of the staff came around to say that there had been problems with the electrics last night, not that I'd noticed, and they were asking the campervan owners if they would mind moving to another part of the campsite. So I went to the reception and sorted out a new pitch, which turned out to be in a quieter area, before vacating my previous pitch and heading off to Pegwell.

It wasn't easy to find the sea at Pegwell, it was there, but it was hidden behind walled estates and caravan parks. By the time I found it I'm not sure if I was actually still in Pegwell or at one end of Ramsgate. Leaving the van on the road, I walked along the cliff top, past an industrial area of the harbour and down the road into Ramsgate, where loads of yachts were moored in the main harbour area. There was a smallish beach just outside the harbour, in front of a pavilion that was boarded up and for sale, and an amusements arcade that had been emptied of any machines. I'm not sure whether this was due to a decline in tourism, or a season that hadn't yet started, or maybe an impending change of image. Much of Ramsgate sat behind a road above the harbour, supported by red brick at one end and white concrete at the other.

North of Ramsgate was Broadstairs, which was quite a nice little place if you ask me. A crescent beach in Viking Bay was dotted with people on what had turned out to be a fairly quiet day, overcast for the most part with a few spots of rain in the morning. I walked down to the beach and along a short breakwater, where several fishing boats had moored, before finding a cafe to sit down for a while and have some lunch.

Next I headed for Margate, stopping briefly along the way at Joss Bay, Botony Bay and Walpole Bay, and looking out to an offshore wind farm as I came around onto northern facing shores. I drove through Margate, past various amusement arcades, and stopped just after the main beach. As I walked back towards the beach I could feel the place sucking my very soul from my body, like some kind of coastal Dementor. Rather than continue any further I turned around and walked to a second area of beach, before returning to the van and moving on to Westgate on Sea to find two bays separated by a promontory, covered by a high tide.

I got back to the campsite fairly early in the afternoon and parked in my new pitch, had the first decent shower of the week and am currently watching my washing going round and round in a tumble dryer. This time I checked the washer for stray socks first, obviously.

Oh... my... God... I have just glanced at the basket that I used to move my laundry from the washer to the dryer. There's only a freakin' sock in it! I kid you not. Could it be possible that it's the same sock?! I may have to segregate it from the other clothes, what if it tries to persuade some of my undercrackers to escape too?

Reculver to Rochester
Sunday, 8th April

I covered a fair bit of ground today, partly because the weather wasn't great at times, and partly because, well, I didn't really find much to see. Things started well though as I unwrapped an Easter egg and a box of creme eggs that I'd been carrying with me since I started out (thanks Mum).

My first point of call was at Reculver to see the twin towers of the ruined St Mary's Church. Most of the church was demolished in the early nineteenth century, but the towers were considered to be an important navigational aid and were restored by Trinity House, the corporation that own and operate many of the British lighthouses.

Next I stopped at Herne Bay. Three quarters of a mile out to sea was the stranded end of a lengthy pier, the rest of which was destroyed by storms in 1978. The main point of focus of the seafront was a clock tower built in 1837.

Moving on again, I drove around Whitstable for a while, getting increasingly annoyed by all the car parks with height barriers, until I eventually found a spot on a street just outside one of them. I walked into the harbour area to find a small market, selling various things from shellfish to olives (neither of them high on my list of nice things to eat), all sold from black huts of various sizes, similar to the Stade at Hastings.

From Whitstable I passed through Faversham and Sittingbourne and over a bridge across the Swale to the Isle of Sheppey, continuing most of the way to the east of the isle to Leysdown-on-Sea. The traffic through Leysdown was fairly heavy so I turned around and parked just outside the village, not far from Warden Point. I had a quick look back along a shingle beach towards Leysdown before walking along a road, which became a potholed track, towards what I believe was Warden Point. The track and everything around it came to a fairly abrupt end, subsiding into the sea, along with a concrete structure below. This was supposed to be a good spot for watching the shipping along the Thames Estuary, but there wasn't much going on, although there was a massive container ship just visible in the haze.

Back at the van again I travelled west, through Minster, towards Sheerness at the other end of the isle. I stopped in a small car park below a high wall and clambered up the steps to drop down the other side to a shingle beach that ran towards the industrial looking docks. I was beginning to lose the will a little by now, to be honest, the Thames Estuary is understandably not the most inspiring stretch of coastline, so I sat in the van for a while, made some lunch, and had a look for a place to stay, picking one near Gravesend but not getting any answer on the phone.

Leaving the Isle of Sheppey, I stopped briefly at Lower Halstow at a sailing club on Halstow Creek, backed by views of dock cranes and power stations, before passing through Chatham and stopping in Rochester. I drove around a car park near Rochester Cathedral, with no height barrier this time, but no real space to stop either, gave up again and parked on a road between the Cathedral and Rochester Castle instead. If anyone had told me I couldn't park there they'd have got an earful about how campervans were persecuted just because they were different. I then crossed the River Medway and stopped in a quiet area on the other side to look back to the Castle and Cathedral.

I still hadn't got in touch with the campsite so I decided to head straight there rather than go to Gravesend. There was no sign of the place being open so I phoned once again from just outside and finally got through, only to find that the owner was away. I wasn't exactly spoilt for choice in this area so I closed my Camping and Caravanning Club book and had a look at the Caravan Club book, which has plenty of sites but many of them don't have any facilities such as showers, toilets and washing up sinks. I found a couple nearby on the map, but couldn't for the life of me find the details in the book, so I drove to the general area on the map without spotting any Caravan Club signs. I eventually found one of them on the Caravan Club website, gave them a call and booked myself in.

Today has probably been the least interesting day so far, but that's not bad considering I've been going for just over a month now. I'm hoping for better things once I get north of the Thames and start up the east coast.

My left shoe has started to squeak.

Gravesend to Burnham-on-Crouch
Monday, 9th April

It was one of those days today.

I headed north, through drizzle, back to the coast at Gravesend. What can I say about Gravesend? Uhhh, well, not much really. Except that it had a statue of Pocahontas. Yeah, seriously. She married John Rolfe, one of the early colonists, and came to England with him in 1616, but died the following year from a fever. Her statue stood in the grounds of St George's Church, not far from the waterfront. By the way, totally unrelated, how do you get Pikachu on a bus?

Pokemon.

On the other side of the Thames from Gravesend was Tilbury. It didn't look any more inviting, but it had a fort, so I thought I may as well head there and use my English Heritage membership, or at least sit in the car park there and plan the rest of the day. A short distance up the Thames, I pulled up to a booth just before the Dartford Crossing and paid a toll. When I emerged from the tunnel, into Essex, I pulled up to another booth and was handed some white stilettos and a bottle of spray tan. While congratulating myself for thinking up that last sentence, I forgot to pay attention to my SatNav and missed my exit from the M25, adding a further 10 miles to my journey.

I parked at Tilbury Fort and flashed my membership card at the staff, who were far too cheerful considering they were working on a rainy Bank Holiday and would probably only see a handful of people today. The fort was first built in 1682 to defend the entrance to London along the Thames. From the walls I could see across to Gravesend and the towers and cranes of Sheerness, among other places. Not being much of a rainproof, indoors kind of fort, I didn't stay particularly long.

I made sure as early as possible this morning that I had somewhere to stay tonight, with a shower, which I was looking forward to, and I couldn't really be bothered to hug the coast today, so I took the main roads straight to Southend-on-Sea. After passing through the sprawling suburbs and narrowly avoiding being channelled into a multi-storey car park I found somewhere to park in a one hour zone on a street and walked to the seafront. What I found there was a mass of funfairs, amusement arcades and motorbikes. I guess there was some kind of biker convention going on today, the place was crawling with them, wandering around in their Hell's Angel style leather jackets proclaiming their various chapters and allegiances. Stretching out into the sea for a staggering 1.3 miles was the Southend pier, where most people no doubt choose to take the electric train to the end and back.

After stopping for some lunch I returned to the van to find a parking ticket under the windscreen wipers. I'd had a bit of a brain fart and not noticed that below the one hour notice was another notice saying 'Except Feb, Apr, Jun, Aug, Oct, Dec', and on the other side of the road the sign said 'Except Jan, Mar, May, Jul, Sep, Nov'. No wonder everyone else was parked on the other side of the road. But seriously, alternating sides of the road, who does that?!

Instead of getting angry I just swapped all of the signs to the opposite sides of the road, that'll teach those smug right hand side parkers (I didn't really, that would be wrong, and I didn't actually think of it at the time).

Moving on again I skipped the coastline of Foulness Island and Wallasea Island and instead drove through Rayleigh and around the River Crouch to Burnham-on-Crouch. Along the way I came off an A road on one of those exits that sends you around in a tight 270 degree circle, a little too fast, and ended up with the drawer, bowls and small plates on the floor again. I've just glued a corner back onto the drawer for the second time. I parked at the Burnham-on-Crouch marina, capable of mooring about 350 boats, and walked along the quayside to the main part of the town, passing several neglected looking boats in the boat yards. By the time I got back to the van the drizzle was coming in horizontally.

I'm staying at Mark Farm tonight, near Tillingham. The Bank Holiday campers all left earlier today so I once again have a campsite to myself, apart from several goats. The whole landscape today has been pretty flat, and the field that I'm in is pretty exposed to the elements. I washed up this evening at an outside sink with the wind blowing the soap suds out of the bowl. I'm fully expecting a startled goat to slam into the windscreen any minute now.

Bradwell Waterside to Tollesbury
Tuesday, 10th April

It's amazing how some decent weather, and some more pancakes, bacon and maple syrup, can improve your outlook. The rain had gone and I decided to slow things down again and spend less time in the van than I have done the past two days.

Just north of Tillingham was Bradwell Waterside, where a marina and a small collection of houses overlooked a narrow stretch of water between the mainland and the small Pewet Island, and beyond to the wide mouth of the River Blackwater. To the east was Bradwell Power Station. The mud at low tide appeared to be covered in oyster shells.

West of Bradwell, where the Blackwater became a regular size river, was the town of Maldon. I parked the van on a street, making sure there were no parking restrictions this time, and walked to Hythe Quay. The river was mostly mud while the tide was out. The quayside was quite a nice area, with parks behind it and a number of small cafes, and an array of boats including old Thames sailing barges. I sat outside one of the cafes for a while with a drink, before returning to the van and stopping at the local Tesco to stock up.

Not far from Maldon, on the northern banks of the Blackwater, I stopped at Heybridge Basin and made myself some lunch. The car park was next to a canal, the Chelmer & Blackwater Navigation, which led to a lock at the entrance to the Blackwater and another pleasant area with several pubs and cafes. I spent a bit more time sat in one of the cafes, looking out to the water. Out in the middle of the wide body of the Blackwater was Osea Island. The island is owned by a record producer and was, until 2010, home to a rehab centre, The Causeway Retreat, which treated many a rock star (including Amy Winehouse), aristocrat and burned out city banker, for around £10,000 a week. It was shut down for not having the appropriate license. The island is now open to the public (the wealthy ones) as a holiday retreat, accessible by a causeway that's only passable for four hours in every twelve.

I got back on the road again and headed for Tollesbury, the other side of the river from where I started this morning at Bradwell Waterside. Tollesbury was another boating centre with a marina that could hold a few hundred craft. The salt marshes, with their maze of water and boardwalks, could hold several hundred more.

My stop for the night was to be in West Mersea on Mersea Island, so I drove through Great Wigborough and Peldon on my way to The Strood, a stretch of road that crossed the Strood Channel onto the island. When I got there, however, cars were starting to queue up and I could see that part of the road was underwater. A number of cars and lorries continued to cross in both directions, making bow waves in front of them, while some turned around and others remained where they were. Not wishing to risk flooding my accommodation, and not knowing how long the road would be covered for, I picked up my Camping and Caravanning Club book and found a site 15 minutes back the way I had come from Tollesbury, gave the place a ring and turned around.

So I'm now in Springfields, a very picturesque little campsite, but with no facilities apart from water and electric. It turns out The Strood is not always covered at high tide and I was just unlucky today. I could have waited an hour to get across, but the tide should be low if I go back again tomorrow morning.

West Mersea to Clacton-on-Sea
Wednesday, 11th April

The Strood was clear this morning, and the Strood Channel was one large mud flat with a narrow stream of water running through it. I drove to West Mersea and into an area of boat yards and houseboats, with many other craft moored out in the shallow channel waters. To the south was the seemingly ever present sight of Bradwell Power Station. If I had been staying here last night I may well have had a meal at the West Mersea Oyster Bar, but as that wasn't an option this morning I instead settled for a bacon baguette and a cup of tea at one of several nearby cafes.

Many years ago my great grandparents owned a houseboat here called the Hispania. The Hispania was originally a racing yacht owned by the King of Spain, Alfonso XIII, winning many races in the early twentieth century. After ending up and serving as a floating home in West Mersea she was purchased by a foundation dedicated to restoring vintage boats and moved to Southampton. I don't actually know what has become of her, but her sister ship Tuiga has been fully restored and won a regatta at Cowes in 2010.

While on the subject of my family, I left Mersea Island

to travel the short distance north to Abberton and St Andrew's Church on the banks of Abberton Reservoir, to find the graves of both my great grandfather and great great grandfather. Abberton was one of three reservoirs used by 617 Squadron, more commonly known as the Dambusters, to test Barnes Wallis' bouncing bomb.

In order to cross the River Colne, I travelled north through Colchester to come back south again and stop at Brightlingsea, a mix of yacht clubs and modern waterfront apartments, before finding a campsite at Grange Farm in Thorpe-le-Soken. Once I'd had a shower and smartened myself up a little I headed off again to Clacton-on-Sea, parked up and walked to the beach and pier. I wandered along the pier, past amusements and funfair rides, to get a clearer view of the offshore wind farm, several miles out to sea. When I turned around and looked back down the pier I found myself staring into an angry black sky building up over the town, so I got myself indoors for a drink while the worst of it passed.

I had recently heard from a friend, Julie, that her parents had been following the blog and I was welcome to drop in for a meal when I was passing through Clacton. As things have worked out, Julie was currently staying with them with her kids, Jonathan and Lucy (I say kids, Jonathan is wayyy taller than me and Lucy probably won't be far behind). So I gave Julie a call and three and a half minutes later I pulled up outside George and Margaret's house, who very kindly welcomed me into their home for the evening. Julie, Jonathan and I went for a walk along the seafront before we all sat down for a delicious meal. Afterwards we put a road atlas on the table and looked at the coastline from here all the way home to Bristol.

Man, I've got a long way to go, but thanks to the kindness of friends, and strangers alike, I'm getting well fed along the way!

Frinton-on-Sea to Mistley
Thursday, 12th April

Not far from Clacton-on-Sea was a sandy beach at Frinton-on-Sea, backed by the now customary colourful beach huts. Behind and above the beach ran a wide stretch of green known as The Greensward. Frinton had so far managed to remain devoid of the amusements and funfairs that feature in many of the other resorts.

After a quick look at Frinton I moved further along to Walton-on-the-Naze, which had embraced the amusements and funfairs on its pier. At only three-quarters of a mile long, the pier was a mere baby compared to Southend-on-Sea. Behind the beach, which ran continuously from Frinton, the beach huts were stacked above each other on the cliff side.

From Walton I could see a tower to the north, on The Naze itself, which was my next stop. The brick tower was built in 1720 by Trinity House as a navigational aid, but was now used as an art gallery, museum, viewing platform and tea rooms. I walked beyond the tower along the crumbling cliff tops of The Naze, down to marshy beaches that looked towards Harwich and a number of large dock cranes at Felixstowe.

From there I drove around Hamford Water, with its many little islands, to Dovercourt, just south of Harwich, parked the van and walked onto a sand and shingle beach. A couple of disused lighthouses on stilts decorated the beach, one of them high up the beach, the other just out in the sea. The promenade became a narrower concrete walkway as it snaked around the headland to Harwich old town and some small beaches. Across the body of water that flowed from the Rivers Stour and Orwell, large container ships were being unloaded in Felixstowe. The quay at Harwich was home to a number of light ships, and a Trinity House building and large warehouse stocked with red buoys and yellow and black wreck markers. Across from the quay was Shotley Gate, at the tip of a peninsula that lay between the Stour and the Orwell.

Once I'd walked back to the van I drove along the southern banks of the Stour, stopping at Mistley, a small commercial port and home to a large population of swans, all strutting around as if they owned the place. The twin Mistley Towers were the remains of a church built in 1735, the nave between the towers was demolished in 1870 when a new church was built on another site. The Mistley Quay Workshops were used to make pottery and musical instruments, and also had a cafe, where I sat down for a while with a book and a cup of hot chocolate so large that I could have swam in it, using the little marshmallows as life rafts to paddle between the whipped cream ice burgs. Or something like that.

I have now crossed the border into Suffolk, leaving my white stilettos and what's left of the spray tan at the exit booth, and am staying at Tomcat Farm just south of Ipswich.

Shotley Gate to Felixstowe
Friday, 13th April

Although I'd seen Shotley Gate and Felixstowe from Harwich yesterday, I wasn't exactly in a hurry today so I figured I'd work my way up and down the Stour and Orwell rivers to take a closer look at them.

So after a slow start to the morning I bought an LPG bottle from the campsite to replace the first of the two bottles that I had left home with, tried to put some fresh water in the tank, but gave up as the site's hose was so long that there didn't seem to be enough water pressure to push the water to the end of it, and set off towards Shotley Gate. I was also getting low on fuel and cash so I kept my eyes open for a garage and a cash point.

Shotley Gate was very quiet this morning, its main features being a marina and a jetty for a foot ferry over to Harwich. Across the Stour I could see Harwich quay and the lightships, and a large ferry at the ferry terminal, probably bound for Hoek van Holland. Across the mouth of the Orwell I could see the big cranes and container ships at Felixstowe.

If you follow the Orwell you get to Ipswich. I've worked in Ipswich and I had no particular desire to go back, but I'd never had a look at the harbour areas there so I decided to go and have a look around, rather than cross the Orwell on the A14 bridge. I drove around for a while, looking for somewhere to park, before temporarily giving up in order to find some fuel as I was running worryingly low. Once I'd filled up and returned to the harbour I was pleasantly surprised to see that Ipswich had quite a nice, modern harbour area. Whether or not it was like that while I was working there, I'm not sure.

I set off again, down the other side of the Orwell, towards Felixstowe, stopping on the way at the huge Suffolk Yacht Harbour, just beyond Levington. It was a private marina, so I only walked just inside the gate to have a quick look around.

A little later I arrived in Felixstowe and parked at Landguard Fort, just short of Landguard Point. The fort was originally built in 1543 to guard the deep waters of Harwich Harbour, and had been rebuilt or remodelled several times since. There seemed to be more English Heritage staff in the fort than punters, milling around and chatting loudly. Today the fort just provided a slightly higher ground from which to watch the container ships being loaded and unloaded, or to look over to Harwich, the beach at Dovercourt, and The Naze.

Felixstowe was not how I imagined, I thought it would be a run of the mill industrial docks, but it had several parts to it. The docks were vast and lined the landward side of Landguard Point from the fort onwards. The seaward side of Landguard Point was a long beach that ran past the main town and beyond. On the southern side of the pier were amusement arcades and funfair rides, and even some donkeys, but on the northern side of the pier these were replaced by houses, cafes and restaurants, and a pedestrian high street leading away from the sea, where I finally found a cash machine.

Before parking up and walking along the promenade I pulled into the only caravan site in Felixstowe, having made a snap decision to spend the night there, but they were holding a rally tonight and were completely full. So instead I went for my walk and then found a campsite called Woodward Park, 15 minutes away near Bucklesham, where I've stopped for the night.

Woodbridge to Snape

Saturday, 14th April

I think I may be starting to get the hang of this travelling business, spending less time on the road and more time sat on my butt in cafes.

I headed straight to Woodbridge first thing this morning, on the River Deben, had a bit of a look around the waterfront and then found a cafe on the high street to spend a while uploading the last few blog entries and sorting a few things out.

On my way to Bawdsey Quay I passed signs for Sutton Hoo. Not wishing to pass up the opportunity to visit one of England's most important Anglo-Saxon burial grounds (not to mention it has a funny name and was another chance to 'spend' my National Trust membership), I pulled over to take a look. To the untrained eye, Sutton Hoo is a collection of grassy mounds. To the archaeological eyes of Basil Brown, in 1939, it was a collection of grassy mounds with a bunch of stuff under them. The 'stuff' turned out to include a burial ship containing the body, and treasures, of Raedwald (possibly), King of East Anglia, laid to rest in 625 (possibly). Next to the burial ground was a holiday site for pigs, where they came to relax, socialise and lie in the mud, but they stayed for the view of the burial grounds.

Bawdsey Quay lay at the mouth of the Deben, across the river from Felixstowe Ferry, a couple of miles north of Felixstowe town. Funnily enough, you could take a ferry across at this point. It was quite a nice area, with a tempting looking cafe overlooking the river, and who was I to resist such temptations. The weather was quite warm, Liverpool were losing in the FA Cup Semi Final (I'm a Manchester United fan), and as I took my seat on the cafe balcony what sounded like a Spitfire was flying overhead. All was well. I ordered some tea and a warm scone with cream and jam, which was all very nice, but the cream was not clotted, so had there been such a thing as a Suffolk cream tea I suspect the other Cream Tea Counties would have taken umbrance at this and had Suffolk expelled.

Within seconds of getting back in the van it had started raining and Liverpool had equalised, proof if any is needed that life is better in cafes.

It looks as though you can't really 'follow' the Suffolk coast in the same way that you can along most of the south coast, the main roads that run parallel to the coast are a couple of miles inland, with the occasional road branching off towards a spot on the coast. From Bawdsey I skirted around the Butley River to Orford, on the banks of the River Alde. Across the Alde was Havergate Island, home to an RSPB Reserve, and beyond that was Orford Ness, a 10 mile spit of vegetated shingle. In the twelfth century Orford was a major sea port, prior to the growth of Orford Ness, hence the presence of a large medieval church and a castle.

Further up the Alde was Snape Maltings, a collection of Victorian buildings that were originally used to process barley for brewing. In 1967 they were converted into a complex that includes shops, a craft centre, a pub, a cafe and a concert hall that hosts the Aldeburgh Music Festival. Playing tonight is The Barber of Seville. There was also a

School for Advanced Musical Studies, dedicated to the founders of the festival, Benjamin Britten and Peter Pears. In the grounds were several sculptures, including 'The Family of Man' by Barbara Hepworth and 'Perceval' by Sarah Lucas, which appeared to be a horse (no doubt called Perceval) pulling a gold trimmed cart containing a couple of massive cheesy Wotsits, minus the orange colouring that represents the decline of civilisation in the post modern era, juxtaposed against man's eternal struggle with the material world (probably). Must try harder Sarah, see me after class.

Tonight I am staying at Mill Farm, near Saxmundham, which has its own little fishing pond, a Spitfire flying overhead (surely not a coincidence) but no toilet paper in the gents, and I'm not even going to start on how I found that out!

Aldeburgh to Walberswick
Sunday, 15th April

There was a chill wind blowing along the beach at Aldeburgh this morning. After examining a nearby sculpture on the shingle beach, based on a clamshell, I walked south towards the town, lying just behind the beach, where fishing boats had been winched up and their catch was being sold from little huts. The Tudor Moot Hall, half timber, half red brick, was still being used these days for council meetings. In 1948 the annual Aldeburgh music festival was created by Benjamin Britten and Peter Pears, now held at Snape Maltings. Walking beyond the town, I came to a large Martello tower sitting on a narrow stretch of land. On one side were the beach and the sea, on the other side the River Alde flirted with the coast before turning inland towards Snape.

Walking back through the town I stopped at a cafe for some brunch. No sooner had I taken my seat than it started to hail, just for a minute or two. One of the waitresses spoke to the customers in a strange sing-song Cockney accent, I half expected her to hitch her thumbs into some braces, leap into the air and click her heals together. When I left the cafe the sun had come out from behind the clouds and a group of people were playing boules on a couple of purpose built courts near the Moot Hall.

Driving north behind the beach, I soon reached Thorpeness. At the centre of the village was The Meare, a manmade boating lake, quite popular amongst people wishing to get in some rowing action today. Not far from the lake was the House in the Clouds, which could be seen from Aldeburgh. The seven storey house was originally a water tower and can now be hired as a holiday home. Next to the house was a windmill, minus its blades, which used to be in Aldringham two miles away but was moved here and restored. Thorpeness was mostly made up of weatherboard and timber houses from a range of different periods.

Also visible from Aldeburgh, and about a mile and a half north of Thorpeness, was Sizewell Power Station. I drove to Sizewell and wandered out onto the same stretch of beach, in front of the block and sphere structures of the power station and not far from a couple of platforms standing just off shore. Several kite surfers were milling around on the beach while one of them headed out to sea several times, before racing back towards the beach and catching some air.

From Thorpeness I came back inland for a while before returning to the beach at Dunwich, just north of Minsmere RSPB Reserve, then back inland again before once more heading for the coast at Walberswick, where the beach was finally interrupted by the mouth of the River Blythe, marked by a couple of breakwaters on either side. The river could be crossed by a rowboat ferry to Southwold harbour.

I've stopped a little ahead of myself this evening, at Kessingland, but will return to Southwold tomorrow morning. I got a bit confused when I reached the campsite as it shares an entrance with the Africa Alive safari park. The touring field lies between two huge wind turbines, which make a deep swishing sound as the blades rotate. It could be an interesting night, I may wake up to the sound of anything from wind turbines, to lions, to Arnold the Aardvark sniffing around outside.

Southwold to Lowestoft
Monday, 16th April

I wasn't woken up by any strange noises during the night, but something had pooped down the side of the van, probably African in origin.

I made my way to Southwold and parked near a pier, next to a boating lake and a row of colourful beach huts. Southwold pier is my favourite so far, it was littered with metal works of art, from simple things like signs and noticeboards, to an elaborate water clock and a quantum tunnelling telescope, which in hindsight I wish I had tried. There was also a building exhibiting 'The Under The Pier Show', a collection of coin operated pier amusements with a difference. You could try your hand at crossing a motorway using a Zimmer frame, be frisked using the Autofrisk, view an instant eclipse, or decide the fate of a cute little lamb with 'Pet Or Meat', to mention a few. I tried the 'Gene Forecaster 2012', which had a pair of scissors hanging from it that you could use to cut some hair to place in the machine's sensor (I figured it would probably work just as well without). It informed me that I was human, although it did hover over weasel for a while, I had the musical ability of the fifth Beatle, and it was 100% certain I would die sometime before 2133. Once it had finished I collected my '3D printout' from a chute, a fortune cookie containing a piece of paper stating "share your happiness with others today". I felt cheated.

I walked along the promenade, beneath the gaze of a large white lighthouse, to Gun Hill, where I could see towards a harbour and beyond to Sizewell. On the way back to the van I walked through the town, complete with market stalls, and stocked up on groceries.

A little way north of Southwold was Covehithe, where the road towards it took a sharp hairpin and scarpered back inland again almost before I knew it. I stopped just before the hairpin and walked to the remains of the Church of St Andrews, built in the fifteenth century. The church was so large that eventually the parishioners could not maintain it and instead constructed a smaller church inside it, using the remains of the original, but keeping the tower. A footpath near the church led to an attractive stretch of sandy beach and low cliffs, within the Benacre National Nature Reserve, with another porcine holiday camp behind it.

Moving on again I headed north towards Lowestoft and stopped in the southern suburb of Pakefield, a couple of streets in from the beach, and walked along the beach to Lowestoft, the most easterly town in Britain. Lowestoft sat either side of Lake Lothing, a narrow strip of water that ran inland for about a mile and a half. North of the lake was the main town and high street, south of the lake was a harbour, South Beach, and a pier. Walking back along the beach I passed a family walking their dog. Whenever they threw a ball the dog would take a running dive onto it, throwing up a cloud of sand.

Tonight I have taken leave of the coast for a while, crossed the border into Norfolk and headed inland to Norwich, where I shall be taking a 'city break' tomorrow.

Norwich

Tuesday, 17ᵗʰ April

Happy Birthday to me,
Travelling by the sea,
I've seen a lot of coastline,
But today's all city.

Thank you, I wrote that myself, but feel free to use it if you ever find yourself celebrating a birthday in a city while travelling around a body of land along its coast.

I have to admit that I've missed certain aspects of city life, such as cinemas and certain restaurants, all things that I got used to while working away from home for many years. So, once I'd unwrapped a few presents and cards that I'd brought with me, had some more bacon, pancakes and maple syrup, showered, put my hair up and grabbed my umbrella, I walked the 20 minutes or so into the centre of Norwich and straight to an Apple Store, to see if I could find an iPad. Which I did, and I think we'll be very happy together. I spent a while in the store, using the WiFi to set up the iPad and trying to figure out why my laptop had stopped communicating with the interwebnet recently. Both missions accomplished, I headed for a cinema.

Movie Review No 1: The Hunger Games - I haven't

really kept up to date with the recent releases, but I'd heard good things about this one, so I thought I'd give it a go. It was an interesting idea, and fairly well done, with a few weak bits here and there, I didn't really buy into the love interest side of it. I understand it's the first in a series of teen books, similar to Twilight, so the end was left sufficiently hanging to allow the next film to pick up from. Overall, not bad, but not a classic.

Next I headed to Starbucks for some coffee and cake and uploaded the last few days of blog entries, all in just enough time to head back to the cinema again. I know, I've OD'd on movies today!

Move Review No 2: The Cabin in the Woods - I only heard about this film yesterday, and all I knew about it was that Joss Whedon was the producer and it was possibly a horror film. As one of the finest writer/directors alive today (in my opinion), if Joss Whedon saw fit to produce it, that was good enough for me. Now I'm not really a fan of horror films because, well, they scare me, and as a rule I don't like being scared, so I was a little apprehensive to begin with, but was soon comforted by the presence of familiar actors from The West Wing and Dollhouse, among others. And I have to say I thought it was excellent, a few scares here and there, but not always in the obvious places, and a completely original (as far as I know) spin on the horror genre, very clever and very funny in places. If you liked Shaun of the Dead or Drag me to Hell, both horror comedies (homedies, comedors?), I think you might like this one.

All that was left to do was stuff my face, so I found a Pizza Express and (very predictably for me) indulged myself with a sloppy giuseppe and a tiramisu, before walking back home again to spend some quality time with my iPad. Happy days!

Oh yeah, Norwich. I couldn't really tell you much about it as I didn't spend much time outside today, but it has several shopping centres, a very neat looking castle, at least one big church, and a cathedral that I only saw the spire of. Seemed to me like it warranted a closer look sometime.

Still Norwich
Wednesday, 18th April

The temptations of the city have been too great.

Late last night, while still synching the iPad with my laptop, I decided that there was still plenty of lazing around to be done, plus I'd forgotten to pick up a few things that I wanted yesterday. So I extended my stay at the campsite for another night and walked back into the centre of Norwich.

I figured it would be wrong not to take a closer look at Norwich's fine cathedral, so after spending a while browsing iPad covers in John Lewis I found the cathedral and walked around it while the heavens threatened to open up (with rain, not fire and brimstone or anything biblical like that).

From the cathedral I walked to The Forum, an impressive large glass building where I'd spent a bit of time yesterday in a cafe and Pizza Express. It also housed shops, a library, a tourist office and BBC East among other things. The area and steps outside are often used for public performances, including skaters and free runners. If only I'd found space to bring my rollerblades. Opposite The Forum was St Peter Mancroft Church and to one side was City Hall, with its columns and tower.

I took the opportunity to sit in the same cafe as yesterday for a while with my laptop, but not wishing to spend the entire day there I headed back to Starbucks in The Castle Mall for lunch (no drink), then to Costa Coffee in the Chapelfield centre for a drink. I like to think that I don't favour any particular global capitalist coffee house chain. To round off the afternoon I thought I might go and see a film for a change.

Movie Review No 3: The Pirates - The latest stop motion offering from Aardman Animations, guaranteed to be packed full of more than you can take in in one go. You kind of need to watch their films in slow motion to spot all of the things going on in the background. I personally think that Aardman have yet to better the Wallace and Gromit films, but this wasn't a bad effort, most of the jokes worked and the characters were likeable enough, apart from a Queen Victoria that looked disturbingly like Stewie from Family Guy and did things that are not in any of the history books that I've read.

All in all, the centre of Norwich was quite nice, a mix of the new and the old, seemingly with a church or cathedral around every corner, and enough cinemas, cafes and restaurants to keep a passing traveller happy.

Anyhoo, I'd better head back to the coast tomorrow, otherwise I'll end up as a penniless film critic living on the streets of Norwich.

Gorleston-on-Sea to Horsey
Thursday, 19th April

By 9:30am this morning my feet were back on sand and the sun was poking through the clouds. I'll be honest, after two days being re-immersed in the ways of the city it had seemed a bit strange to be coming back to the coast again, but as I stood on the wide sandy beach at Gorleston-on-Sea, with a few patches of blue in the sky and waves breaking in front of me, I couldn't help but smile. A smallish dog, a pit bull terrier I think, ran up to me and buried its head between my feet. Its owners said it was just trying to get its muzzle off, but I took it as a 'welcome back'.

The journey from Norwich had brought me across The Broads, I could see for miles across the flat countryside, and around the top of Breydon Water. Along the way I'd passed what looked to be several windmills, but I believe they were windpumps. More on that subject later.

Before setting off from Gorleston I phoned Southend County Council to pay my parking fine from the other week, I'd already tried several times to pay online or using their automated payment system, neither of which worked, but that's computers for you, who needs them?! In some way it seems I had pleased the Gods of parking. I was about to curse the four hour minimum payment on a street at the seafront in Great Yarmouth when I noticed that there was already a ticket in the machine. When I picked it up I found it was good for another three hours. Somebody had very kindly used an hour of their ticket and put it back in the machine for the next person to find.

Blimey, Great Yarmouth had a big beach! It also appeared to be trying to compensate for something, having not just one but two piers, neither of which actually reached the sea on account of the size of the beach. I can't say I've ever walked to the end of a pier at beach level before, you could maybe try it at Weston-super-Mare but you'd probably be up to your neck in mud by the time you reached the end. I walked along the beach from one pier to the other, the second one was considerably shorter but had obviously been longer in the past, with the wooden supports still standing in the sand.

Great Yarmouth had clearly seen better days, but it was still a slumbering giant waiting to be woken by an influx of summer holiday crowds. It had some interesting old buildings, many of which had been spoilt by turning them into amusement arcades or crazy golf centres, and the Marina leisure centre was a pretty monstrous building, particularly when seen from the beach. With nearly two hours left on the parking ticket, I put it back in the machine in the hope that someone else would make use of it.

Much quieter was Caister-on-Sea, with nothing much more than a beach, a lifeboat station and a small beach cafe, looking out to an offshore wind farm. Great Yarmouth had been one of the places I had wanted to see, for no other reason than it had a wind farm, but by the time I got there I'd already seen plenty of them.

It was pouring with rain when I pulled into a car park next to a cafe at Winterton-on-Sea, so I went into the cafe to pay the parking fee and sit down with a cup of tea. The owner waived the parking fee as the weather was miserable. By the time I finished the tea the rain had eased up and I walked out onto a very nice beach, backed by grass covered dunes. Most of the pebbles on the beach had little ramps of sand behind them, sheltered from the wind that must blow fairly frequently. Not far inland from the beach was the church of Holy Trinity and All Saints, with a 40m tower that could be seen for miles around.

Next I stopped at Horsey Windpump, and I'm so very glad that I did. The pump was a National Trust site, it was built in 1911 to pump surplus water away from the surrounding agricultural land, into Horsey Mere. In 1938 Horsey was flooded after high tides and strong winds created a half mile breach in the sand hills. The floods covered 15 square miles for three months before the breach was plugged. The salt water killed many of the fresh fish and the land could not be farmed for five years.

Next to the windpump was a small National Trust shop and tea rooms, with just enough room inside for a small round table that a single group of people could sit around. While presenting my membership card for access to the windpump the guy inside told me a little about the pump and mentioned a walk to a nearby beach where sixty to seventy seals were currently in residence. After looking around the pump and walking to a viewpoint on Horsey Mere I returned to the shop and ordered a toasted tea cake while he found a little laminated map of the route to the beach to lend me. Much to my dismay, as he put the tea cake in the toaster the electricity all went off. I was about to panic, "what about my tea cake?", when he executed a practiced sequence of standing on chairs, opening cupboards and flicking switches, followed by digging a burnt currant out of the toaster before switching it back on again, this time without tripping the power.

Buttered tea cake in hand, I set off for the beach, where

I was assured I would find seals three minutes to the right. The path brought me to a concrete sided gap in the sand hills, like walking into a stadium. As I emerged on the other side I saw a head bobbing around in the sea in front of me, then I noticed half a dozen seals lying on the beach in front of me, then I noticed more, and more, in front of me, to the left and to the right. I couldn't believe my eyes and laughed out loud, it was a feeling that's hard to describe, but I'd felt the same while on a boat surrounded by dusky dolphins, or stepping out of a helicopter onto virgin snow high in the New Zealand Alps, a feeling of amazement and joy to be so close to nature.

There must have been a hundred or more seals, some of them in the water, most of them lying on the beach, a couple of them playing Swingball. One of them had the hiccups. I got as close to them as I dared. Every time I moved forward, left or right, a number of heads would come up and watch me for a few seconds, then sink back down again. Only one young seal seemed spooked and moved away, the rest continued with their playing or sunbathing. At one point I realised there was a small seal by some rocks, half the distance away than the others. They were all different colours, some white, some brown, some mottled grey, some black, some a mixture. I must have spent nearly an hour there, moving between several groups on different parts of the beach. What a fine way to end an afternoon.

Back at the tea room I handed in the map, thanked the man profusely and drove a few minutes down the road to Walnut Farm, my stop for the night just short of Waxham, at the end of a very satisfying day.

Waxham to Overstrand
Friday, 20th April

Passing through Waxham first thing this morning, I stopped briefly at the Waxham Barn, the longest thatched barn (54m) in all of Norfolk by all accounts, before parking at Sea Palling.

A friend had recommended a bacon and egg bap at Sea Palling, after a walk or some jet skiing. Jet skiing struck me as unlikely, not in these heels, but a walk I could do. I foolishly paid for an hour's parking before glancing around and realising that nothing was open, not the jet ski centre, not the cafe, not the ice cream parlour or pub. I tutted at myself and walked towards the road that rose up and dropped down again as it passed through a gap in the sand hills.

As it turned out, an hour wasn't enough. The beach was another lovely sandy affair, with breakwaters not far from shore that must provide a pretty calm area of water to practice your jet skiing. I walked a while in both directions, passing several people out walking their dogs. By the time I got back to the van, with my fingers crossed, the cafe was open and served up a very nice bacon and egg bap with a cup of tea.

I drove towards Eccles on Sea and was nearly crushed as a dustbin truck tried to pull out of a junction that I was turning into, swinging around my nose as I hurriedly reversed to get out of its way. Eccles on Sea was also a collection of narrow roads that ran around a community of bungalows and chalets, nestled below the sand hills. There was nowhere obvious to stop, and with another dustbin truck heading my way I left the area and instead continued to Cart Gap, where I walked out onto another fine stretch of beach. Several fishermen were casting a couple of rods each from the beach, one of which reeled in a small flatfish while I was returning from walking back towards Eccles on Sea.

Onwards again, this time stopping at Happisburgh (pronounced 'Hazeborough') and first taking a look at the Church of St Mary and its 30m tower. You get used to seeing large church towers as you pass through Norfolk. Walking along a road towards the beach I came across a little kitten on one side of the road. Ignoring the car that was slowly heading towards us it crossed the road half way and rolled over on its back for a good ticklin'. I half encouraged and half dragged it out of the road while the driver kindly avoided running the dozy little bugger over.

At the end of the road, beyond a new car park, a striking red and white striped lighthouse stood in a field to warn ships of dangerous sands about seven miles from the shore. Walking down a sand ramp onto a beach, I entered a slightly surreal and eerie world. Happisburgh was disappearing into the sea at an alarming rate. Parts of the beach were strewn with the remains of buildings that used to stand on top of the cliffs. Looking up at the cliffs I could see pipes and hoses emerging from them, or the dangling ends of fences overhanging them. A flight of stairs on the beach led up to nothing, standing alone behind the remains of failed sea defences. What at first glance look like rock in the beach and the cliff turned out to be clay that crumbled when touched. After centuries of fields, a lighthouse, and the entire village of Whimpwell sliding into the sea, the steel and wood sea defences were built in the late 1950s and new bungalows and caravans started to appear on the cliff top. In the 1980s and 90s the defences began to fail and homes were lost. I spoke to a couple on the beach that been here earlier this year and claimed to have climbed the flight of stairs and walked onto the cliff. If anyone is in any doubt that we are merely tenants on this planet, and Mother Nature is the landlord, Happisburgh is a prime example.

I kept an eye out for kamikaze kittens as I walked back to the van and continued along the coast road, stopping briefly at Walcott, passing a blot on the landscape that was Bacton Gas Terminal (where gas was being piped ashore from North Sea wells up to 65 miles away), taking a quick walk onto a beach at Mundesley, and parking up in Overstrand, hoping to be rewarded with a cafe. When I reached the top of the cliffs, with a path leading down to a beach, the Cliff Top Cafe shone like a beacon. But first I walked down to the beach for a stroll around one of many small sections separated by fences running into the sea.

While looking towards the pier at Cromer I spotted something on the beach, near the sea, which turned out to be a radio controlled flying wing, drifting around in the surf. I picked it up and set it down on the steps at the edge of the beach, intending to leave it there, when I noticed it had a name and phone number written on it. Unfortunately I had no signal on my phone, but the area code was a local one, so I decided to take it with me and call when I got a signal. Having put the wing in the van I grabbed my book and returned to the Cliff Top Cafe for some coffee and cake (lemon cake, homemade, very nice). Before I left I asked the cafe owner if they would be happy to keep the wing if I called its owner later and told him where it was, which they were, and they offered me their landline to call from, which I did and left a message. Retrieving the wing from the van, I took it back to the cafe and set off for a campsite in West Runton, where I'll be spending the next two nights.

Along the way my SatNav tried to take me down a track ending with a stile, but a wise old man with a dog spotted my predicament, realised that I was probably looking for the campsite, advised me to throw my SatNav in the bin, and set me off again in the right direction. Back in signal range I called the owner of the flying wing again, who had just arrived home after looking for it. Apparently he'd lost it at about 10:30am this morning when he reckons it got up to about 2,000 feet and disappeared into cloud.

Cromer, West Runton and Sheringham
Saturday, 21ˢᵗ April

I eased myself upright this morning, had some breakfast, did the washing up and went to the back of the van to take the bike off.

When I arrived at the campsite last night I had pulled up to the entrance barrier, hoping it would lift so that I could drive in and stop near the reception. It didn't, so I reversed back out and aimed just off the road so that I didn't block it. Then I hit something. It wasn't a solid hit or a crunching stop, so I figured I had just caught the curb.

At the back of the van today I found that the rearmost of the three 'trays' that you slot the wheels of a bike into had been bent towards the van and up a little. I guess that's what I must have hit. Oh well, my bike was in the middle tray, so no real damage done. I may leave the third tray as a reminder or just take it off completely some time.

The campsite was at the bottom of the only hill in Norfolk, which I struggled up, with the chain jumping around on the sprocket, something was clearly wrong. I pulled over on the main road into Cromer and examined the bike. I would never describe myself as a cyclist, but nevertheless I am a disgrace to cyclists, and my bike is a disgrace to bikes, through no fault of its own as I've neglected it for nearly the entire time I've owned it, leaving it unwashed to rust and gather dust. One of the chain links had seized up and wasn't running over the sprocket properly. I worked it to loosen it up a bit and smugly congratulated myself as I cycled off again with everything seemingly okay.

Within half a mile it was playing up again, but I locked it up when I got to Cromer and resisted the temptation to throw it into the sea. The seafront at Cromer had a quiet dignity about it. It did have an amusements arcade and a funfair, but both were small and innocuous. Curved steps at the entrance to a pier lay at the bottom of two paths that criss-crossed each other up to the Hotel de Paris. Near the end of the pier was the Pavilion Theatre, and behind it was a lifeboat station. To the east of the pier a number of small fishing boats sat on trailers, attached to their own personal tractors, and beyond them were beach huts beneath the cliff.

I got back on the bike and cycled west through East Runton to West Runton. I smiled ruefully as I passed a sign saying 'West Runton, please drive slowly'. There wasn't much danger of my disrespecting this, unless I managed a Marty McFly manoeuvre and grabbed the back of a pickup truck. The beach at West Runton was wide and largely covered with chipped rocks and chalk, which in turn were largely covered with seaweed. It's a popular area amongst beach fishermen and fossil hunters. I only had a boy look and didn't find any fossils, although as I was leaving I stumbled across the remains of Delia Smith's career at the bottom of a broken wine bottle. I thank you.

I continued west to Sheringham, where I cycled east along a promenade and back, before locking up the bike and noticing a sign saying not to cycle along the promenade, but hey, if I'm ever to become a proper cyclist I must learn to ignore all road signs and pay no regard to pedestrians. I walked into the Submarine cafe, which stank of chip oil, and walked straight back out again. Instead I tried the Funky Mackerel cafe, which was much nicer and offered a sofa with a view of the sea. I topped up my reserves with coffee and cake (carrot, lovely), though I was sorely tempted by the Bombay mix flapjacks, while hoping that the drizzle that had started since I'd sat down would soon stop.

It was still raining when I left, but within a couple of minutes the sun was out as I walked onto the beach and west along the promenade to a lifeboat station. A bank of grey rain clouds was heading towards me at speed, so I turned back towards the bike, taking a look at some of the murals and sculptures along the seawall that formed part of the Sheringham art and sculpture trail. As I got back on the bike it started to rain, and quickly got heavier, so I stopped again to put on my waterproofs and pull the hood over the top of my crash helmet as the heavens opened up. I was thankful that I had had the common sense to pack leggings, as well as wear waterproof walking shoes, and lenses instead of specs. To be fair this was the first drenching that I'd taken since leaving home, I'd not been caught outside in anything heavier than light rain for more than a couple of minutes up until then. Truth be told, it felt pretty good, kind of liberating. I pedalled as hard as I could while motorists - my kin, my brethren - neither soaked me from puddles nor outright killed me.

I smiled gleefully as I passed a sign saying 'Cromer, come in and get dry son' and within a minute or so of stopping the rain faded away. I did a lap of the town while I dried off, passing an impressive church with its 'mine is larger than yours' 49m tower, before finding another cafe to sit in for a while. When they closed at 5:00pm I went to find something to eat.

My Norfolk dietary advisor had recommended fish and

chips in Cromer, so I did a quick Google search for Cromer's best fish and chip shop and Mary Jane's Fish Bar and Restaurant came out top. The restaurant side of it was full, so I ordered cod and chips from the takeaway and took them onto the pier. And very nice they were too.

I managed to get back to the campsite without getting wet again and had a second triumph when I counted all the socks into the washer and counted them all out of the dryer. I think it's fair to say I've quashed that particular uprising.

Weybourne to Wells-next-the-Sea
Sunday, 22nd April

I got going a little earlier today and had a look at the shingle beaches at Weybourne and Salthouse, with a brief stop in between at Weybourne Camp, home of the Muckleburgh Collection of military equipment. I don't think it was open, and even if it had been I wanted to move on to other things today, but I was able to drive into the car park and have a quick look at some of the tanks, planes and rockets on display outside. I do like a nice bit of military equipment, me.

Just short of Cley next the Sea (pronounced 'Cly') I stopped at the Cley Marsh visitor centre, slowly filling up with twitchers armed with cameras and telescopes, and asked where the best place was from which to walk to Blakeney Point. As it turned out there was a car park visible behind the beach, just across some of the reed beds and lagoons that made this area one of the foremost nature reserves in the country.

I drove the short distance to the car park, put on my walking boots and trousers, packed my waterproofs in my rucksack and set off along the three or so miles of shingle spit that was Blakeney Point. Walking on shingle was hard going, so wherever I could I kept to the landward side of the beach and walked across any grassy areas that I could find, passing a rusty old boat along the way, but my calf muscles were soon burning. After nearly an hour I came to some firmer ground leading up to sand dunes that took me back towards the sea. As I came over the top of the sand dunes I found that I had been walking parallel to a nice firm sandy beach for some time, but hadn't been able to see it because I was on the other side of a rise. I walked out onto the sand and carried on going until I could make out a large number of seal shaped objects lying on the beach ahead. To my left a fenced off area prevented access back onto the sand dunes, which was presumably a breeding area for Turns that had been mentioned in the visitor centre. There was nobody at all in front of me as I carried on towards the seals, and I'd only seen three other people since I'd started walking.

The beach was pretty vast and there were groups of seals all over it, some much further away beyond a channel of water. I didn't get particularly close to the nearest group, but many of them started moving away from me towards the sea. They clearly weren't as comfortable in my presence as the seals at Horsey, and with no-one else around I felt that maybe I shouldn't have been there. Most people will see the seals from boat trips, run out of Blakeney and Morston. I backed away a little and took a handful of photos from a distance, before starting the three miles back to the van. This time I kept to the seaward side of the beach, which remained sandy for about half way before becoming shingle, but still a little easier going than the other side of the rise.

The sky was a mix of blue, fluffy white clouds and angry black clouds, but the rain pretty much held off. When I got back to the van I returned to the visitor centre for a pot of tea and a Norfolk pasty. I'm not entirely sure what was in the pasty, it may have been seal, but it was quite nice. I noted the crinkly top seam design, as opposed to the Cornish side handgrip.

I was feeling a little tired after my exertions, and had some visiting to do later, so I made a couple of brief stops at Blakeney Quay and Morston Quay before finding the Pinewoods caravan park at the far end of the sea wall in Wells-next-the-Sea. Showered, shaved, and looking vaguely respectable, I walked a mile and a half back along the sea wall and past a quay to meet some of my distant relatives, John and Diana, in a bungalow that John was born in, in a yard where they once owned and operated a small soft drinks business. Diana is my second cousin once removed, uhhh, I think, or something like that. I spent a few hours with them and consumed plenty of tea and homemade ginger cake and scones (regular and cheese) before walking back to the van as the sun went down. The boats that had been lying on the sand earlier were all now floating.

I will drop in to see John and Diana again tomorrow, to return the Tupperware that I came away with containing more cake and scones, and possibly to pick up the half loaf of homemade wholemeal bread that I forgot to take with me.

Wells-next-the-Sea to Hunstanton
Monday, 23rd April

I wasn't particularly impressed with Pinewoods, it was much more expensive than most places I'd stayed at so far, the facilities were nothing special, and the reception wasn't open when I went walking at 8:30am, wanting to ask if I could extend my stay an hour until midday. What it did have going for it, however, was that if you turned left out of the entrance you were a short walk from a beach, just beyond an inner harbour that had been built to house boats that serviced the wind farms along the coast.

Anyone that has been to Wells-next-the-Sea and didn't at least pop their head around the end of the sea wall to have a look at the beach has missed half the charm of the place. The beach was backed by forest and beach huts, raised on stilts to try to protect them from storms, which together with their verandas and staircases make them unique amongst the many beach huts that I'd seen so far. A small lagoon had been formed behind a couple of sand dunes with a large sandy beach running off to the west. It was a beautiful place to be as the clouds started to break up a little.

I walked along the beach until it became Holkham Beach and the main body of it turned into salt marshes within

Holkham National Nature Reserve. During the summer the Household Cavalry bring their horses to the beach and gallop them through the surf, which must be a sight to see. I walked through the forest to a car park and a driveway that led to the main road and towards Holkham Hall. I had intended to carry on into Holkham Hall so I gave Pinewoods a ring to ask about extending my stay. They were going to charge me £8, which would allow me to extend until 6:00pm, even though I only needed an extra hour and they weren't exactly busy. So I told them to forget it, made my way back along the main road and along the sea wall to complete a square circuit, and drove off at 11:00am.

I dropped into John and Diana's again to return the Tupperware and have a cup of coffee, before driving to Holkham Hall and parking just outside the grounds. As I walked into the grounds I came across several hundred fallow deer, in two large groups under several trees. They were just off the driveway in an open area, but if I got too close to them they would leap up in unison, ready to run off until I backed away again. Holkham Hall was a Palladian mansion built for the Earl of Leicester in the eighteenth century, set in vast grounds with a lake, the deer park, a walled garden, a cafe and the Bygones Museum, where you could see antique cars, tractors, steam engines and tools, among other things.

From Holkham I drove to Burnham Overy Staithe, a creek that ran off Burnham Harbour, sat on a bench and dined on a packed lunch of scones and cake, before moving inland a little to see how the other half lived in the leafy little market town of Burnham Market. Originally three separate villages, Burnham Sutton, Burnham Ulph and Burnham Westgate, the central village green was flanked by shops and cafes, and was also a bit of a car park. Burnham Thorpe, to the southeast, was the birthplace of Lord Nelson (he was just known as Nelson at the time).

I had a quick look at a small muddy harbour at Brancaster Staithe then headed for a beach at Brancaster. Parking was £4 for the day, but when I told the attendant I only needed half an hour, if that, he gave me a 'nudge nudge, wink wink' kind of look and charged me £1 if I promised not to tell anyone. £4 for a day was probably a good deal, the beach was ma-hoo-sive, stretching about a mile and a half in both directions. But being a man of my word I took a few photos and was on my way again to make one more quick stop at Holme next the Sea, where I walked across a golf course to a beach from where I could just about make out the coast of Lincolnshire across The Wash.

I'm spending tonight in Hunstanton, where the choice was pretty much limited to holiday parks. The first one I tried did not accept single occupancy campervans (huh?), the first time I've come across that particular prejudice, so instead I ended up next door to it at Manor Park and have paid only £5, half the price quoted on their website. I'm hoping I won't suddenly find out during the night why it was so cheap.

Hunstanton
Tuesday, 24th April

It was a pretty miserable start to the morning today, raining constantly, so I decided to take an extra night in Hunstanton and spend most of the day indoors.

I packed my waterproofs, laptop, iPad and some books in my rucksack and set off towards the seafront, walking north along a promenade in the wind and rain until I could no longer feel my head. When I reached the cliffs (more on those later) I turned inland to find the Golden Lion Hotel to see if it had somewhere to have a coffee, which it did, and to thaw my face. This was not a location plucked out of thin air, I have an app that tells me where all of The Cloud WiFi spots are, and this was the only one in Hunstanton.

A comfy sofa in the bar became my very relaxing home for the next four and a half hours, including coffee, lunch and a pint, while I mercilessly hammered the WiFi uploading the recent blog entries and downloading stuff onto the iPad. When I eventually left, it was starting to become a decent day outside, so I carried on walking north along the top of the cliffs, past an old lighthouse and onto Old Hunstanton beach, which I walked along heading back south.

The cliffs at Hunstanton were formed of three distinctly different coloured horizontal layers, known as the White Chalk, the Hunstanton Formation (red chalk) and the Carstone. On the beach I found the remains of an iron hulled ship, encrusted in barnacles. I sat on the beach at the base of the cliffs for a while, listening to fulmars and pigeons nesting in the cliff face behind me, writing today's entry.

When I stood up again I realised that the rock I had been sitting against, and those around it, had all at one time been part of the cliff face, and as I walked up the steps to the promenade I noticed a sign saying not to sit at the base of the cliffs. Oh well, I do like to live dangerously now and again. I walked around the centre of Hunstanton assessing the restaurants, which didn't take long, before I settled on the Northgate Indian Restaurant, which I can recommend if you're in the area and have a hankering for an Indian.

When I came out again, sufficiently full of chicken biryani, it had turned into a nice evening. Hunstanton isn't the most attractive place, the promenade is backed by the usual amusements and funfair rides, but it's not a bad place for walking along the beach on a warm sunny evening. On the way back to the van I passed a couple of amphibious vehicles, one of them called 'The Wash Monster'. As I sat in the van writing this I noticed the sky turning orange outside, so I grabbed my camera and walked back to the promenade, but had missed the best of the sunset by a good 10 or 15 minutes.

My right walking shoe has started to squeak.

Heacham to Sandringham
Wednesday, 25th April

It was raining again this morning, and has been pretty miserable all day. I got up a little earlier than yesterday but sorted myself out with a bacon sandwich rather than rushing to leave the campsite.

I travelled a short distance to Heacham and had a quick look at the beach, then continued to Snettisham where I sat in the van for a while, a few hundred yards from the beach, but couldn't be bothered to get out in the rain. Instead I got going again towards my main stop and ultimate destination for the day, Sandringham.

I had intended to get settled in at the campsite within the Sandringham Country Park before wandering around the grounds, but it wasn't even midday yet so I went straight to the visitor centre car park and sat in the cafe for a while. It was still raining when I came out, so I had a quick loop around the shop and decided I may as well pay the entry fee to go into the gardens, house and museum. I stood in the shelter of the entrance gateway for a minute or so waiting for a little blue shuttle car thingy to save me getting wet on the way to the house. I and five others that were waiting squeezed into the six seats and were driven a winding route to the house entrance. One side of the car was open, so I still got wet.

Sandringham, if you didn't already know, is the Queen's Norfolk country retreat, and the private home of the British monarchs since 1862. The Sandringham Estate covers 8,000 hectares, of which the Country Park takes up 240 and the house and its gardens take up 24 of those. Overall responsibility for the management of the estate, which employs over 200 people including farmers, foresters, gamekeepers and gardeners, lies with The Duke of Edinburgh, since 1952. The gardens have been open to the public since 1908 and the house has been open since 1977. The house was built in 1870 by the Prince and Princess of Wales, later to become King Edward VII and Queen Alexandra.

On entering the house I was asked to switch off my phone and not to take any photos, but there were no security checks or fuss. The rooms were grand, as you would expect, full of family portrait paintings and tapestries, as well as armour and weapons from India and Afghanistan, presented to the Prince of Wales in 1876. One of the corridors contained gun cabinets full of shotguns and rifles, many of which have presumably been used by royal hunting parties, and several excellent candid sketches of the Queen, The Duke of Edinburgh, The Princess Royal and Prince Charles, among others, out on such hunts. It was kind of weird to stand in the rooms where the Royals congregate en masse at Christmas, to dine and open their presents, where the Queen puts on a plaid Slanket and plays Angry Birds, The Duke of Edinburgh complains about the quality of the jokes in the Tom Smith crackers, and Prince Charles puts on one of the gold party crowns, dreaming of the real thing.

The museum housed several miniature cars, some of them used by the Queen and Prince Charles when they were young, a number of royal automobiles, including wooden panelled 'shooting brakes' that were used for transporting hunting parties around the estate, as well as other royal memorabilia. With the rain still coming down when I left the museum, I had some lunch in a tea room next door. By the time I had finished the rain had finally stopped for a while and I spent a bit of time wandering around the gardens.

I've been in the campsite since mid afternoon, keeping out of the rain showers, which have given way to patches of blue sky at times, and performing some of my occasional chores, such as emptying the toilet. It's not all glamour, you know.

Castle Rising to Freiston Shore
Thursday, 26th April

I didn't really see much of the coast today, the southern shore of The Wash tended to hide away from the road behind sea walls and acres of marshland and mudflats.

I started the day at Castle Rising, with a quick look around Castle Rising Castle, which by all accounts is one of the most important twelfth century castles in England (to whom, I'm not entirely sure). The largely intact castle stood behind earthworks and a dry moat.

Continuing south, I stopped for a while in King's Lynn, on the banks of the River Great Ouse, which flowed into the southeast corner of The Wash, mostly to sit in a cafe. I also spent five minutes in an O2 shop waiting for a torrential downpour to pass. I didn't find a huge amount to see in King's Lynn, nor did I look particularly hard, if I'm honest. Purfleet Quay was a small, quiet quay, and the docks at the northern end of the town were hidden behind closed gates and fences.

I crossed the Great Ouse and watched the trip meter tick over to 2,000 miles, just two and a half miles before I crossed the border into Lincolnshire. Just before crossing the River Nene at Sutton Bridge I turned north and drove a couple of miles along the east bank to what looked like a small lighthouse, but together with its twin on the other bank was actually built to mark the opening of the channel of water. From there you could follow the Peter Scott Walk for 10 miles along the banks of The Wash and the Great Ouse to West Lynn. I took a few photos of the area, including three geese not far from me and returned to the road, where I met an amateur birdwatcher, excited because we'd both just seen three Barnacle Geese. I was very happy for him.

The bridge over the Nene to Sutton Bridge stood out as an unusual looking design, and the same design was carried into the village in the park benches, notice boards and anything else it lent itself to. I headed up the west bank of the Nene and back towards The Wash just above Gedney Drove End, where I was able to walk to a sea wall and just about see as far as The Wash. There were several rusty looking ships out on the sand banks, which looked like wrecks, but were actually placed there as targets within a bombing range that made up part of RAF Holbeach. That maybe explained why I'd seen or heard several fighter jets overhead the last few days. The single track roads in this area caused me some concern as they were flanked by wet grass, which I spun my wheels and nearly got stuck in while passing the one and only other car that I came across.

From Gedney Drove End I travelled a fair distance, across the River Welland, which flowed into the southwest corner of The Wash, turning north through Boston and past the cranes that lined its busy docks. As I headed towards an RSPB Reserve at Freiston Shore a strong wind blew in and swept rain across the road. I sat in the van in the car park for a while until a break in the clouds brought the rain to a stop, for a while at least, and I chanced a walk toward the sea wall. Once again The Wash was still some distance away across the marshes, but I could see back to one of the bombing range ships. Along the path was a hide, with a door that made a sound like a goose when I opened it (I mean when I opened the door, not when I opened a goose). Now you've probably already noticed this, but ornithology isn't really my bag. I can tell the difference between a bird and, say, a dog, but making out individual varieties isn't my strong point. Anyway, there were some ducks, some gulls, a few sheep (I know, I know, these are more like dogs), a couple of condors and I believe I saw a phoenix in the distance, steaming slightly.

Tonight's campsite, The Chestnuts, is just up the road from Freiston Shore, but they neglected to tell me on the phone that I needed a special adapter if I wanted to use their power, which I don't have. Oh well, this will be my first night without hookup, it will be interesting to see whether I can make it through the night without running out of electr

Wainfleet All Saints to Gibraltar Point
Friday, 27th April

I think I may have passed a milestone this morning by bringing up the half century of banging my head against different parts of the van. The cumulative effect could render me brain dead before I make it home again.

Without too many options for seeing the coast today I instead headed straight for Wainfleet All Saints, best known in these parts as the home of Batemans, at Salem Bridge Brewery. When I arrived there was still an hour or so before the visitor centre opened, and a couple of hours before the first tour, so I decided to carry on to Gibraltar Point National Nature Reserve to see if I could find the sea.

Although Gibraltar Point was several miles south of Skegness, I got to it by driving into Skegness and out again to the south, but I didn't spoil anything to come as it didn't take me past the Skegness seafront. It was raining when I got to the visitor centre, so rather than get wet walking out to the beach I sat in the cafe for a while, passing some time before I went back to Wainfleet All Saints.

I paid for the brewery tour and sat in the bar at the bottom of an old windmill until my tour guide turned up for my own personal tour. This was only her second tour, so she read most of the information from her notes. We spent half the time talking about travelling, she had raised a daughter as a single mum and was now taking a tourism degree and intended to move to California in four years time. The tour was therefore pretty informal and one of the brewers joined us at one point to give a bit more information about the vats of wort, where the yeast fermentation was forming a thick foam. I put my nose over the top of one of them, took a deep breath and nearly passed out from the CO_2, before the guide showed me the 'regal wave' used to waft the smell towards your nose with your hand. The brewery was founded by a local farmer, George Bateman, in 1874, when he sold his nearby farm in order to rent a building for brewing, buying the lease a year later. Today the brewery has passed through four generations of the Bateman family. In 1998 Batemans entered into a partnership with the local council and brewed a range of beers named in honour of Jolly Fisherman, the official 'mascot' of Skegness, who was 90 that year.

Once I'd had my free half pint of XB, plus an extra sample for being such a good touree, I made myself some lunch in the van and, with the rain having stopped, drove back to Gibraltar Point. I walked through the nature reserve to a beach, and the sight of yet another wind farm. I've noticed a strange phenomena with the wind turbines over the last few weeks, when I first see them they appear to be fairly close, but by the time I've reached the beach they appear to be smaller and further away. I can't really explain this, unless they're shy and not yet used to being around humans. I couldn't walk south towards Wainfleet Harbour, the beach was roped off to protect the many species of birds that inhabit the area, so instead I wandered aimlessly north, following a stream for a while. By the time I got back to the visitor centre I'd seen several albatross, a family of sea pipits and a nervous looking dodo. Just behind the visitor centre several yachts and fishing boats were moored on the banks of the Steeping River, winding its way towards Wainfleet.

I drove back through Skegness again, stopping a mile and a half south of it at the Pine Trees campsite.

Skegness

Saturday, 28th April

What a lousy morning, for once the weather forecast was wrong in a bad way, it wasn't supposed to rain in Skegness today but it rained all morning. All I managed to achieve by midday was to move from the grass pitch that I was on last night to a hardstanding pitch at another site just over a mile away. I didn't want to risk getting stuck in the sodden grass, and a change is as good as a rest, apparently.

I've made no secret of my dislike for the holiday parks, and come the summer I will do my best to avoid them, but I couldn't help but be impressed by the scale of Southview Leisure Park, from the waterfalls at the entrance, to the large hotel, to the size and neatness of the whole place. Shortly after I'd parked up I grabbed my umbrella and walked the mile and a half or so into the centre of Skegness, trying most of the way to prevent the umbrella from turning inside out. When Jolly Fisherman was introduced to Skegness in 1908, he came with the slogan 'Skegness is SO bracing'. If by bracing they meant wet and windy, then yes, yes it is.

Not wishing to spend the whole afternoon exposed to the elements, I found some lunch and headed to the Tower Cinema, which was a bit of a blast from the past. A queue steadily formed at the box office within an amusements arcade, which didn't open until about five minutes before the film was about to start, and I took my seat in an old fashioned auditorium that reminded me of the Gaiety in Bristol, many years ago.

Movie Review No 4: Avengers Assemble - If a bit of mindless, noisy, effects driven nonsense is what you're after, this does the trick nicely, bringing together many of the Marvel comic characters that have had their own films up until now, such as Ironman, The Hulk, Captain America and Thor. It's a bit confusing at times, not helped by the sound quality in the cinema being a little poor, with plenty of 'that would never have happened' moments, but the special effects are stunning and there were a few laugh out loud moments. Having previously bigged up Joss Whedon, this wasn't his best project (director and co writer), but this isn't his usual kind of fare, and I'm willing to bet he did a better job than Michael Bay would have done. Most notable (and annoying) moments were the film coming to a sudden stop for an intermission (seriously? they still do that?) and being switched off while the credits were still rolling, which for a Marvel film probably meant missing something at the end of the credits.

As I ventured back out into the sunlight the rain had stopped but the wind had picked up, so I took a quick sandblasted stroll along the seafront, past a funfair and amusements and out to the end of a pier, which fell somewhat short of the sea, possibly less so when the tide is in. I then found myself a Chinese restaurant, ate as much as I could eat from the 'all you can eat' buffet, and got a stitch while walking back to the campsite.

The squeak from my right walking shoe has got louder, I may have to consider earmuffs, or hopping.

Ingoldmells to Mablethorpe
Sunday, 29th April

I'm pretty used to the sound of the rain during the night, my bedroom at home is in a loft conversion with two skylights, but my bedroom doesn't generally rock around in the wind, which was a new experience in the van last night. The good weather of a few weeks ago seems like an age away at the moment.

Back on the road again, in the wind and the rain, I made my first brief stop of the day at Ingoldmells, at a car park with access to a windswept beach. Driving through Ingoldmells I passed a large Butlins, site of the very first Butlins in fact, built in 1936.

A little further north was Chapel St Leonards, which for the most part was a solid mass of funfairs, amusements and caravan parks, which I passed through before eventually coming to what seemed to be the village itself. I parked near a green and walked past a couple of smaller amusements flanking an entry ramp to a beach. It was getting difficult to walk into the wind without getting blinded by sand, and by the time I'd walked a short distance on the beach and back I was brushing the sand off my jacket.

I stopped again just down the road at Chapel Point,

where I had a cup of tea and a tea cake in a cafe just below a sea wall. I seem to have developed a taste for tea cakes, if I see them on a menu I can't help myself. The owner didn't charge me for the car parking, and was getting a bit fed up of going outside to put the parking sign upright, just to watch it blow over again.

I followed the coast road for a few miles, with the sea wall not far to my right. Now and again a road would branch off towards a car park and a gap in the sand dunes, so I stopped at one of them, the imaginatively named Huttoft Car Terrace. The coast road came to an end at Sandilands, where I again pulled over for a quick look at the beach.

The road dipped inland briefly before coming back to the coast at Sutton on Sea. I was going to have lunch in the Beach Bar on the promenade, but it had that kind of 'local' feel to it where everyone stopped and looked at you as you walked in, so I backed out again, couldn't find anywhere else open, and made myself a sandwich in the van.

It was barely 1:30pm, but I'd had enough of the weather by now so I headed straight to a campsite at Mablethorpe and settled myself in to spend the rest of the day lounging around in the van.

Mablethorpe

Monday, 30th April

Sunshine. Glorious sunshine. I knew it was only supposed to last for today, but it was nice to wake up to the sun shining through the skylight, rather than rain falling on it.

My dad and his partner Christine were coming to see me today, from my sister's in Coventry, so I had most of the morning to lie in, cook some breakfast and make myself vaguely presentable. I even cleaned the van (inside, not out) before they arrived at about 11:30am, bearing gifts.

My laptop ran flat several days ago and refused to recharge, but fortunately in time to ask my dad to get hold of a new power adapter, which he did, and thankfully it worked, otherwise that would have been the end of this blog. In reality I'd have probably got on a train to London to visit the Apple Store, which would have been no bad thing. They also brought some birthday presents from my sister and her partner Steve, and my mail, which contained another Premium Bonds cheque and a reissue form for a previous Premium Bonds cheque that I never cashed, because I either lost it or it was stolen out of my car along with my SatNav. At this rate I'll be a millionaire in, uhhh,

3,333 years.

After a cup of tea my dad drove us to the beach at Mablethorpe, which we walked along from north to south. I'd noticed a large ship close in to the shore when we arrived, which by the time we got nearer had been joined by a small tug. The tug hitched itself to a boom floating in the sea and towed it towards the larger ship, which picked up a cable attached to the boom and drew it in, eventually drawing the end of a large pipe into a connection at the bow. By this time we'd reached an area of the beach that was closed, with a digger and a couple of bulldozers waiting by another length of pipe on the beach. This was all part of the Lincshore beach nourishment scheme, which has been going since 1994 at a cost of around £6 million a year. The large ship was a dredger, which sucks up sand from defined areas of the seabed, around 20 miles out to sea. It then returns to the shore, connects to the pipeline and pumps a mixture of sand and seawater through the pipeline onto the beach, where the seawater runs off back into the sea and the sand is moved around the beach by the bulldozers. The sand is used to change the profile of the beach to ensure there is a certain depth of sand above the clay, thereby preventing damage to the sea defences and reducing the risk of flooding to a coastal plane that stretches along 20km of coast and up to 15km inland.

We had some lunch in a cafe behind the beach, next to a boating pond and miniature railway, followed soon after by a 'treble 99', unique to that particular rock and ice cream emporium, with vanilla, strawberry and (blue) raspberry ice cream, before returning to the campsite. My dad showed me some of the photos from their recent 'around New Zealand in a campervan' trip before they set off for King's Lynn for the night, from where they'll continue on to visit John and Diana in Wells-next-the-Sea.

I'm expecting to wake up to rain again tomorrow.

Mablethorpe to Cleethorpes
Tuesday, 1st May

DANGER
DO NOT TOUCH ANY MILITARY DEBRIS IT MAY EXPLODE AND KILL YOU

I was right, it was raining when I woke up, but it had cleared by the time I got underway and didn't come back until the afternoon.

I had a quick look at a beach at the northern end of Mablethorpe, which was largely untouched by civilisation, before heading into an area known as the Saltfleetby Theddlethorpe Dunes and stopping at Crook Bank. As I walked from the car park and along a track out onto a beach I walked straight into the wind. Fortunately it was blowing sand along the surface of the beach rather than up into the air, which made the large beach look alive with clouds of drifting sand, fleeing the sea to hide in the dunes and bushes.

A little further on I stopped at Saltfleet and walked along marshes to get to another windswept beach lined with sand dunes. The beach was at the southern edge of another bombing range and the red flags were flying. I was hoping to see the beach suddenly explode in a burst of napalm, but no such luck. I did come across a dead seal though, assuming it was a seal and not one of the local naturists that I had been warned about, with a leathery hide tough enough to protect them from the weather.

Further on again I came to Donna Nook, near RAF Donna Nook, right in the middle of the bombing range. It was pretty obvious that you couldn't walk out towards the beach, and not wishing to be exploded or killed in any way I surveyed the area from dunes above the car park. Now I'm not a military expert, but I'm pretty sure that the 'tanks', made from what looked like driftwood and netting, were probably no match for a fighter jet, it didn't seem like a fair fight.

I headed towards Horse Shoe Point and was turned back by a private road before coming across the proper route a little further down the road. By the time I got there the rain had started again, so I made myself some lunch in the van and abandoned the idea of another walk to another windswept beach with pretty much the same view as the others. Instead I continued on to Cleethorpes. Driving into Cleethorpes from the southeast, I passed a theme park, the Lakeside leisure park, a shopping area, cinema etc, before coming to the traditional seafront, promenade and pier. I parked on the promenade and walked towards the pier. My umbrella wasn't helping much in the wind, so to get out of the rain I ducked into a nice looking cafe and took refuge behind the largest slice of banoffee pie I'd ever seen.

Once the rain had cleared (and the banoffee pie was no longer offering any protection anyway) I came back out and wandered around the seafront. Several large ships were working their way along the Humber estuary and there were a couple of fixed structures out in the mouth of the river. These were Haile Sand Fort and Bull Sand Fort, built during WWI and used as anti-submarine defences during WWII, when they were regularly attacked by the Luftwaffe.

I've travelled a few miles inland for the night, to Prospect Farm near Waltham.

Grimsby to Barrow Haven
Wednesday, 2nd May

I spent most of today looking for the River Humber, kind of. I made my way into Grimsby, parked on a street not far from the docks and walked towards a marina and the Dock Tower, only to realise it might be easier to drive a little closer. As I was parked outside of a Post Office I spent a bit of time doing some 'admin' before parking nearer to the marina. It wasn't very easy to get to the river, from what I could see, so I instead moved inland for a stroll around the People's Park, before moving towards the town centre, where I found myself a cafe with WiFi and settled in with a coffee. I stopped at a few other places to take in some more of Grimsby's 'sites'.

From Grimsby I drove to Immingham, from where the Pilgrim Fathers set sail in 1608 to Holland, on their way to the New World. Today Immingham was mostly a massive docks and industrial complex, which I drove around aimlessly in search of the river bank, only to be turned around each time by the entrance to a dock yard or private complex. I eventually gave up and headed for New Holland.

On the way I happened to pass Thornton Abbey, so I pulled over to make some lunch and took a quick look at the English Heritage site. Not much of the abbey remained, but a large ornate gatehouse still stood at the entrance.

At New Holland I came across another docks area so I passed on through and stopped instead at Barrow Haven Wharf, where I was able to follow a footpath and finally stand on the banks of the River Humber. On the far side was Yorkshire and Kingston upon Hull. To my left was the Humber Bridge, looking very similar to the Severn crossings back home.

I'm finishing the day in Scunthorpe, not strictly on the coast, but I'm catching up with a friend, Jane, and staying a night. We reminisced about work days gone by, Jane cooked a lovely meal, which I've stolen the recipe for, watched a film on a TV almost large enough to be a cinema screen, tried without success to replicate a scene in a photography magazine, and sat up late drinking Dr McGillicuddy's Fireball Whisky in honour of a ski trip to Big White in Canada just over five years ago now.

Hull to Spurn Head

Thursday, 3rd May

I left Scunthorpe just after 10:30am this morning, after a breakfast of croissants with raspberry and kirsch jam from the rather delicious Tregunter range (www.tregunter-online.co.uk), which I may have mentioned before. I said my goodbyes to Jane and left with a goody bag full of chocolate and beer, woohoo!

Once I'd stocked up on groceries and diesel I was soon on my way across the Humber Bridge and into the East Riding of Yorkshire, working my way through the outskirts of Kingston upon Hull, better known as just 'Hull' to its mates. I drove around the centre for a while before I found somewhere to stop, not far from a park that stretched out in front of the treble towers of the Hull Maritime Museum. From there I walked along the side of Princes Quay, a shopping centre set on stilts in the former Princes Dock, to a marina (formerly the Humber Dock), a lock and the riverside. There were a number of interesting structures in Hull, such as some of the bridges over the River Hull and in particular The Deep, an award-winning angular aquarium capped with a pyramid of glass.

In 2005 Hull was named the worst place to live in the

UK, based on crime, education, employment, environment and lifestyle. I'm not sure how much of the city I saw today has been redeveloped since then, but it didn't seem like such a bad place to me, the city centre area was quite nice.

The van was still intact when I got back, another plus, so I set off through the many roundabouts on the eastern exit from the city and eventually found myself driving through fields, many of them vivid yellow with oilseed rape, until I reached Stone Creek. From there I could look out from the creek across the Humber to the docks at Immingham and the Dock Tower at Grimsby.

From Stone Creek I moved on towards Spurn Head. The Spurn peninsula jutted out at a right angle into the mouth of the Humber, three miles long but only about 10m wide in places. You could walk along the peninsula for free, or pay to take a car to Spurn Head, but no dogs were allowed, not even in cars, to help protect the wildlife. The road to Spurn Head was not the best I've travelled, the first mile was a kind of paved track that juddered the hell out of myself and the contents of the van, at times almost covered by sand drifts that nearly brought me to a standstill. The road covering the remaining distance was okay, with speed bumps and passing points. An old lighthouse stood amidst the sand dunes, flanked on either side by sandy beaches. Right at the end of Spurn Head was a jetty where the pilots that guide larger ships into the Humber depart from, and a lifeboat. The crew of the lifeboat are the only full time crew in the country, living at Spurn Head with their families.

I've now started working my way up the coast and away from the Humber, stopping for the night at Elmtree Farm at Holmpton, where I have a small site to myself again.

Withernsea to Hornsea
Friday, 4th May

I made my first stop this morning at Withernsea, where I parked on a side road and walked to a lighthouse that I had seen above the houses. The lighthouse was a little unusual in that it was in the middle of the town, rather than on a cliff or headland, and had been converted into a tearoom and a museum for the RNLI, coastguard and local 1950s actress Kay Kendall. A beach in front of the town was a long sandy affair below a seawall, upon which sat a turreted folly.

Not far up the coast was another example of the territorial struggle between land and sea. Seaside Road at Aldbrough came to an abrupt end at a barrier of concrete and red road signs. Just the other side of the barrier the road disappeared, fallen away along with the cliff that it rested on. I took a walk along the top of the cliff and came across fissures several metres from the cliff edge. It's only a matter of time before they become the new cliff edge. In addition to the signs warning of coastal erosion were MOD warnings of unexploded ordnance, due to the RAF Cowden bombing range to the north. All in all, Aldbrough was not a good place to hang around for too long.

At Mappleton, attempts had been made to preserve the cliffs and protect the village by piling lots of rocks along the base of the cliffs. Time will tell whether these do the job or not.

It wasn't yet midday when I arrived in Hornsea, so I walked along the seafront before finding myself a table at The Marine pub for a drink, some lunch, and some quality comfy seat time. Unfortunately it was drizzling with rain when I emerged and headed for Hornsea Mere, the largest natural freshwater lake in Yorkshire. The eastern shore near the town was home to the Hornsea Sailing Club and a cafe, where you could sail or hire rowing boats. I had to have a bit of patience when driving in and out of the car park, to allow the geese time to decide which direction they were going to amble out of my way.

When I reached Skipsea and drove towards the sea I came across another barrier across the road, and again at Barmston, so I called it a day and retreated half a mile back along the road to Rectory Farm, home for the night.

Bridlington to Reighton Gap
Saturday, 5th May

Today started with rain, followed by hail, before it settled down into a pretty nice, sunny day, if a little chilly in the wind.

I turned off the main road at Fraisthorpe (another of the many 'thorpes' in this part of the country) to head towards a beach, and saw several kites in the air as I approached, no doubt whisking kite surfers across the waves, but I didn't like the look of the parking charge when I got to the end of the track so I turned back to the main road.

Not much later I entered the town of Bridlington, looking for somewhere to park on the street, but not too far from the seafront, eventually finding a spot a short walk from the harbour. The harbour neatly divided the seafront into the North Beach and South Beach. Most of the town along North Beach, and the harbour itself, sat upon and behind a sturdy stone seawall, overlooking a large sandy beach. There were plenty of fishing boats and a handful of yachts moored in the harbour, but not a huge amount of people around given it was a bank holiday. After walking around the harbour area and taking a look at both beaches I found a cafe to sit in for a while. I'd only intended to have a drink, but I caught a whiff of a toasted tea cake and couldn't help myself from ordering one. I am weak.

A couple of miles north of Bridlington I stopped at Sewerby, where a land train ran along a path through a large grassy area at the top of the cliffs, before moving on to Flamborough Head. I parked by a lighthouse and spent a couple of hours wandering along the coast in both directions. All around the headland the sea had shaped the chalk cliffs, creating little bays, stacks and holes. Steps led down to a little beach at Selwicks Bay, where you could play a giant game of othello with the chalk and rock boulders. I was standing on the beach, taking a photo of a chalk stack, when a man asked me whether I had noticed the seal, which I hadn't. Very close in to the beach, a grey seal was swimming back and forth in the foaming surf, watching the people on the beach, who were in turn watching it. A little further north, walking along the edge of a links golf course, the cliffs were covered in birds, perched along the horizontal striations.

Next I decided to stop at an RSPB visitor centre at Bempton Cliffs, where there were no doubt even more birds, but for the second time today I was put off by the parking charge. The signs even had the cheek to suggest that £5 was a bargain 'for everyone in your car'. Fine if you're a large Catholic family on a day out. Anyway, I had major lens envy from some of the massive zoom lenses being carted around, so probably best I didn't stick around. I suspect that the best views, and varieties of birds, would be seen by boat from Bridlington during the summer.

I made one last stop at Reighton Gap, which seemed to be slowly sliding into the sea judging by the amount of concrete and brick lying on the beach, and the dirty brown surf washing off the muddy cliffs.

My stop for the night is near Hunmanby Gap. As well as a small campsite, Springfield House is a home, a cattery and dog kennels. I expect I will hear more from the dogs than I will see of them, but I have met Leo, the owner's Springer Spaniel, who was very keen on taking a good look around the van.

Filey to Scarborough
Sunday, 6th May

I spent a very pleasant morning in Filey today, a lovely little place to be in the sunshine. There weren't many people around as I walked along the promenade, and most of those that were out and about were towards the northern end of the beach, on their way towards Filey Brigg. On my way to the beach I passed a 12ft high rust coloured sculpture of a fisherman. Entitled 'A High Tide in Short Wellies' and created by Ray Lonsdale, a steel fabricator from Durham, the sculpture was bought by a local philanthropist, Maureen Robinson, at a reported cost of £50,000.

Filey Brigg was a promontory about a mile long, the first half of which, known as Carr Naze, was high cliffs, and the second half, known as the Brigg, was low rock that is covered at high tide. Once I got off the beach and onto the Brigg there was a concrete path to follow out to the end, although I could pick my own route across the rocks and through the rock pools. The Filey Bay side of the Brigg was fairly calm, with a few fishermen trying their luck, but the other side was being battered by the waves, sending spray high into the air in places and streaming water across the surface of the rock. From the Brigg I could look back across

Filey Bay to the town, or north to Scarborough.

I spent a while on the Brigg before walking back along the beach, which was a lot busier by then. The RNLI had brought their lifeboat down onto the beach for people to take a look at. Just after I reached it they towed it back up onto the seawall, past little gift shops and amusement arcades, and manoeuvred it back into the lifeboat station, where quite a few people were milling around. I got myself a cup of tea and a tea cake from a nearby cafe and sat outside in the sun. Seeing as it was nearly lunchtime I also treated myself to a Nutella and banana crepe, which I took down onto the beach while watching some donkeys plying their trade.

I wanted to get to my campsite in Scarborough fairly early in the afternoon, so I made one more stop at Cayton Bay. The sea was fairly busy with surfers and kayakers, while people walked their dogs or played ball games on the beach, or explored a couple of gun emplacements looking out to sea. In the next bay around, the stacked houses of Scarborough were bathed in sunlight.

When I got to the campsite I had an overdue shave and a decent shower, sorted a few things out and set off for a mile and a half walk to see Diz, another friend. Once again I have been fed very well and got to spend some time catching up and talking about travelling. Diz's son, Kieran, dropped in for a while too and we talked about photography and set the world to rights.

Scarborough (campsite)
Monday, 7th May

So, what can I tell you about Scarborough? Well, nothing yet, because I didn't leave the campsite today.

I'm staying at one of the Club Sites that are run by the Camping and Caravanning Club. They're generally large sites with good facilities and cheapish WiFi (which may or may not reach wherever you happen to be parked), so you know what you're going to get and I generally stay at them if I'm passing one. The staff are friendly and usually endearingly confused when it comes to their computer system.

When I (loosely) planned this whole trip I had a number of things that I wanted to spend time doing, one of which was studying photography, both in using a camera properly to take the photos and then using software to edit them. I've been going for two months now and I haven't done any of these things. I've taken hundreds of photos but I've not learnt anything new yet, and as far as I'm concerned they've all been holiday snaps rather than photos to be proud of.

While at Jane's in Scunthorpe the other night, trying to recreate a photo in a magazine, I decided that I needed to set some time aside to at least do some post processing, and

I bought a magazine the following day with some techniques and tutorials. Listening to Kieran talk about photography last night reinforced my decision to spend today doing almost nothing but some good old fashioned learning.

So once I'd done my occasional chores, which are pretty easy on the Club Sites, I settled down in the van to learn some stuff. It's fair to say I have soooo much to learn, and I suspect that I won't end up spending a whole lot of time learning much more while I'm travelling around, but it's at least got me started and I'll hopefully do a lot more once I'm home again.

Normal service shall be resumed tomorrow, I'm intending to spend the day looking around Scarborough, and I can't write an entry without mentioning food, so I shall just say that I made use of the onsite chippy (some of the Club Sites have fish and chip vans that turn up, though I've not used them, and this one has a proper chip shop cafe that also serves breakfast) to grab some sausage and chips. The homemade steak pie looked very nice, I may have to consider going back again tomorrow.

Scarborough

Tuesday, 8th May

It was supposed to be a decent day today, so I packed my rucksack, crossed the road outside the campsite and walked through a couple of fields to the coast, where Scarborough lay before me to the south, beyond a small headland.

Scarborough was spread out along two bays, separated by a larger headland with a ruined castle on it. As I walked onto the first headland I could see down into North Bay and the large beach stretching across it. I continued past a Sea Life centre and a row of the cleanest, most vividly coloured beach huts that I'd come across, before stopping and sitting outside a cafe half way along the bay. No need to tell you what I had. A little further along from the cafe was a larger than life sculpture of a man entitled 'Freddie Gilroy and the Belsen Stragglers' sitting on a park bench. The sculpture was in the same style as the fisherman at Filey, and not surprisingly was also by Ray Lonsdale, and had also been purchased by Maureen Robinson after it had been temporarily loaned to the town. I got talking to an older couple about how this kind of sculpture had so much more meaning to us than 'modern' art.

Royal Albert Drive, which ran along the seafront, became Marine Drive as I walked around the central headland, with the castle hidden by the high cliffs above me, bringing me to a harbour and South Bay. I've had a squeak free day wearing my walking boots today, but I walked past a woman with two squeaky shoes. I felt her pain.

The harbour was split into two sections, with Vincent Pier running between them. At the end of the pier were a lighthouse and a statue called the 'Diving Belle' of a woman about to dive into the sea. Erected in 2007 by the Civic Society, the statue represents Scarborough's regeneration and future in the 21st century, while a sister statue in the town centre, the 'Bathing Belle', represents Scarborough's past as the first sea bathing resort in the UK.

Overlooking South Bay was the impressive Grand Hotel, built in 1863 and once a Butlins Hotel. It boasted four towers, 12 floors and originally 365 rooms (to represent the seasons, months and days of the year) and was built in the shape of a V to honour Queen Victoria. After looking around the harbour I walked up onto the headland to take a look around the castle, and get some great views across both bays. While in the grounds of the castle it started to rain, which typically hadn't been forecast, but shortly after walking back down to South Bay the sun had come out again.

I walked along the seafront, past a couple of groups of donkeys and the Grand Hotel, underneath an ornate footbridge, past the Rotunda Museum and turned back on myself to head into the town centre, where I wandered through the main shopping street and back across the neck of the castle headland to the same cafe in North Bay that I'd stopped at in the morning.

After I'd had a late lunch, and written most of this entry, I walked back along the cliffs to the campsite, nearly getting back to the van before it briefly rained again. I like

Scarborough a lot, what I saw of it had a nice feel about it and made for a nice day out in the (mostly) sunshine. My day would have been finished off nicely with a steak pie from the campsite chip shop, but I found it wasn't open on Tuesdays. Dagnabbit!

Cloughton Wyke to Robin Hood's Bay
Wednesday, 9th May

I got back in the driver's seat today and headed to a small car park at the end of a lane at Cloughton Wyke. From there I walked a mile or so along the coast back towards Scarborough, to Long Nab, site of a disused coastguard lookout point and a view of Scarborough Castle. It was the first time I had exerted myself for a while, with a few small dips and rises in the path, on a fairly warm and muggy morning.

I moved on to Ravenscar, parking at a National Trust visitor centre near the entrance to Raven Hall Country House. The visitor centre had displays and information about the nearby Peak Alum Works. Alum is a chemical, made from shale and used to cure leather and fix the dye in textiles. I walked down a track from the visitor centre and came upon a fine view across Robin Hood's Bay. Beneath the shale quarries in the cliffs were the remains of the alum works, which were used from 1650 to 1862. Creating alum is a lengthy process, part of which requires ammonia, which was provided by shipping in barrels of human urine. It was said that poor people's urine was better as it was not the product of such strong drink. Good to know.

Ravenscar was renamed from Peak in the early twentieth century when an entrepreneur decided that a town should be built around the village to take advantage of a railway line being built from Whitby to Scarborough. The construction of roads and sewers commenced and plots of land were sold, but less than a dozen houses were built because the location was too exposed and precarious. They clearly didn't think it through.

Once I'd walked back to the van, my legs having lost any fitness they gained on the southwest coast, I drove to the delightfully named Boggle Hole. From a small car park I walked down a road past a YHA to a little bay. Walking out onto a beach, I had Ravenscar to my right, with the country house high up on the cliffs, and the village of Robin Hood's Bay to my left. I pottered contentedly around the beach for a while, on and around shelves of rock and across many streams and pools. I had intended to drive to Robin Hood's Bay, but it was so close it would have been crazy not to walk there along the beach.

Robin Hood's Bay was at one end of Wainwright's Coast to Coast walk, the other end being St Bees, about 190 miles away. It reminded me of Cornwall, set around narrow streets on a steep hill, with people milling around the cafes and ice cream parlours. I fancied staying awhile, but I hadn't brought a book or my iPad with me, and I wasn't sure whether the route back to Boggle Hole would be cut off by the tide, so I took my time climbing up through the village looking for a suitable cafe and parking spot before walking back to the van. It took me as long to drive through the winding lanes back to Robin Hood's Bay as it had taken to walk there, but I parked up at the top of the village and found my preferred cafe for the rest of the afternoon. The owner noticed me using the iPad and switched on the WiFi for me, which was nice of him.

I'm spending tonight at Beacon Farm in Sneaton. From

my pitch I can see across fields and forest to Whitby and the ruins of Whitby Abbey overlooking it.

Whitby to Runswick Bay
Thursday, 10th May

It was a bit grey this morning, and some heavy rain overnight had turned my grass pitch into a bit of a swamp. Fortunately I was able to get off it without spinning my wheels and drove into Whitby, parking above the cliffs to the north of the town. One of the first things I noticed about Whitby were the imposing ruins of a Benedictine abbey overlooking the harbour on the southern side, along with the church of St Mary.

I walked down the side of the cliff to some beach huts overlooking a beach largely hidden by the tide, then along to the harbour area. Above the harbour was a statue of Captain Cook, who trained as a seaman there, and an arch made from the jaw bones of a whale, a sign of Whitby's whaling past. The original arch was erected around 1853, with a replica donated by Norway in 1963 and the current bones by Alaska in 2003.

I walked out onto the harbour wall before heading into the town and over a bridge across the River Esk. Leading from the harbour up to the church and abbey were 199 steps. I counted them on the way back down again, but on the way up I took them two at a time and was cheerfully accused of cheating by an elderly woman sitting on a bench half way up.

The abbey, now an English Heritage site, must have been an incredible sight when complete, even as a ruin it was impressive. Bram Stoker was inspired to use it as a backdrop to Dracula, a fact that Whitby does not shy away from using for tourism, particularly among the Gothic community, playing host to the bi-annual Whitby Gothic Weekend for the past 17 years. After wandering around the abbey and up and down the harbour streets I made myself comfortable in the Hatless Heron for a relaxing lunch.

After lunch I moved on and stopped just up the road outside Sandsend and walked along a beach towards a row of houses perched up on a sea wall. I crossed a stream on a small road bridge before returning to the beach and walking between the remains of some groynes, long since rotted away by the sea.

On the way back to the van I stopped at the Woodlands Cafebar near the road bridge, for a cup of tea in a very mellow atmosphere to the sounds of Hotel Costes. It started to rain when I left the cafe and was coming down fairly hard by the time I was on my way to Runswick, where I encountered the worst moments of the trip so far, and hopefully the worst overall.

I've mentioned before that my SatNav occasionally throws me a curveball, but in general has been fine. Well, while looking for the Runswick Bay Caravan and Camping Park I turned into a road into Runswick Bay that was the steepest I'd been down by far. If I'd have been skiing I would have tightened my boots, and probably my sphincter, before proceeding. At the bottom of the hill was a mini roundabout where I was instructed to turn left into a narrow road in the middle of the small village. I should have bailed at this point but this took me down another short steep dip and up the other side into a dead end with a lorry parked at the end of it. I had no obvious way of turning around so I started reversing along the narrow road, with a fence and a drop off to my right. As I was reversing the lorry started towards me so I pulled into a small passing spot to let it pass, thinking it must have been able to turn around at the end of the road. In hindsight I think it must have reversed all the way up, but I found a small turning spot and proceeded to do a 73 point turn. At one point I heard what sounded like a crunching sound from either the bike rack or the fence, or possibly both, and for a while I thought I was going to get wedged at an angle that I couldn't get out of. If you've ever seen the original Austin Powers film, there's a scene where he tries to turn around a golf buggy type cart in a narrow corridor, which I found hilarious. Not so hilarious today. Anyhoo, I managed to get it turned around and approached the short dip before the mini roundabout in second gear, which wasn't going to work, so I ground to a stop and changed down to first, but the handbrake wouldn't hold at that angle and I rolled backwards (in a controlled manner, I would like to think) into the dip before I could stop and try again in first. Finally, to get back up the hill out of Runswick Bay I had to keep in first gear and pray that I didn't come to a halt.

I found the campsite on the main road outside the village. There were no staff around so I parked up on an empty pitch and kind of hoped to get a free night as compensation for having to accommodate my heart in my mouth while trying to get here. The right hand side of the rear most tray of the bike rack is ever so slightly bent, which led me to wonder whether the fence came off worst.

Someone from the campsite turned up in the rain and took my payment, unfortunately, but once I'd had some dinner, washed up and had a shave, the rain had stopped. Seeing as I hadn't actually taken much notice of Runswick Bay, and I'm at one of the few campsites so far that's an easy walk from the coast, I decided to walk down to the bay to take a proper look around. Even walking down the hill was vaguely alarming, but considering the place is a death trap, it was quite a nice little bay, with a bunch of houses clustered around the bottom of the cliff at one end, and a couple of isolated buildings at the other end. I climbed some stairs up to the road that had been the scene of my troubles earlier on, and along to the turning circle and fence. When I found a little piece of red plastic sticking out of the top of the fence I realised with dismay that it hadn't been the bike rack that had made contact (I must have done that somewhere else). Below me on the other side of the fence was a slightly larger piece. The walk back up the hill was a complete bugger.

At first I couldn't see anything wrong with the rear lights on the van, until I noticed a hole in the plastic on the side, but not in an area that had any effect on the lights. Just for the hell of it I superglued the little bit of plastic back into place.

Staithes to Redcar
Friday, 11th May

It was a pretty miserable day today, weather wise, raining or drizzling for most of the day. The Scandinavians have a saying, "there's no such thing as the wrong weather, just the wrong clothing". True enough, but I prefer "there's no such thing as the wrong weather when you're sat in a cafe".

I made my way towards Staithes, but I knew it was a narrow, steep little village so I avoided any similar mishaps to yesterday and parked in a car park at the top of the hill down to the harbour. Walking down into the village there were very few people around, giving the impression that the place hadn't really woken up yet. Staithes was a nice place, set around a narrow valley and river that ran down to the sea, ending at the harbour, with a lifeboat station and several fishing boats. I can imagine it would be very nice on a sunny day.

I drove on towards Skinningrove, passing a large potash mining complex at Boulby, but pulled over in Loftus to get some groceries and sit in a cafe for a while. When I arrived at Skinningrove there wasn't a whole lot to see, and my umbrella was turned inside out by the wind, so I got back in the van and carried on to Saltburn-By-The-Sea. It was still raining a bit when I got there, but I walked a little along the seafront, to a pier and a funicular railway that ran a short way up the cliff to the town, the oldest hydraulic cliff lift in the country, by all accounts, built in 1884. A handy cafe provided a coffee and a dry view over the beach.

At Marske-by-the-Sea the rain had eased up so I took a walk along the beach, which stretched to Saltburn to the east and to Redcar to the west. Another shower on the way to Redcar cleared the air for a while and patches of blue sky started to appear. Major construction work was underway all along the seafront at Redcar, building new sea defences, so much of the seafront was behind fences or scattered with cranes and diggers. Redcar was certainly not the best place I'd seen in Yorkshire, but it was the only place where I had seen a group of penguins stood in front of a bandstand. Coatham Sands to the west of Redcar was a fairly nice stretch of sand, it was just a pity that it had a backdrop of chimneys and steel structures spewing fire and smoke. I believe the fire was from a blast furnace at the SSI steelworks and was relit in April, bringing steelmaking back to Teesside. Former owners Tata shut it down two years ago.

It started to rain again, so I sat it out in a popular high street fast food chain (not that one... or that one... yup, that one) for a late lunch before returning to the van and driving to Margrove Park campsite near Boosbeck, where the heavens opened once again.

Middlesbrough
Saturday, 12th May

The rain had passed by the time I got up and a nice day was on the cards, so I celebrated with a bacon sandwich before leaving the campsite and heading into Middlesbrough.

I had plenty of time so I parked in a cinema complex and walked through some very quiet roads to take a look at Middlesbrough's 'sight', the Tees Transporter Bridge, not far from the Riverside stadium, home of Middleborough F.C. I'd been told by several people to go and see the Transporter Bridge, and they'd all given me descriptions of it that I didn't really understand. As I walked towards it and saw the bridge like structure suspended high above the River Tees I figured that the whole thing must be raised and lowered, but as I got closer it didn't look as though that could be the case. When I stood by the river bank and looked beneath the structure I finally understood how it worked. Suspended below the 'bridge' was a yellow gondola that could be loaded with up to 200 people, nine cars, or six cars and a minibus, and winched across the river. On reflection, it was a lot of bridge for not a lot of load, but it's one of only about a dozen of its kind in the world. The bridge celebrated its centenary last year, but was closed after some structural defects were discovered, although it should be open again soon.

I spent a while sat in a cafe on the high street before it was time to go and visit some friends, Greg and Alison, at their home in Eaglescliffe about 15 minutes away. Ali's kids, Bailey and Amara, whom I'd met at Greg and Ali's wedding almost exactly a year ago, were around when I arrived but were both going away for the night, so I was kindly offered accommodation. I had planned to finish the day near Hartlepool, but I was tempted by the offer. Also in residence was Cornelius the Miniature Schnauzer, or Cornie for short.

Greg, Ali and I went for a late lunch in nearby Yarm, a very nice place with good restaurants, cafes and mostly independent shops, and busy with cars as a result. In the sleepy afterglow of a good meal and a pint of beer I made my mind up to stay the night. The rest of the day was spent drinking cups of tea in the garden, before having a curry and relaxing in the living room with a few drinks, where we were joined by Glen from next door, whom I'd also met at the wedding and had been spending the afternoon building a shed while being teased by Greg and Ali across the fence. Cornie spent his time either curled up and snoring in his bed or moving between whoever would pay him the most attention.

Seaton Sands to Hartlepool
Sunday, 13th May

After a leisurely breakfast with Greg, Ali and Cornie, I set off again late in the morning, crossing the River Tees into County Durham and passing the Transporter Bridge on the Port Clarence side of the river.

I drove along the edge of Seal Sands, which was part urban wildlife haven, home to birds and seals, and part petro-chemical works, which dominated the landscape along with a nuclear power station. I stopped at a car park at Seaton Sands and walked across a golf course to a beach at the mouth of the Tees. Once again the beach had a backdrop of the steel works at Redcar and the full glory of industrial Teesside. There were quite a few people out and about on the beach, on a windy but decent morning, walking dogs or riding horses.

Just up the road I stopped briefly at Seaton Carew and stepped out onto a beach before carrying on to Hartlepool and parking up. Hartlepool seemed to be largely supermarkets and retail parks, but with a large marina. Permanently moored in Hartlepool was the HMS Trincomalee, a frigate built in the early eighteen hundreds and now fully restored. I didn't find a whole lot else to see on a quiet Sunday so I sat myself in a cafe for a long lunch.

With kick-off of the final day of the Premiership looming, I decided I would head for a campsite at Crimdon and settle down to listen to the inevitable outcome of Manchester City taking the title away from Manchester United, they only needed to match United's result, although there was still a faint glimmer of hope for United. I accidentally overshot the turning for the campsite but found that the next turning went towards a beach, so I parked at the end of the road and grabbed my radio. Just as I stepped out of the van, United scored at Sunderland. Early days, but I paced nervously up and down the beach until, just before half time, City scored at home to QPR. Surely that was it, QPR weren't going to get a goal back. So I got back in the van and drove back up the road to the campsite. There was no-one around to take my money, so I parked in the field but realised there were no electric hookups. I consulted my Camping and Caravanning Club and Caravan Club books and found another campsite just up the road. Just before I set off again QPR did the impossible and equalised, advantage United. I missed the turning to the campsite, so drove a little way up the road to find somewhere to turn around. As I got back heading in the right direction again, Joey Barton, the utter clown, got himself sent off for QPR, surely it was now just a matter of time before City went back in front. I reached the campsite and had a chat with the owner, who thought the grass was probably too wet, so I set off back towards the first campsite. As I turned back onto the main road, QPR scored! In my state of joy and disbelief I drove past the entrance to Crimdon Dene Holiday Park, so I turned around and came back again, quickly got out of the van, checked to see if they had a spare pitch, which they did, paid and parked on the pitch in time to listen to the end of the games. United were still 1-0 up, City were 2-1 down, I couldn't believe it, United were going to retain the title after seemingly throwing it away in the last few weeks... and then City scored twice in injury time.

Numbness.

I kind of lost the will to do anything for some hours after that, apart from general moping and sulking. A lot of chocolate shall be consumed this evening.

Horden Beach to Whitley Bay
Monday, 14th May

By 'eck, that was a long day, with plenty seen and done. Campsites are a bit few and far between along the coast in Durham, so I got up and got going this morning with the intention of getting as far as Whitley Bay.

My first stop was at Horden Beach, where the sea was gradually clearing the beach of colliery waste that was dumped there from Horden pit until the mid eighties. I found further reminders of Durham's mining past at Easington Colliery, where a path from a car park led up a hill to an old pit lift cage. Along the length of the path were plaques showing the timeline of the pit, including an explosion in 1951 that killed 83 men and the closure of the pit in 1993.

Next I stopped above the cliffs and a couple of small beaches at Nose's Point, just south of Seaham, and in Seaham itself, which sat above a longer beach, from where I could see the tower blocks of Sunderland to the north. On the edge of a small village green in Seaham was, rather bizarrely, the first electric vehicle recharging point that I'd ever seen.

From Seaham I passed through Ryhope and drove into

Sunderland, not really knowing what to expect. The coastal area of Sunderland seemed pretty industrial, with a large docks at the mouth of the River Wear, so I drove a little way down the southern bank of the river before stopping and walking to the riverbank. The river area looked quite nice, with a lot of modern developments, particularly on the northern banks, but also a number of fishing boats moored in the river, which looked a little out of place. I walked west a short distance until I came to the Wearmouth Bridge, which if I'm honest looked like a slightly poorer cousin of the Tyne Bridge at Newcastle/Gateshead. I climbed up the side of the cliff by the bridge, which was next door to a smaller railway bridge, and into a shopping area to have some lunch.

After walking back to the van I crossed the Wearmouth Bridge, drove back to the coast in the northern side of Sunderland and stopped at a couple of places in Roker and Seaburn to see the harbour and beaches, before stopping again at the northern end of Whitburn Bay. Just above Whitburn I stopped for a while to take a look around Souter Lighthouse. The lighthouse was maintained by the National Trust and was quite an impressive place. Opened in 1871, it was the first lighthouse to use alternating electric current, generated onsite, which powered a carbon arc light producing an 800,000 candle power light and an air pump that fed a pressure tank used for the foghorns. I climbed the stairs in the lighthouse to take a look at the lamp and lenses, which weighed four and half tons and rested on a bed of one and a half tons of mercury, which offered so little friction that you could push the whole assembly around its axis using one finger. The view from the top was clear for miles to the north and south. Once I was in the lighthouse it was quite hard to get out again, the staff were very keen to tell me everything they could about the place.

Moving on again I drove to South Shields, stopping at a

couple of beaches that lay either side of a break water that projected a mile into the mouth of the River Tyne. Across the Tyne I could see the remains of Tynemouth Castle and Priory. I stopped again above the Tyne to see a little of the river before entering the Tyne Tunnel and travelling under it, into Northumberland.

At Tynemouth I made use of my English Heritage membership again to take a look around the castle and priory. Set atop a promontory, the Benedictine priory overlooked small bays on either side and another breakwater in the mouth of the Tyne. A coastal defence battery was also constructed in the grounds during WWII. Tynemouth itself was quite a nice place, with a large sandy beach north of the priory, including an abandoned rock filled lido at the southern end. Just beyond the beach was another attractive little bay at Cullercoats.

It was getting late in the day as I rounded a corner and Whitley Bay came into view. I stopped to take a few photos but by then I just wanted to get settled in to the campsite at Old Hartley, just beyond the far end of the bay. I was rewarded for my lengthy day with a campsite right on top of the cliffs, overlooking St Mary's Island and Lighthouse, a beautiful location to end a fine day.

Whitley Bay and St Mary's Island
Tuesday, 15th May

It was a windy day for the most part today, raining at first but clearing up mid morning and becoming very nice in the evening.

I didn't really get going until late morning when I started walking along the coast to Whitley Bay, past St Mary's Island. The tide was in and the causeway to the island was covered, so I continued until I could drop down onto a thin sliver of beach at the northern end of Whitley Bay and walk pretty much the length of it into the town at the southern end.

The wind was a bit of a pain and the seafront was largely deserted, so I wandered up and down streets full of seemingly empty hotels and restaurants, before finding a bit of life on the main shopping high street, where I spent a couple of hours surfing t'internet, reading my book and having some lunch.

After lunch it was time to face up to something that I wasn't particularly looking forward to, a haircut. I've been travelling before for three months and came back with a mop top / shaggy bowl affair because I didn't want to risk getting scalped by a stranger. If only my hair grew with any kind of dignity I could get away with some flowing locks, but it just seems to grow out thick and directionless, which will just not do for another three months. So, I found the first hairdresser I came across, checked for signs of blood on the floor or trap doors under the chairs and enquired about an appointment in the near future. Half an hour later, after a long lap of a few surrounding streets, I was sat in a chair, chatting and having a load taken off my mind, literally. She did a decent job, but in hindsight I let her leave it far too long at the front, so I'll either be taking a pair of scissors to it myself or I'll be back in a similar chair sooner rather than later. But at least I'd lost some of the fear.

Within minutes my new, tidier barnet was being blown around back on the seafront as I headed back towards the campsite. The causeway to St Mary's Island was now clear, so I walked across and around the base of the lighthouse. I felt drawn to this lighthouse, there's something about its location on an island that makes it visually appealing. I can see it through the window in the van and I keep looking up at it. It was decommissioned in 1984, which is a shame as it would have been nice to see it working as the sun goes down on another very pleasant evening.

Collywell Bay to Alnmouth
Wednesday, 16th May

I seem to have covered quite a lot of ground again today, without really expecting to. I started off on foot with a walk along the road into neighbouring Collywell Bay, where I found a couple of sandy, rocky bays backed by sturdy (some might say ugly) concrete seawalls. Walking back to the campsite along the coast I came across a field that was home to a small group of alpacas, busily munching away at the grass. Funny looking things. I got going in the van and almost immediately pulled over in Seaton Sluice, where I took a look at a small harbour at the head of a stretch of water called Seaton Burn. The water flowed into the sea at the southern end of a beautiful sandy beach, on a beautiful morning, which ran all the way to the industrial looking Blyth.

I stopped at several points along the beach before stopping at a quay in Blyth, where a P&O multipurpose vessel lay at anchor near a sculpture called 'Spirit of the Staithes', which apparently looked like a steam train if you viewed it from the right angle (I didn't realise that at the time). The other side of the quay was lined with wind turbines and storage silos.

Just north of Blyth, across the River Blyth, I stepped out onto Cambois Beach before crossing the River Wansbeck and stopping for a while at Newbiggin-by-the-Sea. Out in the bay at Newbiggin, standing on a structure erected on a breakwater, was a 5m high sculpture of a man and woman, called 'Couple'. A smaller version of the same sculpture stood on the seafront. I kind of understood the sculpture out in the bay, but the structure it stood on looked out of place to me. At the northern end of the bay was the Church of St Bartholomew. I stopped for lunch at the Newbiggin Maritime Centre and had a cream tea. I know, long time no see. It was okay, but the scone was too small, the cream was practically squirty cream, and the jam was nothing special. I felt a pang of longing for Fowey.

From Newbiggin I drove through Lynemouth, passing various ponies tied to lengths of rope in and around the fields and dunes along the coast, before stopping briefly at Cresswell at the southern end of Druridge Bay, and again on the beach a little further up the bay. Just south of Amble I stopped behind the dunes again at High Hauxley. A mile or so off the coast was Coquet Island, an RSPB nature reserve that's off limits to the public, with a small lighthouse. At Amble I sat in the van for five minutes while a heavy shower passed before wandering around the shore and harbour. A fairground was being built near the harbour, which seemed a little pointless given there was hardly anyone around. I guess there must be a big weekend coming up in Amble. A cafe just behind the harbour proved too tempting to pass up.

Across the River Coquet from Amble I could see Warkworth Castle, which I stopped at next to take a look around. The castle was once home to Harry Hotspur (nope, me neither), 'hero of many Border ballads and the bane of the Scots raiders'. I guess the family moved south and changed their name to Redknapp over the years.

I made one last stop at Alnmouth where the mouth of the River Aln was flanked by more sand dunes and stretches of sandy beach, then made my way inland to Alnwick for the night, where I'm staying in the nicely maintained backyard of the Shepherds Rest Inn. While I was looking for somewhere to stay in the Amble area I found plenty of reviews of this place referring to the warm welcome and fine cooking of 'Bob', the owner, so I thought maybe I might treat myself to a pub meal tonight. Unfortunately, when I booked it yesterday 'Bob' told me he had a hospital appointment to attend in Newcastle, so wouldn't be around this evening, so no food. Oh well. When I arrived this afternoon, 'Bob' (who wasn't a girl disguised as a man) was just about to leave, so I had a quick chat with him before he went. Seemed like a nice guy, I'm hoping he knocks on the van door tomorrow morning offering free bacon stotties.

By the way, 'Bob', Blackadder, girl dressed as a man? Didn't watch it? Shame.

Addendum: I guess I should point out that Harry Redknapp was still the manager of Tottenham Hotspur on the 16th May 2012.

Alnwick to Beadnell Bay
Thursday, 17th May

Today, I have mostly visited castles. The fellas in the northeast have always liked a bit of ruffty tuffty, usually on a Friday night in the 'toon'. So many years ago they started building castles as a bit of a come on to anyone that thought they were hard enough.

I had another quick chat with 'Bob', (I say chat, I could barely get a word in edgeways) before driving just up the road to Alnwick Castle. The castle didn't open until 10:00am so I walked the streets of Alnwick for a while and came across a statue of Harry Hotspur, he obviously gets around in this area. Alnwick Castle was impressive, if you've seen any of the Harry Potter films you'll have seen parts of it. It was originally built following the Norman conquest and has been modified several times since. Today it was the residence of the 12th Duke of Northumberland, Ralph Percy, having been in the Percy family for seven hundred years. Harry Hotspur was in fact a nickname for Henry Percy, son of Henry Percy, the 1st Earl of Northumberland, father of Henry Percy, the 2nd Earl of Northumberland (originality when it came to names was not their strong point, there have been many more Henrys in the family). He gained fame as a great warrior while battling the Scots and the French, and was written about by none other than Shakespeare in Henry IV, Part 1. The Percy family owned land in Tottenham, hence the name Tottenham Hotspur. Who knew!

The castle was full of museums, displays and hands-on activities for school classes, overseen by costumed guides. You could even learn to fly a broomstick. The opulent State Rooms at the centre of the castle were full of art and furniture collected by the Percy family over many years. Together with the castle gardens, which I didn't view, and the town itself, there was plenty to spend a day seeing. But with other things to do today I had an early lunch and rejoined the coast, first at Boulmer, then Howick, before stopping for most of the afternoon at Craster.

Craster was set around a small harbour, but the main reason for stopping there was to walk a mile or so along the coast to Dunstanburgh Castle, built in the thirteen hundreds. The castle was the complete opposite to Alnwick, set in isolation next to the sea, rather than in the middle of an inland town, and in ruins rather than preserved. But for these very reasons it was equally impressive, at least from a distance. The forecast was for rain all day today, so I prepared myself for a wet walk, but it never really got much beyond drizzle at any time. Beyond the castle, to the north, was a golf course above a rocky beach and beyond that the sandy beach of Embleton Bay.

On the way back along the coast I reached a gate surrounded by cows, at the same time that a delivery van reached it from the other side. The driver hopped out and said "why aye pet man, cannie get tha gate, tha cows escape like when ahh dee it, divint thee", or something like that, so I kept the cows away from the gate and closed it behind him, then stuck around to chat with the cows for a bit. Didn't understand a word they said. Back in Craster, I dried myself off in a cafe with a cup of tea and a tea cake, which came with jam! I gave it a go, but it wasn't right, jam has no place on tea cakes in my humble opinion.

I set off again and quickly poked my head into Low Newton-by-the-Sea and High Newton-by-the-Sea, both with sandy beaches, before reaching my campsite at Beadnell Bay. I had a shower and chopped a bit off my fringe. If you've ever seen the movie Tropic Thunder, think Simple Jack.

Seahouses to Lindisfarne
Friday, 18th May

Man, there are a lot of castles around here. I've had to view a stretch of coast in reverse today, clockwise, due to the tides. I had until 12:20pm to get onto and back off the Holy Island of Lindisfarne, otherwise the causeway would have been closed and I'd have been stuck there until 5:00pm.

As the castle on Lindisfarne didn't open until 10:00am I didn't rush to get there, which is just as well as it was further from Beadnell than I thought. I passed through Beal and onto a causeway across Holy Island Sands, to an island that was larger than I had imagined. I parked in a car park just outside a village at 9:45am, thinking maybe I should have rushed a little more as it looked like at least a mile walk to the castle and two hours to see everything didn't seem like so long now. As I was putting on my waterproof trousers a castle shuttle bus turned up, so I quickly sorted myself out, paid for the parking and jumped on the bus.

The bus drove a group of us through the village and past a harbour to the foot of a whinstone hill, called Beblowe, with the castle perched high atop it. The castle was built in the late fifteen hundreds, using stone taken from the nearby

Lindisfarne Priory, to protect Holy Island harbour, the last deep water port before the Anglo-Scottish border. At the beginning of the twentieth century the castle was acquired by Edward Hudson, the founder of Country Life magazine. It changed hands several times and was eventually given to the National Trust in 1944 and opened to the public in 1970. I climbed a path up the side of Beblowe, into the wind and rain, before entering into the comparative warmth of the castle. The interior was largely as it was after Hudson commissioned Edwin Lutyens to convert it into a holiday home.

Lindisfarne was part of a spectacular stretch of coast, from the upper battery of the castle I could see the Farne Islands and Bamburgh Castle to the south. I could also see two navigation obelisks and a colony of seals on Ross Sands. The rain had reduced to drizzle so I walked from the castle back to the village, past the harbour and several sheds made from cutting upturned boats in half. Three more of these sheds sat just outside the castle, but only one of them was an original herring boat from Hudson's time as owner. Once I'd walked through the village and had a look at the remains of the Priory, I found that I still had time for a coffee and tea cake, hurrah! Again with the jam, maybe it's something peculiar to Northumberland?

I drove back over the causeway, stopping briefly to look back across to the island, and made my way towards Bamburgh but took a side road towards Ross. At the end of the road I came across a sign requesting visitors to park considerately near the small collection of buildings that made up Ross. From there I walked for a mile or so, firstly to the very end of the road, past a coastguard building, then along a designated path through a nature reserve and dunes until I found myself on a three mile stretch of sandy beach. And what an awesome place it was, to my left was Lindisfarne Castle, to my right was Bamburgh Castle, and out to sea before me were the Farne Islands. If you ever find yourself in this area, it's well worth taking the time to find this beach, Ross Back Sands. It's not a particularly well known beach, so it's likely to be quiet, but beware, apparently this makes it popular with naturists. Not on a day like today though, there is most certainly such a thing as the wrong weather if you're not wearing any clothing, let alone the wrong clothing.

Once I'd sorted myself out with some lunch in the van I continued towards Bamburgh but made another last minute detour towards Budle Point at the end of Budle Bay, where a sandy, rocky beach lay beneath the gaze of Bamburgh Castle. When I finally reached the car park at Bamburgh Castle I parked next to a campervan that I recognised, I'd spoken to its owners at The Shepherds Rest at Alnwick, and had also seen it parked at Craster. I noticed a few other people today that I saw at Alnwick and Dunstanburgh Castles, and I'm pretty sure there's a campervan on the campsite this evening that was on the campsite in Scarborough. Small world.

Bamburgh Castle was another huge, imposing fortification, right on the coast. The castle that stood there today began its life at around the start of the second millennium. It now belongs to the Armstrong family after it was bought by the Victorian industrialist, William Armstrong. The Armstrong and Aviation Artefacts Museum based in the castle laundry was largely dedicated to Armstrong's manufacturing companies, responsible for designing and building many bridges, ships, locomotives, automobiles, aircraft and armaments. The State Rooms were also open for public viewing. You have to be careful when walking around some of these properties, the guides have obviously spent a lot of time learning a lot of facts about their respective rooms and buildings, and they can latch onto unsuspecting tourists, particularly on quiet rainy days, with a kind of factual tourettes.

On the way back to the campsite at Beadnell I stopped at Seahouses, firstly to take a look around, secondly to get some groceries, and thirdly to see if I could find out some information about boat trips around the Farne Islands tomorrow. None of the booths at the harbour were still manned, but most of them had leaflets to take, so I came away with a handful.

Beadnell Bay to Berwick-upon-Tweed
Saturday, 19th May

The weather forecast was looking a bit better today, and I was hoping to catch a boat out to the Farne Islands some time after 10:00am. But first I had a quick look at Beadnell Bay, having spent the last two nights there but not actually having seen much of it. From the bay I got a view south to the ruins of Dunstanburgh Castle.

I got to Seahouses at about 9:45am and walked down to the booths at the harbour where I'd picked up the leaflets yesterday. The mood was not a hopeful one. A dive boat was going to go out and report back, but they weren't expecting to know for at least an hour whether the other boats would go out. It hadn't been a good start to the season since April, with the weather stopping most of the trips so far. Not to worry, I decided to get some breakfast instead and make use of the extra few hours to have a more relaxed day. I feel I will be back in Northumberland someday, the coast around this area is stunning, particularly wherever you have views of one or more of Dunstanburgh, Bamburgh and Lindisfarne Castles.

After a cup of tea and a hefty bacon, sausage and egg bap, I stepped onto the beach at Seahouses before continuing and stopping in Bamburgh to take a look around the village, which I didn't really see yesterday. I think I may base myself there if I do come back, it was a nice little village with several pubs and cafes set around a green, with another large green at the base of the castle. I had a look at the church of St Aidan, where I found a monument to local heroine Grace Darling. Only three weeks after being born in Bamburgh, in 1815, Grace was taken to live on Brownsman Island, in the Farne Islands, where her father was the lighthouse keeper, and in 1826 the family moved to a new lighthouse on Longstone Island. On the 7th September 1838 the steamship Forfarshire struck a rock, with the loss of 40 lives. Grace and her father rowed against the tide and wind to rescue five survivors and take them back to the lighthouse, her father and two of the rescued crew returned to rescue the remaining survivors. Grace became a national heroine but tragically died of tuberculosis only four years later. Bamburgh also has a museum dedicated to Grace, run by the RNLI.

Moving on from Bamburgh, I stopped to look at beaches at Cheswick and Cocklawburn before reaching Spittal, at the mouth of the River Tweed. I parked and found a promenade to walk along behind the beach. Just by chance I had parked on a street outside one of the Club Sites belonging to the Caravan Club. I was going to stay inland at a campsite just north of Berwick-upon-Tweed tonight, but this would give me a view of the sea in walking distance of Berwick. They were able to accommodate me for one night so I checked in and cancelled the other booking. Once I'd selected a pitch and parked up I set off along the banks of the Tweed until I came to a narrow road bridge and crossed into the walled city of Berwick-upon-Tweed. Once I'd walked someway around the city walls I headed into the centre and found a cafe to sit in for the rest of the afternoon.

I've pretty much run out of England, it nearly all lies to

the south of me. Being a southerner, a trip to the north generally involves getting in a car, driving for at least three hours, and getting out of the car somewhere 'oop north', where everybody speaks funny. It's a bit like getting the geographical bends. But this time I've risen up the country gradually, decompressing sufficiently along the way. My mind has been on the coast, so largely without realising it I've passed above Birmingham, Manchester, Leeds and York. By the time I reached Scarborough, Middlesborough, Sunderland and Newcastle, the accents were morphing gradually and I was being called 'duck' and 'love'. Over the past couple of days I've noticed the occasional soft Scottish tones, including a gentleman who struck up a conversation with me today and proceeded to tell me random stories from his past, based around this area. Nice enough bloke, probably just wanted someone to talk to.

Did Chelsea really just become European Champions? Seriously?! Strange times.

Eyemouth to Dunbar

Sunday, 20th May

At 8:21am, I crossed the border into Scotland. No fanfares, no marching band, just a quiet sunny Sunday morning. Shortly afterwards I parked in Eyemouth and walked around the beach, harbour and small town centre. What I at first thought was the hull of an old ship, called the Phoenix, turned out to be a building, the Eyemouth Maritime Centre, designed to look like a ship. Set in a small village green were two memorials related to a storm in 1881 that claimed the lives of 189 east coast fishermen. The first, a large white stone sculpture, dedicated to those that lost their lives, of which 129 came from Eyemouth. The second, a bronze sculpture, dedicated to the women and children who were 'left behind', having lost their husbands and fathers.

Moving on From Eyemouth, I stopped next at Coldingham Sands, a beach in a small bay popular with local surfers. I walked for a while to the southeast, through a smaller rocky bay and towards a larger rocky beach. Once back at the van I moved on a short distance to St Abbs. Overlooking a little harbour I found another bronze sculpture dedicated to the women and children left behind.

The harbour was busy with a number of divers, wandering around in their drysuits. Apparently the marine reserve off St Abb's Head offers some of the best diving in Scotland. I walked down into the harbour and sat outside a cafe with a cup of tea and a tea cake (no jam this time, normality has been restored). Just before I finished, a family seated near me got up from their table to leave. Within seconds a seagull had swooped down and stolen a piece of toast, followed by a flurry of other gulls looking for scraps. As I left my table, a seagull landed on it and swallowed two foil wrappers from the butter that came with the tea cake. That's gonna chafe on the way out.

I moved the van just up the road to a car park next to a National Trust of Scotland visitor centre, cafe and art gallery. From there I set off on a walk along the coast to St Abb's Head. It was getting warm by then and I had to put on some suncream as I walked down to a small bay before climbing up towards a lighthouse on the Head. As I stood above the lighthouse it was warm and still, taking me back to Golden Cap in Dorset. I could see for miles, across the North Sea to the coast of Fife, and along the current stretch of coast, taking in the Torness Power Station, Bass Rock and North Berwick Law, a mountain just outside North Berwick. On the rocks below were hundreds of nesting birds. I continued around the coast until the bay of Pettico Wick lay far below me, and a beautiful stretch of coastline lay before me. I returned to the car park via a route that took me along the side of Mire Loch, which was as still as a millpond and flanked by patches of yellow gorse. What an awesome walk, deserving of a cold drink and a slice of cake while sat outside the cafe.

I got going again and followed a track that branched off the main road, but which seemed to end up heading towards a farm, though I was able to get out before turning around and look along the coast again. My next stop was at Cove, where I found a third bronze sculpture, all three of them created by Jill Watson. I followed a track down the side of the cliff which brought me around to the outer wall of Cove harbour, protecting a very pretty little bay and beach. To get to the beach I walked back up the track a little way and through a dark 55m tunnel dug through the cliff, just wide enough for a horse and cart. After walking across the beach and back I headed back up the track and along the top of the cliffs until I could look down to Pease Bay, a larger bay and sandy beach with a small town of static caravans.

Once I'd got back to the van I crossed from Scottish Borders into East Lothian and made a quick stop at Thorntonloch, where a sandy dune backed beach lay beneath the gaze of Torness Power Station. I'm not averse to these power stations, on an aesthetic level, they may not be the most attractive buildings, but when seen from various points along the coast, as I saw this one today, I think they can add something to the view rather than spoiling it.

My final stop for today was at Dunbar. I passed the entrance to the campsite on the way into the town, parked up and walked to the seafront. The town was stretched along several small beaches and a multi sectioned harbour, with the remains of a castle at the end of it that was pretty much 'knocked through' to create the harbour. I returned to the van and drove back to the campsite, selecting a pitch that looked across Dunbar, and out to Bass Rock and, much further out, the Isle of May. What an excellent first day in Scotland.

I believe that the notion that Scotland suffers from terrible weather has been made up by those that wish to keep Scotland to themselves. It's been a glorious day today, and as I come to think about it I'm not sure I've ever really experienced particularly bad weather up here. I shall be baking a pastry hat, just in case.

Belhaven to Edinburgh
Monday, 21ˢᵗ May

It seems that bigging up the Scottish weather yesterday had brought on a little shyness this morning, the cloud was low and most of what I saw yesterday was hidden from view. But let's be clear that this does not constitute bad weather and I shall not be eating my still warm pastry hat.

I started the day with a quick stop at Belhaven, just around the corner from Dunbar, where a large expanse of sand disappeared into the murk, before making another quick stop roughly above Canty Bay, where I looked over the gate of a private driveway at Bass Rock, of which the bottom half was just about visible. It was kind of hard to tell, but Bass Rock was home to literally thousands of gannets, turning most of it white, as well as a lighthouse and the ruins of a chapel and fort.

Continuing on I parked up in North Berwick, and had I not seen it yesterday I would have been almost completely unaware of North Berwick Law, rising into the clouds behind the town. I walked around the harbour, which jutted out into the sea between the sandy beaches of Milsey Bay to the east and North Berwick Bay to the west, then along the high street until I selected a cafe to sit in for a while with a coffee, catching up on various things. I had a quick look at the route of the Olympic Torches, but I don't think our paths will cross. They will only be travelling around the country for 70 days, the lightweights.

From North Berwick I moved into the woodlands of Yellowcraig and out onto a lovely stretch of dune and forest backed beach that I explored for a while in both directions. In front of me was a lighthouse on the island of Fidra and to the east I could see the bases of Bass Rock and North Berwick Law.

I made brief stops to see a beach at Gullane Bay and mud flats at Aberlady, before finding a height restriction free lay-by (as opposed to the car parks) at Longniddry and walking along a stretch of the beach, as the clouds broke and the warm rays of the sun shone through. The twin chimneys of Cockenzie Power Station were to my west. Just beyond the power station I stopped for a look at Prestonpans, which didn't seem to have much to offer, so I moved on to the much more pleasant Musselburgh, set back from the coast along the grassy banks of the River Esk, where I found myself some lunch on the high street.

After lunch I drove on into Midlothian (or if you wish to be current, the City of Edinburgh) and stopped at Portobello. Named by its founder after the 1739 battle of Puerto Bello in Panama, at which he fought, Portobello is Edinburgh's seaside resort. I walked most of the length of the beach along the promenade. By that time the clouds had largely gone and visibility was good again. I could clearly see North Berwick Law holding up the 'Loser' sign, having won this morning's game of hide and seek. The weather called for an ice cream, and I am but a humble servant to such demands.

From the seaside to the docks, I stopped next in Leith, where I aimlessly wandered around, looking for the Royal Yacht Britannia, moored there somewhere. Leith has undergone a lot of restoration and development, and I have to say I quite liked the area, at times the waterways lined with cafes, restaurants and bars reminded me of Amsterdam, which I really hadn't expected. I eventually found the Britannia in a large shopping mall, kind of. It was moored behind it, but the only real way to get a look at it, apart from through a fence, was to begin a tour on the third floor of the mall and cinema complex, Ocean Terminal. Now why hadn't that occurred to me to begin with? I didn't take the tour, but I got a kind of sideways downward glance at its bow through the large glass wall of a food court.

I carried on along the Edinburgh coastline until I found my stop for the night, on the northwest outskirts of the city, a pretty impressive Caravan Club Site. The Club Sites of both the Caravan Club and the Camping and Caravanning Club have started to get pretty busy now, particularly at weekends, so I've started booking ahead wherever I find them, and am now trying to book every campsite at least the day before, rather than leaving them to chance on the day.

In the evening I walked out of the campsite and strolled along the banks of the Firth of Forth at Cramond. I could just make out, through the glare of the low sun, the top of Forth Bridge over the trees on Hound Point. Out in the Firth was Cramond Island, connected to the mainland by a tidal causeway, and St Colm's Abbey on Inchcolm Island.

Edinburgh
Tuesday, 22ⁿᵈ May

I took a day off today, to explore the centre of Edinburgh, starting with a lie-in followed by breakfast.

The day started cloudy again, but as I walked from the campsite to the nearby bus stop it was getting warm and the sun was burning off the clouds.

I hate buses, I find them the most complicated form of transport to use in foreign cities. Metros are usually easy, you get a ticket from a machine and check the map to see where you need to get on and off, trains aren't too bad either, but buses usually involve talking to someone who you may or may not understand and trying to figure out a ticketing system that often includes zones and time spans. Now I knew which bus to get, and where to get on and off, but I'll be honest, my brain has started to fall a little behind the Scottish accents now, just enough to cause a slight delay in comprehension. I asked for a return, but learnt that there were singles or a day saver, which was only worth it if you needed three or more singles. I offered my money to the driver, he pointed me to a hopper to my left. I put my money in the hopper and looked at the driver expecting my ticket, he pointed me to a ticket dispenser to my right. I took my seat with the embarrassed look of a stranger in a new city, and attempted to replace it with the smug look of someone that would know what to do next time.

Edinburgh was looking mighty fine as I stepped off the bus, with the castle high on Castle Rock in front of me. There were a lot of roadworks going on along Princes Street, which spoilt the view a little, but plenty of people were wandering along the street in the sunshine.

I love Edinburgh, I'd been there before but I was still taken aback by how nice the Princes Street and castle area was. I had most of the rest of the day to wander around so I decided to take some time to reacquaint myself with an old travelling buddy, the Starbucks white chocolate mocha (with cream, obviously), with roughly 10,000 calories of sickly sweet goodness, which I savoured while sat on a sofa in a large bay window, soaking up the sun and looking out over Princes Street Gardens.

I walked around Princes Street Gardens for a while before climbing up the hill to the entrance of the castle, arriving just as the two man guard at the gates was changed. Preparations were underway for the Queen's Jubilee, with the seating usually used for the Edinburgh Tattoo being erected. I didn't go into the castle, I'd been around it before and I think I've seen plenty of castles recently. Instead I walked down the Royal Mile until I came to the Scottish Parliament Building at Holyrood. It was an interesting building, but much criticised for its cost, late delivery, design, choice of materials etc. In front of the building was a landscaped park area with water features.

From there I couldn't fail to notice Holyrood Park, where a long high ridge hid most of Arthur's Seat, rising to a height of 250m. Arthur's Seat was higher, further away and with a larger number of paths to the summit than I remembered, but I chose one of the paths and walked up to the top. What a view, in all directions, on a stunning day.

After spending some time on the summit, happy like a giddy child, I came down a steeper route and then up again onto the ridge, overlooking the Parliament Building.

When I got back to the Parliament Building I had three things on my mind; I wanted to lie in the park area with my book, I was desperate for a pee, and I needed a cold drink. There was a sign for a cafe in the Parliament Building so I decided to go in to get a drink and use the facilities. Which was simpler than it sounded. I first had to empty my pockets and take off my belt to go through a metal detector. I wear a belt for a reason (to keep my trousers up, duh), and without it the seat of the Scottish Parliament very nearly got to see the seat of me. With belt refastened, bladder emptied and cold bottle of Irn Bru in hand, I went back outside and lay in the park with my book for an hour or so.

Feeling the need to sit inside and write some of this up, I returned to the Starbucks on Princes Street, for a cold drink this time, for another hour or so, before walking around to Rose Street, which ran parallel behind Princes Street. There I found a restaurant that had been recommended to me, Miros Cantina Mexicana, and had some delicious slow cooked lamb with a cool bottle of beer.

Once back at the bus stop I waited for the bus to turn up, got on with my change ready to put in the hopper to my left, while asking the driver for a single at the same time (just in case he had any kind of role in the transaction), and looked to my right to collect the ticket from the... uhhh, no ticket dispenser. Looking quickly back to my left I saw the ticket dispenser next to the hopper. I think I got away with it, so I settled into my seat with a look of nonchalance. There was a guy on the bus wearing a cloak. You don't see enough cloaks these days, mostly just professors and wizards, I guess.

If Edinburgh was like this every day, I could quite happily live here.

Queensferry to Lower Largo
Wednesday, 23rd May

The sun was out before me this morning. I'd forgotten I was on the outskirts of a major city, so the traffic was fairly heavy as I made my way to Queensferry, which was a lot busier than I had expected. I think there was a mixture of coaches coming in for boat trips from a jetty below the Forth Rail Bridge, towering high above, and passengers coming ashore from the Caribbean Princess, moored out in the Forth, to take coaches into Edinburgh.

It was time to cross the Forth, so I got back on the road and onto the less impressive Forth Road Bridge, forever living in the shadow of its big brother, and into Fife. On the other side I swung back on myself to North Queensferry and stood below the bridge looking back to the other side.

Moving on again I was heading through Dalgety Bay, a large housing estate with more than its fair share of roundabouts, when I took a detour to St Davids Harbour, again looking back across the Forth. I spent a while trying to find the actual bay at Dalgety Bay, but the most obvious road to get to the bay was a private road and everywhere else just took me into cul-de-sacs in the housing estate. So I gave up and moved on to Aberdour, a really nice little sandy bay, looking over to Arthur's Seat and to St Colm's Abbey on Inchcolm Island.

At Burntisland I found a stretch of beach below the town that looked like it was probably quite narrow at high tide, but with the tide out there was a massive expanse of sand in front of it. I found a cafe and sat down for a while for some late morning coffee and cake (the time is kind of irrelevant, no time is bad for cake).

After Burntisland I stopped at Kinghorn, another nice sandy bay with a small hard standing at one end where the boats from the local sailing club were stored. On top of a railing by the boats someone had written handy pointers to the various locations and islands in and across the Forth. I stopped again at Kirkcaldy, a larger town with a beach and harbour but without the charm of the smaller bays.

Beyond Kirkcaldy were Dysart and West Wymss (pronounced 'Weems'), back in the realms of small harbours and stretches of beach, really nice places to wander around in the warmth of the sun. It seemed almost Mediterranean at times today.

Not nearly so nice, or indeed nice at all, were Buckhaven and Methil, which seemed very industrial and vaguely scary, so I passed on through pretty quickly to Leven. I stopped at a couple of places along the beach at Leven, but it was a bit more of a resort than some of the smaller places I'd been through today so I decided to carry on around Largo Bay and stop at Lower Largo. There I found another small harbour and several collections of houses, either right up against the water or along the back of a sandy stretch of beach, which ran all the way along Largo Bay to Ruddons Point.

After spending some time walking among the houses and along the beach, I returned to the van and set off through Upper Largo to Forth House, a small campsite set amongst hillside fields, with one other campervan present.

Earlsferry to St Andrews
Thursday, 24th May

As I stood on the beach at Earlsferry this morning I could barely see more than 50 metres through the fog. It was warm and quite still, and I could just about hear waves lapping against the sand, somewhere in front of me. As I walked along the beach I came across a handful of beach huts, well, sheds more than huts, before eventually reaching a seawall with houses atop it.

Just down the road at Elie I found a sandy harbour separating two other beaches, one small, one larger, or at least it disappeared further into the fog. This was clearly a popular place for watersports, with racks of wetsuits sitting outside one of the buildings at the harbour.

At St Monans the sky overhead was clear and the sun was shining through the low level fog in the harbour. The houses crowded around the harbour reminded me of Cornwall, as they also did at Pittenweem, where the fog was finally starting to clear. Part way down a narrow street that wound down to the harbour at Pittenweem was a cave, or 'weem', where the seventh century missionary St Fillan supposedly lived. If you wished, you could hire a key from the Cocoa Tree cafe and take a look inside. When I got to the Cocoa Tree I opted instead to sit inside with a strawberry milkshake and some warm ginger sponge. Why anyone would spend their time in a cave when there was such a nice cafe just up the street is a mystery to me.

When I got to Anstruther the remaining patches of fog were rolling across the beach near yet another harbour, although larger than the neighbouring harbours. I wandered around the harbour area, past more enticing cafes, which I resisted with very little conviction.

I decided that it was far too nice a day to spend it all outdoors, soaking up the sun, and that what I needed to do was to get myself one hundred feet or so underground. So I went to find the Scottish Secret Bunker. Now, I'm not an expert in secrecy, but it seems to me that if you want something to be secret it's probably not a good idea to put up sign posts and create a website called www.secretbunker.co.uk. Anyhoo, in an area of fields, on the B940 to Crail, was an innocent looking farmhouse. Beneath it, hidden from the general public until 1992, was a staircase that led down to a tunnel, which in turn led to about 24,000 square feet of rooms, over two floors, encased in 15 feet of reinforced concrete. This was a place that secretly observed the Cold War, and where the Scottish Government would have retreated and attempted to run the country in the event of a nuclear attack. The staircase and tunnel were not quite an entrance through a changing room, or phone box, like you might see in The Man from U.N.C.L.E or James Bond, but the whole idea of the place was like something from a movie. It made me think of computer games like Half-Life or Resident Evil. It was an eerie place, a reminder of a time when nuclear war was a distinct possibility. I remember being shown a film called 'Threads' when I was at school, about the lead up to and aftermath of a nuclear attack, and one of two cinemas in the complex was showing a black and white film called 'War

Games', with the other one showing public service announcements about how to prepare yourself and your home for such an event. The audio commentary in the bunker was quite sobering at times, particularly when talking about the large blast doors that would seal the occupants in, and the likes of us out. I can't say I enjoyed being there, but it was certainly interesting.

Back in the warm, fresh air, I headed for Crail, where I found another pretty little harbour and beach. I bought a chicken curry pie from a bakery on the way back to the van, which was too hot to eat straight away (I don't think I paid any extra for it to be heated, or does that just apply to Cornish pasties?), so I took it with me to Craighead, where I drove back into fog. I came to the end of the road at a golf course, but I was able to pay to park there and walk across the golf course onto a beach, which I did after devouring the pie. It was the kind of chicken curry that everyone's mum makes, with sultanas and yellow curry sauce, and very nice it was too!

From Craighead I drove back out of the fog and on to a golden sandy beach at Kingbarns, before moving on again to St Andrews. I didn't really know much about St Andrews, other than the obvious fact that it's the home of golf, and the Old Course is one of the most famous courses in the world. It was larger than I imagined, with two beaches. East Sands ran east from a small harbour, and West Sands ran north along one edge of the Old Course. St Andrews is home to the ruins of the twelfth century St Andrews Cathedral, and St Andrews Castle, and a university, the third oldest in Britain, founded in 1410. I felt a little emotional standing next to the Old Course, which I had seen so many times on TV, but had never really grasped the beauty of the place, or of St Andrews in general, until now. It must be an incredible place to be when the Open is played there under good weather conditions. The only downside was the odour of money, a lot of it American, coming from some of the people leaving the course or sitting outside bars near the course.

One other downside was having to pay £24 for a night at a caravan park nearby, twice as much as I've been paying at most places.

Addendum: Only a few days later the government did a bit of a U-turn on their plans to charge VAT on hot Cornish pasties.

St Andrews to Monifieth
Friday, 25th May

I had an overwhelming urge to return to the Old Course this morning, even though it was foggy again. So I first headed to the far end of West Sands, where I couldn't see anything through the fog, before returning and parking near the Old Course to take another look around. As the fog slowly thinned I eventually got the view that I was looking for, of the small stone Swilcan Burn Bridge with the Old Course Hotel in the background.

I got underway and drove through Guardbridge and Leuchars to head into the Tentsmuir Forest, where I came across a barrier, so I pulled over to see what the cars behind me would do. The first car put some money into the barrier and went through, while the driver of the second car spent some time putting in money, then getting out of the car, fiddling with the return tray, putting in money again, smacking the machine, fiddling with the return tray, then eventually getting through the barrier. By this time a Forestry Commission car had turned up to let some contractors through, so I pulled up to the barrier, put 50p in, which was accepted, followed by £1, which didn't register, followed by another 50p, which kicked all three coins out to the return tray. Luckily the Forestry Commission man retrieved them for me and fed them back in again.

At the end of the road was a car park at the edge of the forest, beyond which were dunes and a beautiful sandy beach, stretching into the distance. I walked north along the beach for some time until I saw what I was hoping for, the familiar sight of a group of seals basking on the sand. They were quite some way away, across a couple of stretches of water running through the beach, but I walked towards the first stretch of water to see what I could see. On the way I found a length of rope lying on the beach, so I stopped to take a photo, then noticed a seal not far from the rope, on its own, motionless, facing the water. I figured I had stumbled across another dead seal. I focused the camera on the rope, but as the camera beeped the seal suddenly darted forward into the water, where it eyed me suspiciously and swam back and forth for a bit before heading off along the water.

The seal wasn't swimming fast and my path along the water took me beyond it, where I took some distant photos of the large group of seals while I waited for it to pass me. Instead of swimming on beyond me, it turned around again and swam back and forth in front of me, surfacing and looking at me now and again, before it swam towards me and flopped out of the water onto the sand, about 20 yards away. I couldn't believe it. It even yawned at one point before splashing back into the water, then swam to the other side, got out on the other bank, then back into the water and swam close in front of me. Eventually it swam away along the shallow channel of water, where I watched it disappear out towards the open sea. There were quite a few people on the beach and in the car park when I walked back, but not one of them had walked out to where I'd seen the seal. I miss the little fella.

I drove on to Tayport, where I walked down to the harbour and looked across the Firth of Tay to Broughty Ferry. On the way back to the van I spotted some pies in a bakery, so I nipped in to get one. They sold chicken curry pies, but I went for a steak and gravy, which was delicious! Full of pie, I crossed the Tay Bridge into Angus and the city of Dundee. There were a lot of road works going on, but I stopped in a car park next to the Discovery Point Visitor Centre, where the Royal Research Ship Discovery was moored. Built in 1901, the Discovery was used by Captain Scott to sail to the Antarctic. Dundee had quite a few ugly concrete buildings, but also had some attractive older buildings in the centre, including the High School of Dundee with a pillared entrance. I found the high street and settled myself in a cafe for coffee and lemon cheesecake.

When I arrived in Broughty Ferry the high street was heaving with people and cars, and I found the beach was pretty busy too. I wandered along the seafront past a harbour, where some kids were jumping off the breakwater, and continued past a little castle and a lifeboat station, until I could see back to Dundee. Monifieth was thankfully quieter, where I found a pitch in the Tayview caravan park before walking out onto the beach.

Tayview is probably the most interesting campsite I've stayed at so far, I've just bought an ice lolly from a guy cycling around the site with a trailer fridge, and two guys have been flying three Harris Hawks around, landing in the trees, on the buildings, and on some of the residents. It's been a good day.

Carnoustie to Inverbervie
Saturday, 26th May

My first stop today was at another golfing heavyweight, Carnoustie. The place was smaller than St Andrews and without any of the grandeur as far as I could see, you could probably pass through it without much thought. I made my way to the beach and walked along to one of the three golf courses, where the day's earlier tee offs were enjoying sunny conditions.

I moved on to Arbroath, parked near a harbour and walked around the harbour and beach area. I considered sampling some of the local 'smokies', haddock cured over beech wood fires, but instead ended up in a cafe and paid a third of the price for coffee and cake.

From Arbroath I took a side road off the main road until I reached the little village of Auchmithie and walked down to a small bay with a pebble beach, before clocking 3,000 miles while continuing on to a busy car park behind dunes at Lunan Bay. On the other side of the dunes was a huge bay and sandy beach.

Moving on again I headed towards the tall spire of the Montrose parish church and crossed the South Esk. The South Esk estuary opened out behind Montrose into the

Montrose Basin, a tidal basin about a mile across and teeming with wildlife. I parked up and walked a loop around Montrose, through one of its golf courses, along a beach, across the town and along one edge of the basin, where I couldn't really get a decent view from behind some train tracks. I had booked a campsite in Montrose, but as it was only mid afternoon I decided I would move further on and try and book a campsite a little way up the coast. However, after getting mixed up with the phone numbers and ending up with two bookings in Montrose, I decided to cut my losses and stay there, but after looking at a few more places up the coast first.

I crossed into Aberdeenshire and followed a road towards a National Nature Reserve visitor centre near St Cyrus, but the car park was full and the road lined with cars, so I ended up passing it and leaving again along a steep, narrow, winding road, praying that I didn't meet anything coming the other way. I stopped just outside St Cyrus itself and walked through the village, past a church and to the top of the cliffs that overlooked another long sandy beach. The cliffs were steep with a zig zag path down to the beach, so I decided to torture myself by walking down just so that I had to walk back up again.

Next I stopped at Johnshaven, where the houses ran down to a harbour, before making one more stop at Inverbervie, with a nice little bay and tiered pebble beach, plus a bowling green that was being put to full use in the afternoon sun. I doubled back, crossed back into Angus and returned to Montrose for a night at South Links campsite. No ice cream trailer or birds of prey tonight. Shame.

Kinneff to Walker Park
Sunday, 27th May

I set off in fog once again this morning, crossed back into Aberdeenshire and made my first stop next to a church at Kinneff. I followed a path behind the church, past some ruined buildings, and nearly fell off the edge of the cliffs before spotting a beach below with some more ruins. By the time I reached Catterline, and walked down to a pretty horseshoe bay with a small breakwater at one end, the fog was starting to clear a little.

A short way up the road I stopped at Crawton at a small car park at the entrance to the Fowlsheugh RSPB Reserve. There was a chance of sighting puffins, seals, dolphins, porpoises and even minke whales, so I followed the cliffs for a while. The fog was drifting around further up the coast but had largely retreated offshore, so that you could see the sea and the sky, but no horizon, which was kind of weird. I reached a sign that suggested the best place to see puffins was on the grass verge below a cave, just in front of me, but I couldn't see any of the comical little fellas. A blackboard in a little RSPB building, last updated on the 25th, suggested that there had been daily sightings of them. Maybe they were all in church at that time. The cliffs were mostly covered with herring gulls and guillemots (I've been learning) and the only things I spotted in the water were more birds and a group of sea kayakers. The smell of guano was ever present, but I don't think that was anything to do with the sea kayakers.

In the distance I could see the remains of some buildings, so I moved on to take a look at Dunnottar Castle, where cars were starting to line the road near it. The castle was built in the fourteenth century, on a high rocky base jutting out into the sea, with bays on either side and separated from the mainland by a ravine. It was quite a sight, but looked even more impressive from an aerial photo that I saw next to the path down to it. I spotted three seals in one of the bays, poking their heads up now and again.

I stopped next in Stonehaven, which was a pretty nice place with a large sandy harbour at the old town and a large bay and beach running in front of the main town. I walked from the harbour along a boardwalk around part of the bay, where I came across a rock sporting a steel sculpture of a fishing boat manned by fish. I love that kind of random thing. I had a look for a decent cafe to sit in for a while but couldn't find one and instead opted to make some sandwiches when I arrived in Newtonhill.

With sandwich in hand I walked through the village of Newtonhill to find a little bay below me, almost out of sight of the village. On the slopes leading down to the beach were some fishermen's huts and some little winch huts used to haul small boats up the beach. I found a similar setting at Portlethen, another little bay and beach with a collection of small boats, also reached by walking through a little village.

I stopped again at Cove Bay, on the southern outskirts of Aberdeen, and walked about half a mile along the coast to Cove Harbour, which seemed to be where the local noisy teens hung out, so I didn't stay for long. On the way back along the coast I continued just beyond the path back to the van to say hello to some cows with large horns. I patted one of them on the nose before it tried its hardest to gore me to death from behind a fence.

Before heading off inland to my campsite, I drove along a coastal road that took me past Nigg Bay and around Walker Park, with a lighthouse at the end of it, giving me my first views of Aberdeen. There were quite a few large ships off the coast, possibly to do with the North Sea oil industry that Aberdeen plays a major part in. The road continued past a golf course and an industrial port with more large ships. From there I pretty much followed the River Dee to the Deeside Holiday Park and a nice shady pitch among the trees, blessed relief from the heat of the day.

Aberdeen to Rattray Head
Monday, 28th May

Today was a little flat, after just over a week of sunny and scenic Scotland. The weather was cool and cloudy and I travelled a fair way without too much to see.

I started the day in a cafe in the centre of Aberdeen, uploading the last few days of entries and doing a bit of housekeeping. I didn't wander around the centre of Aberdeen and instead headed for the seafront, stopping at a few places along a promenade behind the beach.

I then crossed the River Don and passed through Bridge of Don on my way to a car park in Balmedie Country Park, where I just about squeezed the van through some width restriction bollards. There was a big pile of rubbish by the car park, presumably because the bins couldn't cope with the waste from the number of people that turned up over the sunny weekend, which I guess is fair enough. But, when I reached the beach, it was littered with beer bottles and coke cans that people hadn't even bothered to try to carry away. It's at times like these when I wish that global warming would hurry up and eradicate mankind from this planet.

Far more pleasant was Collieston, a small sandy harbour

lined with cottages on the grassy slopes around it, next door to a sandy bay. I made myself some lunch before a brief walk around the harbour. Next I parked at Cruden Bay and walked across a narrow white footbridge to a large sandy beach beneath a golf course set atop the dunes. At one end of the bay was a harbour, where I climbed up a wooden staircase onto the low cliffs and walked a short distance to get a slightly better view of the ruins of Slains Castle. Bram Stoker visited Cruden Bay regularly, so Whitby may have to share some of the credit for his inspiration behind Dracula.

Not far beyond Cruden Bay I stopped at a car park just off the road for a short walk to see the Bullers of Buchan, a collapsed sea cave that forms a 'pot' into which the sea flows through an archway. There were loads of birds nesting on the cliff faces so I walked out to the end of an outcrop on the other side of the archway, where I noticed a lone puffin, looking shifty. I took a photo and cursed myself for leaving my telephoto lens in the van, so I returned to the van, swapped lenses, returned to the cliff, and... it had gone. Ah well, I'm sure there will be plenty more of them to see.

Next I stopped briefly near a lighthouse in Boddam before pulling into a car park overlooking a harbour and marina at Peterhead. Just below me was a campsite, which I'd tried to phone earlier in the day. I drove down and found that the reception was closed until 4:30pm, but there seemed to be plenty of spaces. However, it was only 3:00pm and I wanted to move on if I could, so I called a small five van site near Fraserburgh, who had space. Before leaving Peterhead I drove through the mostly industrial town to a part of the harbour where many of the fishing vessels were moored.

I continued along the A90 towards Fraserburgh and took a side road at St Fergus to Scotstown Beach, another sandy dune backed beach, not far from a gas terminal. I took another turn off the A90 before Crimdon, past one end of the Loch of Strathbeg, which ended with a mile of pot holes that made me wonder how the tyres were coping with that amount of abuse. At the end of the road was an equally pot holed car park at Rattray Head, a mass of dunes. I walked through the dunes and out onto the beach, where a small lighthouse stood just offshore on a sturdy platform.

With another mile of pot holes behind me I headed inland to Smithy Croft campsite at Boyndlie, southwest of Fraserburgh.

Cairnbulg Point to Findochty
Tuesday, 29th May

Today, I have mostly been looking at harbours. Lots, and lots, of harbours.

I returned to the coast at a small harbour at Cairnbulg Point, reached by driving through Inverallochy, where I could see across Fraserburgh Bay to Fraserburgh. Just offshore from the harbour was the wreck of a ship. The wheelhouse was missing and there was a large hole near the bow on the port side, presumably from being slowly salvaged for scrap.

Fraserburgh was another large fishing port, the second largest on the northeast coast behind Peterhead, with a harbour that was jam packed with big fishing vessels. I walked through the harbour to Kinnaird Lighthouse, which was now the Museum for Scottish Lighthouses.

At Rosehearty I found a very quiet harbour next to a bay, before working my way to Aberdour Bay, a mostly pebble beach, with no harbour! When I got to Pennan the road took a steep dive down to a row of houses that lined a pebbly, rocky beach, with a small harbour at one end. If you've ever seen the film 'Local Hero', you'll have seen parts of Pennan, and you'll remember a red telephone box. The telephone box used in the film was actually a prop, placed in a more cinematic position than the real telephone box, which was almost hidden next to a building.

Once the van had laboured to get back out of Pennan, I continued to Crovie, but took the advice on a road sign to park at a viewpoint above the village, rather than drive down into it. Similar to Pennan, Crovie had a row of houses at the base of the cliffs, but no room for a road in front of the houses, instead it just dropped down to one end of the village. From there I could see neighbouring Gardenstown, where a larger number of houses rose up the cliffside. When I reached Gardenstown I again parked near the top, but couldn't be bothered to walk all the way down to the sea, so I observed the small harbour and large rocky beach from above.

Macduff was a larger town, another fishing port, with a correspondingly larger harbour, and the Doune Church overlooking the town from the Hill of Doune. Across the sandy mouth of the River Deveron was Bannf, which had, among other things, a harbour and a sailing club.

Whitehills, rather surprisingly, had a harbour, some may say marina, full of yachts, whereas Portsoy had not one, but two harbours, one of which dated back to the seventeenth century, the oldest on the Moray Firth. The buildings around the old harbour had been restored, one of which was a home to Portsoy Marble, a red and green serpentine that was used in the Palace of Versailles.

Sandend had one of Scotland's smallest harbours. So small, in fact, that I didn't realise it was there until I just looked it up. Instead I was happy to wander out onto a sandy beach, where several surfers were trying their luck with the gentle waves.

I crossed into Moray on my way to Cullen, where I stopped in the upper part of the town and looked down onto a harbour and Cullen Bay. I'd been looking out for a decent cafe all day, and finally found one there, so I stopped for a little while before moving down to a beach near a couple of rocky 'teeth' sticking out of the sand. Running through the town and behind the beach was a disused railway viaduct.

Moving on again I stopped at Portknockie. Apart from the, uhhh, harbour, there were several little rocky bays to the east of the village and rock formations jutting out of the sea, including the 'Bow and Fiddle'.

Fittingly, my campsite for tonight is a stone's throw from a harbour, in Findochty (pronounced 'Finnechty'). It's quite a pretty little place, with the campsite right above a small beach and a hill behind it that provides a great view over the village. The hill has a WWI memorial and a golf course on top.

I have my suspicions as to what I may see tomorrow.

Portessie to Nairn
Wednesday, 30th May

I set off towards Buckie this morning, but stopped briefly on the way at the pebble and sand beach of Portessie. When I reached Buckie I found that it had, rather surprisingly, a harbour, and rows of houses in front of a pebble beach, plus a small gap in a breakwater, for some reason. It also reminded me to lookup the Get Fuzzy cartoon that I used to read daily many years ago.

Portgordon was another village set along a road running behind a pebble beach, with a harbour that had more boats out of the water than in it. I continued on to Spey Bay, at the mouth of the Spey. The village was once a centre for salmon fishing, but today the waters were only fished by individuals, rather than commercial operations. I saw several cars today with fly fishing rods affixed to their bonnets and roofs. A nineteenth century ice house in the village, used for storing salmon, now belongs to the Whale and Dolphin Conservation Society. I was drawn to the sign of a cafe inside the building, but the whole place wasn't yet open, so I moved on rather disappointedly.

At Lossiemouth I stopped by East Beach, reaching it via a footbridge across the Lossie. The sandy beach and dunes stretched for a mile or so to the east. The town itself seemed very quiet, with a wide main street that had a few shops dotted along it, but no cafe, and a harbour and marina that ran around the northeast corner. On the west side of the town was West Beach. RAF Tornados were circling above the town, flying from the RAF's largest fast-jet base, RAF Lossiemouth, next to a golf course just outside the town.

Hopeman was a nice little place, with a harbour flanked by small sandy bays, and a cafe! I stopped for a while for elevenses and to catch up on the latest football transfer gossip. Next I moved on to Burghead, where most of the town lay on a headland. On the west side was the obligatory harbour and a large sandy beach that swept around the length of Burghead Bay to Findhorn, which was where I headed next, passing RAF Kinloss as I drove up the side of the tidal mudflats of Findhorn Bay.

Findhorn was another nice place, a centre for sailing and windsurfing, with several pubs, restaurants and cafes that led me towards a sailing club and a neck of dunes across the back of a beach. To the west, across Findhorn Bay, the trees of Culbin Forest provided an attractive backdrop. As I walked over the sand dunes I could see a number of seals across the beach at the waters edge, so I set off towards them. I wasn't able to get very close before some of them got spooked and headed into the sea, so I backed off again. Across the Moray Firth the eastern coast of Highland had been visible for most of the day.

Next I headed deep into Culbin Forest and parked at a Forestry Commission car park at Wellhill. From there I followed part of the 'Hill 99 Trail' that took me to a lookout tower. The view was pretty good across the Moray Firth and to the Black Isle (which isn't actually surrounded by water) to the west.

My last stop took me from Moray into Highland, and to Nairn. I stopped on the eastern banks of the Nairn and walked out to the eastern beach, then across a footbridge over the river to a marina, and onto the western beach. I found my campsite for the night a couple of miles to the west, in a pleasant wooded area.

Fort George to Rosemarkie
Thursday, 31st May

I wasn't going to travel particularly far today, so I took it easy and started the morning with some bacon and pancakes before setting off to Fort George.

On a headland that jutted out into the Moray Firth, Fort George was a large eighteenth century fortress that was still used as a garrison, most recently by the Black Watch, although part of the fort was open to the public. It was built as the main garrison fortress in the Scottish Highlands after the 1746 Battle of Culloden, which took place eight miles away and that saw the end of the Jacobite Rising.

I drove on into Inverness, but didn't really find an area worth looking at, other than viewing the Kessock Bridge over the Moray Firth. So instead I filled up with diesel and found a cafe for a while before getting some lunch and trying to find a book in probably the last branch of Waterstones for some miles.

I crossed the Kessock Bridge onto the Black Isle and doubled back on myself to North Kessock, on the opposite banks of Beauly Firth to Inverness. There was a Dolphins and Seals centre at North Kessock where you could listen to the dolphins and seals using underwater microphones, but it didn't open until June, which just happens to be tomorrow.

From North Kessock I started up the other side of the Moray Firth and drove to Munlochy, a small village overlooking the head of Munlochy Bay, then to Avoch, a fishing village with a small harbour, before stopping at Fortrose, where I walked down to a beach and harbour. The beach continued along the southern side of a narrow headland, which I drove along through the middle of a golf course to a lighthouse at the end. From there I had great views up and down the Moray Firth, and across it to Fort George.

A short drive down the northern side of the headland brought me to my campsite at Rosemarkie, where I parked up on a narrow strip of grass behind a beach. It was only mid afternoon so I walked along the beach into the village of Rosemarkie, hoping to find a nice cafe to sit in for the rest of the afternoon. Unfortunately one of them had just closed and the other was closing shortly, so I had to make do with an ice cream and a longer stroll along the beach.

Cromarty to Dalchalm
Friday, 1st June

The summer was a little tardy arriving this morning, but eventually turned up a few hours late.

I made a fairly early start and headed for Cromarty, where a ferry to Nigg Ferry should have been running every half hour. I got there just as the ferry was due to depart, but I stopped to look around the harbour and the area where the ferry ran from. Across the Cromarty Firth there appeared to be patches of snow on the hills. As I watched the ferry returning from Nigg Ferry I began to realise that it wasn't a roll-on roll-off, and as it pulled in to shore the crewman shouted for me to turn around and reverse on. Luckily I was the only person waiting, as it would only fit four cars or a couple of motorhomes, which must be why I ended up paying £15 for a one way trip.

It was nice to be out on the water for the 10 minute trip though, across the narrow neck of the Cromarty Firth. There were several oil rigs in the Firth, undergoing maintenance before being floated back into action. As one of the safest anchorages in north Scotland, the Firth was once home to the Royal Navy's Home Fleet. When I drove off in Nigg Ferry, what looked like an armoured motorhome drove straight on, forwards. I hope he didn't get to use the turntable embedded in the deck of the ferry, that wouldn't have been fair.

I watched the ferry leave and got going again, narrowly avoiding a little kamikaze rabbit on the way to Balintore, where I stopped to look at a beach and harbour before moving on to Tarbet Ness, at the tip of a peninsula at the mouth of Dornoch Firth. A short walk from the car park took me past a lighthouse and out to the rocky point of the peninsula. The sky was a mixture of blue and cloud and the sun was warming the air nicely. It would have been nice to have spotted a bottlenose dolphin, but you can't have everything.

Heading back down the peninsula, I stopped at a nice bay and beach at Portmahomack. I had passed a visitor centre with a cafe just before the bay, so I walked back for some coffee and chocolate cake. I'm wondering whether I'll have to go cold turkey on my cafe habit as I progress around the Scottish coast, I don't expect there'll be many of them around in the wilds of the northwest.

Moving on, I stopped briefly by the tidal flatlands of Inver before continuing to Tain and walking through a bunting clad main street, past the fairytale turrets of the Tolbooth. On the way back I dropped into a bakery in search of pies. It seems my desire for tea cakes has abated and been replaced with a desire for lovely round pies. I went for steak, heated, to take with me to a suitable lunch stop.

Leaving Tain, on the way towards a bridge over the Dornoch Firth, I sped past a sign for the Glenmorangie Distillery. I'd like to think that I slammed the breaks on, turned on a sixpence and screeched back up the road in a cloud of tyre rubber, Dukes of Hazzard style, but instead it took me about half a mile to find somewhere to turn around. I pulled into the car park and had a look at the shop, but elected not to take a tour today, or buy a £120 bottle of

Signet, I'm sure there'll be plenty of opportunities to come, maybe on a day when I'm not driving.

Once over the bridge I drove through Dornoch and out to a car park by a sandy beach, where I devoured the pie before taking a look at the beach and a golf course behind it. I then drove back into Dornoch and wandered around its wide streets. Moving on again I drove around Loch Fleet and back down its eastern shore, along the side of a golf course, to Littleferry on one side of a channel of water that ran out of the loch. I walked onto a beach and up to the edge of the water, where something caught my eye and I heard the sound of air being exhaled quickly, like a blowhole, perhaps. I kept my eyes peeled until something broke the water again and snorted. Not a dolphin, but a seal, seemingly labouring against the strong current, but still making its way upstream and out of sight. I wandered up and down the soft beach, up to my ankles in the sand at times, but didn't see anything else.

Passing back up the side of Loch Fleet again I stopped at Golspie to look at a beach and walk out of the eastern side of the village to some pretty cottages near a stream. Behind Golspie was Beinn a' Bhragaidh, standing at 394m, with a huge plinth and statue of the first Duke of Sutherland on top. From Golspie I drove to a beach and harbour at Brora, where bunting marked the location of a fete that was being setup for the Jubilee tomorrow. Before leaving Brora I acted on a recommendation and stopped at Capaldi's ice cream parlour, a family run business since 1929, but now owned by Harry Gow, the 'first ever Scottish Baker of the Year'. I don't know if the ice cream recipe has changed at all recently, but the rum & raisin was very nice!

From Brora I drove about a mile down the road, passing a sculpture of an eagle along the way, to a campsite in Dalchalm, separated from a beautiful sandy beach by a quiet golf course, with a cow infestation.

Helmsdale to Hill o' Many Stanes
Saturday, 2nd June

I started the day with a lie in and some breakfast this morning, while a little early rain passed over.

My first stop was at Helmsdale, nestled under an A9 road bridge that crossed the River Helmsdale. I wandered around the harbour before walking under the bridge to the main part of the village, finding a visitor centre with a cafe advertising Jubilee Cream Teas. Now given that I'd already had a cooked breakfast, and it wasn't even 11:00am yet, I decided to walk up onto the road bridge first, to look at a statue on the other side by a picnic area. The statue was to commemorate all the people of the Highlands that had emigrated to seek new lives elsewhere. By the time I got back to the visitor centre it was 11:00am, time for a cream tea, purely in honour of the Queen you understand.

From Helmsdale I started climbing zig zag roads through an ever increasing number of hills as I moved further north, until I came to a lay-by with a sign post for the Badbea Clearance Village. I'll be honest, when I saw this on the map I pictured an outlet mall selling kilts with imperfect hems, but it was actually a path that led to the ruins of a settlement perched on the side of the cliffs. The Highland Clearances were the forced displacement of many families in the late eighteenth and early nineteenth century, as a result of landowners realising that there was more money to be made from farming sheep in the inland glens than collecting rent. At Badbea the winds were often so high and the cliffs so steep, that the livestock, and even the children, had to be tethered to prevent them from being blown from the cliffs. A monument was erected on the cliffs in 1911 by the son of a family that emigrated from there to New Zealand to escape life at Badbea.

At Dunbeath I dropped below the A9 again to a harbour at the mouth of Dunbeath Water. To the south, right on the edge of the cliffs, was the whitewashed Dunbeath Castle, and out to sea was the Beatrice Oil Field, the closest oil field to the UK. I had a campsite booked just outside Dunbeath, but as it was still early in the afternoon I decided to carry on a little up the coast before coming back again.

Latheronwheel had a tiny harbour and rocky beach, out of sight of the village itself. Quite a serene little place. I drove on through Lybster and turned inland off the A9 for a short distance, following signs for the Hill O' Many Stanes. When I got there I was expecting to find a hillside covered with towering standing stones, but in reality I found what looked like the equivalent of a model village of standing stones, most of them about a foot high, in a small circular area of bracken. Maybe it was a Bronze Age architect's model of what he intended to build, but never got the funding.

I started back towards Dunbeath, but decided to drive into Lybster and down to the harbour, with a small lighthouse at the end, a pebbly beach next to it, and a cafe behind it, what luck. It started to rain fairly heavily, so I had little choice but to take shelter in the cafe for a while before finding the Inver Caravan Park back at Dunbeath.

Cairn o' Get to Dunnet Bay
Sunday, 3rd June

I'd been looking forward to today, it was going to provide one of the little milestones of this trip.

I passed through Latheronwheel and Lybster, past the signpost for the Hill O' Many Stanes, and as I came into Whaligoe I turned inland at a signpost for the Cairn O' Get. I parked a short distance up a narrow track by Loch Watenan and walked along a path through fields, following several black and white marker poles, until I reached the cairn. I had no idea what to expect, and what I found were the remains of a burial cairn, possibly 5,000 years old and the last resting place of at least seven people. Most of the stones from the cairn were removed to build a nearby dam in the eighteen hundreds.

I drove back down the track and straight across the main road to a car park by a cafe. The cafe didn't open until 11:00am, unfortunately, but that didn't really matter as I was there to walk down around 350 steps to a small quay. Herring fishermen used to take their boats there and the women of the village would carry heavy loads up and down the steps. I bet they waited until the cafe was open though, I could have done with a drink by the time I got back to the top.

I drove on to Wick, parked on a street and had a look around the harbour, before wandering across a bridge over the River Wick to the high street, where I found a convenient cafe for some elevenses. Moving on, I stopped briefly at a beach in Keiss where I could look back across Sinclair's Bay to a lighthouse on Noss Head, just north of Wick. I carried on along the A99, stopping briefly in a lay-by looking across Freswick Bay.

As the A99 rose up and then levelled out again I quite literally stopped in my tracks, pulling into a viewpoint, as the Orkney Islands appeared before me. I had driven this road before, but I didn't remember seeing the islands so clearly, or them being so close to the mainland, maybe it had been misty that day.

As I drove into John o' Groats I turned off the main road and out towards Duncansby Head, stopping before I got there above a little sandy beach that I remembered from a previous visit. It was quite a nice day at this point so I fetched my tripod and some filters from the van and spent quite a while playing around taking some photos with a slow shutter speed, to blur the water. After I'd exhausted my limited creativity I drove the rest of the way to Duncansby Head, the most northeasterly tip of the British mainland.

Not far to the south of Duncansby Head were the Stacks of Duncansby, two large pointed pillars of rock, standing in the sea away from the cliffs, the tallest of which was about 60m high. Also near the head was a narrow cleft in the cliffs, where birds were nesting on the vertical faces, including a lone puffin. Fortunately this time I had my zoom lens with me and the little fella stuck around for his close up.

John o' Groats was fairly busy, as might be expected, with people wandering around the small harbour and a collection of souvenir and craft shops. Some were having their photo taken by an official photographer in front of a signpost, identical to the one at Lands End, apart from the locations on the signs, obviously. There were quite a few bikers around, and a few cyclists, but I don't know if any of them had come from Lands End, or were just setting out for there. It had taken me two and a half months to get from one to the other.

My campsite for tonight was at Dunnet Bay, about 20 minutes away, where I had a booking for two nights, so I decided to book myself on a day trip around the Orkney Islands, which I'll come back for tomorrow. I headed straight to the campsite, perched behind the dunes above a large sandy beach, where a horse and rider and a horse and trap were trotting out towards the waves, and a bank of rain was passing over the far side of the bay. Several other banks of rain have since passed directly overhead.

Dunnet Head and The Orkney Islands
Monday, 4th June

I headed straight for Dunnet Head first thing this morning, the most northerly point on the British mainland. From a viewpoint above the lighthouse I could see for miles around. There seemed to be a lot of smoke rising to the southeast, possibly due to some Viking pillaging. To the north, at the far western side of the Orkney Islands, I could see the tall stack of the Old Man of Hoy.

As it started to rain I got in the van and drove east, back to John o' Groats, from where I was going to catch a passenger ferry to the Orkneys. The ferry was a little late, due to strong tides, but after everyone had boarded we pitched and rolled our way to Burwick, on the southern tip of South Ronaldsay.

Most of us boarded a coach, which drove us north across the rolling green fields, pretty much devoid of trees, while the driver imparted titbits of local knowledge. Moving up the eastern edge of Scapa Flow we drove across several causeways to pass through Burray island and two smaller islands, Glims Holm and Lamb Holm, before reaching the main island, Mainland.

Scapa Flow was an important natural harbour for the

Royal Navy during the First and Second World Wars, almost entirely surrounded by the islands, with narrow channels between them. The channels were closed during WWI using booms, or by sinking merchant 'block ships' across them, but this didn't stop a German submarine from slipping through in the first few weeks of WWII and sinking HMS Royal Oak. Fortunately most of the British fleet were elsewhere at the time. Churchill ordered the defences to be improved, so causeways were built between the islands, which also provided communications by road. Some of the block ships still remain.

We stopped for an hour in Kirkwall, the capital of the Orkneys, time enough to take a look at St Magnus Cathedral and the harbour, and to eat some lunch. After lunch we headed to the west coast at Skara Brae, site of a small Stone Age village of eight dwellings. The village lay hidden under sand for around 4,000 years until 1850, when a storm and high tides revealed the tops of the buildings. The buildings and their contents were well preserved by the sand that hid them, and have since been excavated.

Next we moved to a narrow peninsula between the Loch of Harray and Loch of Stenness and stopped for 20 minutes to see the Ring of Brodgar, a Neolithic stone circle, about 100m in diameter and comprising of 36 remaining stones, from 7 to 15 feet in height. The monument was also a henge, having a ditch all the way around it, dug out of the rock. Not far from the stone circle were the Standing Stones of Stenness, possibly the oldest henge monument in the British Isles. Four standing stones remained but the ditch was no longer visible.

Our final stop was on the way back, on Lamb Holm, at an Italian Chapel, the last remaining building of Camp 60, a Prisoner of War camp that was home to Italian soldiers during WWII. The prisoners were provided with two Nissen huts that they placed end to end in order to build the chapel.

From there we returned to the ferry and sailed back to John o' Groats. I couldn't be bothered to cook this evening so I bought a burger from a cafe hut next to the harbour. Throughout the day, whenever we got sight of the mainland, the smoke that I'd spotted earlier in the day had been increasing in volume. According to the woman that served me my burger, a controlled fire had been started yesterday to burn the heather, but it had got out of control, closing the roads to the south. This wasn't the first time this had happened and she was rather scathing about the 'idiots' that had started the fires.

Fortunately I was heading west back to Dunnet Bay, so I ate my burger and returned to the campsite.

Gills to Thurso
Tuesday, 5th June

I was intending to take an easy day today, as I'd decided to spend another night at Dunnet Bay, so I started off with a lie-in and a bacon sandwich before heading off to fill in some of the gaps between John o' Groats and here.

I drove to Brough and parked next to some shaggy black cows above a bay. In the middle of the bay was Little Clett, a sea stack. I walked down into the bay to a slipway disappearing into the sea. While I was stood on the slipway I noticed a buoy in the water to my right, I did a double take but thought 'yeah, it's a buoy', until it slipped under the water and came back up again. It wasn't a buoy, it was a seal. It spent a while popping its head out of the water, looking at me, and dipping back under the surface, before it moved off a bit further out on the left hand side of the bay and was joined by a second seal. I went back up to the van and grabbed my zoom lens (I really should keep it with me at all times) and some other kit so that I could take some more slow shutter photos, while the seals bobbed up and down out in the bay before eventually disappearing.

Once I'd finished taking photos I carried on towards John o' Groats, but kept to the tracks nearer the coast where possible, rather than the main road. I passed by Harrow, above a small harbour, passed the Castle of Mey, and got as close as I could to St John's Point, where the Men of Mey just off the point are supposed to throw up high plumes of water as the tide ebbs. I also drove down to a ferry terminal at Gills, where you could take a vehicle over to the Orkneys. I spotted a campervan belonging to a Welsh couple that I'd chatted to at the campsite, they were going to spend a few days on the islands.

Next I headed back to the west, and beyond Dunnet Bay, to Castletown at the far end of the bay, and to Castlehill just to the north, where I found a small harbour that had been made out of the local Caithness flagstones, which were used through Britain and as far away as Australia and Calcutta until cheap concrete took away most of the demand. Continuing west I stopped in Thurso, hoping to find a cafe with WiFi that I could use to post the last few days of blog entries. I found a cafe with WiFi and ordered a drink, but the WiFi didn't seem to work so I didn't order any lunch. I found another cafe with WiFi but they informed me that it wasn't working either, so instead I found a nearby bakery and bought a chicken pie. I moved from the centre and drove to the mouth of the River Thurso, which also overlooked Thurso Bay and beach. It was raining by now so I sat in the van looking out through a rain streaked windscreen while eating the pie, which was nice but I wasn't expecting it to have carrots in it too. If only I'd had a thermos flask I could have experienced what life holds for me when I'm older.

Just as I was driving away again I came across another cafe, so quickly checked my phone and found a WiFi connection. I didn't intend to sit in a cafe just after eating lunch, as hard as that may be to believe, so I parked the van as close as possible and started uploading the blog. It can take a while to upload, particularly if the connection isn't very fast, so I sat there and watched as the battery on my laptop ran out before it had finished (I can only use the 240V sockets in the van when I'm on hookup), which means it would have only partly uploaded. Seeing as that kind of thing would play on my mind (I hate leaving loose ends), I decided that I would return to the campsite and let the laptop charge while I was shaving, showering, emptying the toilet etc and return to the cafe later on once I'd written today's entry.

And that's what I'm off to do now.

Sandside Bay to Durness
Wednesday, 6th June

It started to rain pretty much at the moment I left the campsite this morning. I drove to Crosskirk, where the twelfth century Chapel of St Mary sat above a bay. It was a bit of a walk to the chapel, so I sat in the van for a while as the rain came down, but eventually decided it wasn't worth getting wet so early in the day, so I moved on.

Just beyond the Dounreay Power Station I stopped at Sandside Bay and walked a short distance through some dunes to a beach. A sign on the path from the car park warned that radioactive metallic particles had been found on the beach, so don't touch anything or you may grow a second head. Nice.

Next I stopped at Melvich Bay and walked out to more dunes behind another beach. Behind the dunes the Halladale River wound beneath a footbridge and past Bighouse Lodge, which used to belong to the Clan MacKay. I drove up the side of the bay to a small harbour at Portskerra before continuing on to Strathy Bay and again walking to dunes behind a beach. And again I drove up the side of the bay, but this time along a couple of miles of headland to Strathy Point. The road stopped some distance short of a lighthouse, and in the wind and rain I decided once again to give it a miss. Apparently on a fine day you can see east to Dunnet Head and west to Cape Wrath, but today was not a fine day.

I was slowly leaving civilisation behind me as the landscape became the greens and browns of grass and heather, mixed with rock and yellow gorse, and the terrain became more mountainous, punctuated by small lochs. Just before reaching Bettyhill I stopped briefly at a viewpoint and surveyed the barren landscape around me, looking forward to whatever was to come. Just down the road I stopped at a visitor centre for some elevenses before leaving the main road and finding a tiny little bay that looked back to a beach, then crossed the small headland that I was on and had my first 'wow' moment of the day. Below me was the mouth of the Naver River and on the opposite side was a spit of sand jutting out into the mouth, surrounded on three sides by clear blue water, with dunes in the middle of it and backed by rugged hills.

After crossing the Naver the A road turned into a single track road, but with plenty of passing places, a further sign of the increasing wilderness. The road continued away from the coast for a while until I caught sight of Tongue Bay, at the head of the Kyle of Tongue. Out in the bay were the Rabbit Islands. Driving down the eastern side of the Kyle of Tongue I could see a causeway snaking across the water, which I crossed and immediately turned north off the main road to drive up the western side. I passed another large spit of sand and carried on until I reached Talmine, a very picturesque bay, beach and harbour. On the beach were the remains of the wreck of a wooden ship, which looked more like the skeleton of a huge fish. Some painted stones had been placed on the bow, like flowers on a grave.

I returned to the main road and crossed another large headland, away from the coast, passed the neck of Loch

Hope and crossed another headland until I came upon another 'wow' moment as Loch Eriboll appeared in front of me and I stopped in a lay-by. The large loch was made more impressive by Ard Neackie, a strip of land protruding into the loch with a narrow neck preventing it from being an island. In the middle of the loch was Eilean Choraidh, an island that was used for target practice by WWII bombers training to attack the German battleship Tirpitz, which was moored in a similar shaped Norwegian fjord. I spoke to a biker in the lay-by who was photographing his mate while he zoomed past. They'd taken about an hour to go one mile, as they couldn't resist stopping to photograph each other in such spectacular surroundings.

There was no way across the loch, so I drove all the way down one side and all the way back up the other, eventually coming to Rispond Bay, where I walked out onto a beautiful sandy beach. I stopped to look at another beach below me as I drove towards Durness, and stopped again to walk down into Smoo Cave. Once inside the cave I walked into a chamber where a waterfall cascaded down through a hole in the roof. While I was in the chamber a boat emerged from a deeper floodlit chamber, passing below a very low bridge of rock.

Once in Durness I found my campsite for the night, Sango Sands, where I chose a pitch on top of the cliff, overlooking a large sandy beach that was split in two by a promontory with a viewing platform built at the end of it. A fine place to stop after a fine day, even if it had rained for a fair bit of it.

Cape Wrath and Balnakiel
Thursday, 7th June

What an awesome day.

I had wanted to get out to Cape Wrath this morning, and up until yesterday I had assumed I could get a vehicle ferry over to a 10 mile road that led to a lighthouse at the most northwesterly point in mainland Britain. But while at the visitor centre I discovered that the ferry was a passenger ferry, not a vehicle ferry. However, once across the Kyle of Durness there was a minibus that would take me to Cape Wrath.

I got to the ferry at Keoldale at 9:00am and spoke to the ferryman and minibus driver. It would take about 45 minutes to drive to the lighthouse and the minibus would make the first return trip an hour later. So I packed some waterproofs and joined a bunch of people, including three Irish lads with bikes, and waited for the ferry to leave at 9.30am. The ferryman took the first group across before coming back for the second group, including myself. I got chatting to a couple that I'd seen on the campsite, who had hired campervans in Australia and Canada for months at a time. It turned out they had been next to me at Dunnet Bay and had recognised my van on the campsite in Durness.

When we got to the slipway at the other side, after a calm crossing on a pleasant but overcast day, we waited for another group to come across so that the first of the two minibuses would be full. The driver introduced himself to everyone and we got underway, along a narrow well worn track, with a total of 56 passing places but only 12 that the driver considered to be safe. Along the way he told us bits of information about the lighthouse and the landscape. The lighthouse was unmanned, but a couple lived there and ran a small cafe. One Christmas the wife had taken their girls to Inverness to do the Christmas shop, but by the time they got back the road had become impassable with snow. It was five weeks before the husband could drive down from the lighthouse to pick them up again.

We passed into and through a military firing and exercise range. Our driver, Alan, originally from Wales, had served in the first Gulf War with the Royal Electrical and Mechanical Engineers. He had previously come to Cape Wrath for six weeks of exercises, and had hated it. But after leaving the forces he started sheep farming, eventually ending up back in this area as a crofter, and started driving the minibus last year.

We drove over several very narrow bridges, up and down and around hills, before reaching the lighthouse, shrouded in cloud. We could barely see anything, so everyone wandered around for 10 or 20 minutes, being careful not to fall off the cliffs, then settled in the cafe until it was time for the return trip. On the way back we stopped to view a rock formation in the sea known as the cathedral. Apparently there was a bothy (a hut for walkers) not far from it, behind a beach. Anyone is welcome to just turn up and stay in it, but it's advisable to take a tent just in case the five rooms are full.

When we got back to the slipway the boat was just arriving with the next group. The ferryman from the morning had gone to the dentist, but his replacement had a friendly dog with him, Tweedy. It was a shame that there had been no visibility at the cape, but everyone had thoroughly enjoyed the whole trip.

I drove back to the campsite and back onto my pitch, then went looking for some lunch, specifically a pie. I tried the Spar and asked in the visitor centre whether there was a bakery nearby, which there wasn't. But I'm getting good at sniffing them out. I passed a small shop and noticed a couple of pies through the window. The only option was a Scotch pie. When I asked what was in them I was told it was a selection of meats. I didn't ask which meats, and I didn't really want to know.

I put my walking trousers on, grabbed my bag, made sure I had the pie and headed out for a walk along a peninsula that ran north from Durness to Faraid Head. The pie was okay, in case you're wondering, but not as nice as the steak, chicken or chicken curry pies. After a while I realised that it was further than I thought to Faraid Head, so I decided to cut across the peninsula towards some sand dunes and Balnakeil Bay, then follow a road back down the other side and complete a square route back to Durness.

The sand dunes were huge, so I looked for a path between them and came across a pretty little lake (possibly more of a pond) in the middle of them, which was the last thing I expected to find. From there the sand became covered with grass for a while, then turned into a sandy grassy mogul field that I worked my way through until I emerged onto an amazing beach. I've had to pinch myself several times on this trip and remind myself that I'm still in Britain, and this was the latest breathtaking beach behind a blue sea. The slightly angry sky ahead made it even more impressive, but there were glimpses of blue appearing too.

I walked along the beach until I reached a car park and the road back to Durness, which was just over a mile away.

By the car park were the ruins of a seventeenth century church. Not far down the road I found a little complex of cafes, craft shops and galleries at the Balnakeil Craft Village, including the Cocoa Mountain. I'll be honest with you, I'd seen signposts to it in Durness, so I was kind of counting on passing it on the way back. I spent a while there while writing this entry, with a hot chocolate 'chaser', which came with two truffles of your choice. Champagne and Darkest Lime, in case you were wondering. Is it me, or is this basically a blog about my eating habits? Ah well, that's not going to change.

By the time I left the cafe it was turning into a pretty nice day. I picked up some groceries at the Spar and drove the van 50m up the road to top up with diesel. I paid wayyy more than I've paid anywhere else for diesel, but I suppose you don't have much option for shopping around up here, and I wanted to be safe rather than sorry before heading further into the wilderness tomorrow.

Kinlochbervie to Clachtoll
Friday, 8th June

It was pretty windy and raining slightly from low grey clouds when I set off this morning, heading southwest on the only road in this area, cutting across the large headland below Cape Wrath. When I reached the other side of the headland I turned northwest up the side of Loch Inchard, to Kinlochbervie.

There wasn't much to see there, apart from the large harbour, so I carried on along narrow roads to see two golden beaches and a turquoise sea at Oldshoremore and Oldshore Beg. At Oldshore Beg I parked by a whitewashed stone cottage with colourful toadstools in front of it. There was also a scale model of the house perched on a wall, and a large dog in the front garden sitting next to a life size model of itself. On the way down to the beach was a gate with a sign saying 'beware of the mermaids'. Peculiar place.

Heading south again I got back onto the A838, cutting across another smaller headland before turning onto the A894 towards Scourie. Part way along I turned north onto a narrow track and followed it until I hit the coast at Tarbet. From there you could take a boat out to Handa Island to see the nesting birds, or to spend a night in a bothy on the otherwise uninhabited island.

Retracing my steps I returned to the main road and on to Scourie, where I found a large bay with a pebble beach and harbour wall at one side and a sandy beach below a grassy bank at the other side. From there I continued south into an increasingly mountainous region, although how high the mountains were I couldn't tell, I could just see them rising up into the cloud. At one point I came over a rise to see Duartmore Forest before me, starting at the banks of a river that ran beneath two small bridges. Once I had passed through the forest I came to a viewpoint that looked down to Loch a'Chairn Bhain. The road wound down to a causeway that flirted with the side of the loch before rising up a little and around a corner to the gracefully curved concrete structure of the Kylesku Bridge. Until the bridge was built in 1984, and opened by the Queen, the only way across was by ferry.

Just across the bridge I dropped off the main road into Kylesku and parked near a small slipway below the Kylesku Hotel. The bar restaurant part of the hotel was quite busy, but I sat at a table to see about some lunch. The menu looked good but was a bit rich for my budget, with mussels and langoustines and the like. The hot smoked salmon was off after a few busy days, so instead I just had a coffee and some chips, which came served in a small rustic bucket, as is the fashion these days, and were very light, fluffy and crispy.

Not far from Kylesku I left the A894 and joined the B869, which would take me all around the North Assynt coast. I was now onto a long stretch of narrow road, twisting, rising and falling. I wouldn't really say it was fun to drive, there was too much concentration involved to make sure I didn't drop a wheel off the tarmac or go too fast around some of the blind corners, but there were plenty of passing spaces for the odd vehicle that I met coming the other way. I stopped briefly at Drumbeg, where a few houses, a hotel and a store were spread along the road, then continued on until I reached a beach at Clashnessie, which had a pink tint to the sand.

Most days, up until now, I've roughly planned where I'm going to stay, or maybe booked somewhere at least the day before, but today I hadn't planned anything and I wanted to see how the day went. The next campsite listed with the Camping and Caravanning Club or the Caravan Club was near Ullapool, which I didn't think I would reach today, so my options were to find a campsite on the way, or to wild camp somewhere. As it turned out, when I arrived in Clachtoll I found a campsite near the beach and got a warm welcome from the owner, so I decided to stay there for the night. Free WiFi too!

Once I'd found a pitch and started uploading the last few days entries I went for a walk for an hour or so along the coast, starting at the beach and making my own tracks around some rocky outcrops, past coastal cows, chickens and ducks, until I got to the top of a small rocky hill and could see some beaches to the south at Achmelvich, which may well be my first stop tomorrow.

Achmelvich to Ullapool
Saturday, 9th June

It was a decent morning today, still cloudy but brighter and calmer than yesterday. I didn't see another vehicle on the road for the first five and a half miles to Achmelvich, where I walked along the sandy beach that I'd seen from the top of the hill yesterday afternoon, in front of another campsite.

I drove the last few miles of the B869, joined the A837 and dropped down into Lochinver, at the head of Loch Inver, funnily enough. I stopped to get a few supplies and took a look at the harbour. Leaving Lochinver I started along the 'Mad Road of Sutherland', as it's known. There were signs at the beginning of the road saying that it was unsuitable for caravans and buses, and had an 8m length limit, presumably because there were some tight corners. Now I know I said I didn't really enjoy the drive yesterday, but I have to admit it was kind of fun today, I couldn't help but smile after some of the twisty turns and rises to blind summits, which was just as well as I was looking to be on this kind of road for several hours.

My first stop along the way was at Inverkirkaig at the head of Loch Kirkaig, a pretty bay with a pebble beach and houses dotted around it. The road continued, often through trees, sometimes with barriers or brick walls along the side of the road. At one point I looked in my mirrors to see how close I was getting to the walls, then decided it was best not to look again. There were signs along the road to beware of runners, but as yet I hadn't come across any. In front of me were three mountains, Cul Mor, Cul Beag and Stac Pollaidh, with their summits brushing the clouds. Eventually I caught up with the tail end runner, and an HM Coastguard truck keeping pace behind her. For a minute I thought I would have to stick behind them for hours, but the truck pulled over to let me pass and I passed the runner, giving her plenty of room. A little further on I passed a couple of cars coming in the opposite direction. The drivers both looked a little twitchy when they had to reverse to let me past, which made me wonder whether they had just been through a particularly traumatic section of road. But nothing nasty lay ahead.

I passed the turning to a road that I would have to come back to later, before reaching a sandy beach at Achnahaird, where I turned north and continued towards Reiff, the most northerly point that I could reach on this section of coast. When I came over a rise I found the view in front of me was full of islands, the Summer Isles. At Reiff, where the road ran out, there was a small collection of houses and a sandy beach, where a small loch fed out to the sea.

From Reiff I headed towards Culnacraig, the most southerly point that I could reach. On the way there, with the Summer Isles to my right, I came to Achiltibuie, which ran for a mile or so along the road, but started with a bay and pebble beach looking out to the islands and across to the distant peaks on the mainland to the southeast. As I passed through Achiltibuie and out the other side the surface of the road deteriorated a little and the landscape became more barren until I eventually reached the end of the road at Culnacraig, where a few buildings lay beneath the gaze of Beinn Mor Coigach.

I could go no further along this part of the coast, so I turned around and returned to Achiltibuie, where I took a different route back to Achnahaird, then further on took the road that I'd passed earlier, which took me along the side of Loch Osgaig, Loch Bad a 'Ghaill and Loch Lurgainn, beneath the summit of Cul Beag, and on to the A835. The road rose and fell again towards Ardmair, where two bays with pebble beaches on Loch Kanaird were separated by a narrow headland with holiday chalets and a campsite. A little further on I drove into Ullapool and headed towards a campsite that I could see at the near side of the town, Broomfield Holiday Park. It was only about 2:00pm, but I fancied stopping and taking the rest of the afternoon off in Ullapool.

I found a pitch, made some lunch and sat eating it on a beach just in front of the campsite, on the shores of Loch Broom. Once I'd taken in the view I followed the beach around a corner to another stretch of beach running in front of the picturesque town, which I walked along to a harbour and ferry terminal, from where you could take a ferry to Stornaway. A couple of guys in front of me at the harbour pointed into the water to our right, where a seal was bobbing around with what looked like a fish in its mouth. I carried on along the last stretch of the beach, with a fine view of the loch, boats and mountains, making a note of a nice looking cafe on the main street.

The reception at the campsite was open by now, so I walked back and paid for the pitch, grabbed my laptop and returned to the cafe to write this up with a cup of coffee, followed by a strawberry milkshake, while sat on a very comfortable sofa in a relaxing atmosphere. I think I might go for a battered sausage and chips this evening.

Corrieshalloch Gorge to Poolewe
Sunday, 10th June

I topped up with diesel again before leaving Ullapool and heading southeast along the eastern side of Loch Broom, then continued along the side of what became the Droma River until I was able to turn right and start heading back towards the coast.

Before I'd gone far I pulled into a car park for the Corrieshalloch Gorge and followed a path that brought me to a bridge over a deep and narrow gorge. Near the bridge the Falls of Measach plummeted 46m into the gorge. Apparently the bridge was only reopened in late May after it was initially closed for wear and tear, but was closed for longer when cracks were found in the support hangers. On the other side of the bridge a path led to a viewing platform that looked back up the gorge to the falls.

I stopped again briefly at Dundonnell, at the head of Little Loch Broom, before continuing along the southern side of the loch and cutting across a headland to Gruinard Bay, where Gruinard Island lay out in the bay. The island was covered with anthrax during WWII as an experiment in germ warfare. I stopped on the road above a beach and walked down to it through the trees and dunes. The sheltered beach had red sand and rocky outcrops at either end. A pretty beach in a pretty bay. I climbed up above a high bank of sand at one end of the beach and across to the other side of the rocky outcrop, where I could see three more sandy beaches. When I got back to the van I drove down to a car park behind the furthest of those beaches.

As I drove around the bay I left the main road and took a single track road up the side of the bay to Mellon Udrigle, where I found possibly the most beautiful beach so far. The sandy beach itself may not have been any more special than many others I've seen, but the overall location was breathtaking. Backed by green and brown hills, and with low rocky outcrops sheltering both ends, the view straight out from the beach was of the sea in front of an almost unbroken line of the Summer Isles and the mountains that I'd driven around yesterday while exploring the coast between Reiff and Culnacraig. I made some lunch and spent an hour or so staring across the sea and exploring the length of the beach. If I was the kind of person that could give up all material possessions, go more than 24 hours without requiring a technology fix, and had the basic skills required to survive by my wits alone, I would build a hut there and live in it.

Obviously I'm not that kind of person, so I got back in the van, dialled my next location into the SatNav and resumed listening to a podcast that I'd downloaded automagically from the big data cloud in the sky.

I returned to the main road, crossed the neck of the headland and came off again at Aultbea, a small village and harbour spread along a pebble beach in a wide bay. I continued along the road towards Mellon Charles, in the hope that it would offer similar riches to its Mellon cousin across the way, but I just found a collection of individual houses dotted around some grassy sand dunes. Having since looked at an aerial map there was actually a beach at Mellon

Charles, but the road was too far back to see it.

From there I rejoined the main road and started down the side of Loch Ewe, with the Isle of Ewe in the middle of it. Near the end of the loch I came to Inverewe Garden, just short of Poolewe. I'd been wondering whether the National Trust for Scotland was affiliated with the National Trust, and indeed it was, so I went for a wander around the 54 acres of gardens, set within the 2,000 acres of the Inverewe Estate. The gardens began their life in 1861 when Osgood Mackenzie inherited the estate. He made use of the mild and humid weather, brought to the northwest of Scotland by the North Atlantic Drift, to grow plants from all over the world, sheltered by trees. A maze of paths wound through the trees and along the banks of Loch Ewe, which surrounded much of the garden.

When I left the gardens I drove a short distance to a campsite in Poolewe, where I found a pitch and went for a stroll along the road to the small village at the head of the loch and the River Ewe.

Gairloch to Lower Diabaig
Monday, 11th June

I started off the day by leaving the coast and heading across to the other side of the headland at Gairloch, spread out along a length of coastline. I came off the main road to part of the village behind a sandy rocky beach and continued on up the headland to the promisingly named Big Sand.

As it turned out, Big Sand did have a large beach, but you could only get access to it if you were staying at a campsite behind the beach. The village itself was a little beyond the beach, with no access. I drove back past the beach and stopped just off the road to walk back to a fence above it. Not far offshore was Longa Island.

Driving back to Gairloch, I rejoined the main road and stopped to take a look at a sandy beach and a sheltered bay with a harbour. I continued along the banks of Loch Gairloch and came off the main road again to follow a wooded single track road along the coast. At Shieldaig and Badachro I stopped to look at sheltered bays with yachts and dinghies moored in them. Trees gave way to open moorland as I passed a beach at Port Henderson and eventually came to the end of the road at Redpoint. From there I could look out across the sea to the many peaks of

Skye and the Outer Hebrides. I walked through dunes down to a sandy beach, where a couple of guys in kayaks were exploring the area.

There was no road around the rest of this part of the coastline, so I retraced my steps back to the main road, which took me inland and east to the southern banks of Loch Maree. I stopped at several car parks, including one where I followed a path to the Victoria Falls, which weren't quite in the same league as their African namesake. Out in the middle of the loch were the Loch Maree Islands, and looming over it to the east was the peak of Slioch. As I drove along the loch the odometer ticked over 4,000 miles.

From the southeastern end of Loch Maree the road turned to the south and into Kinlochewe, where I was considering coming back to for the night. I dropped into the campsite to make sure they had free pitches, but more importantly to see if I could pick up Radio 5 so that I could listen to England's first Euro 2012 game against France in the evening. From there I took another single track road that turned west back towards the coast. The road largely followed a river and took me through a valley between an increasing number of mountainous peaks. I rejoined the coast at Upper Loch Torridon and turned north into the village of Torridon, where I stopped for some lunch in a general store and cafe.

While I was having lunch some guests for a wedding started arriving and using the toilet, promising to come back later to buy something, before they congregated outside and walked along a track out to a bit of land jutting out into the loch. Once they'd disappeared through a gate the bride was driven up the track and walked through the same gate, much to the delight of some locals in the cafe, particularly when the owner produced some binoculars for them.

I set off again with a certain amount of trepidation as I headed along the northern shore of the loch, knowing that the road was going to rise up through steep hairpin bends, supposedly the steepest in Britain, and through the exposed 'Pass of the Winds' before dropping down to sea level again at Lower Diabaig. Before long I was driving up through some hairpins, although they didn't seem that bad to me, then climbing steadily before rising more steeply and finding myself up above a loch, then dropping down to the side of it, passing through Upper Diabaig and finally dropping steeply into Lower Diabaig. It was quite a road, but well worth the journey for the views, particularly when coming down into Lower Diabaig, set in an amphitheatre of rocky hills.

When I parked near the harbour and switched off the engine there was a kind of knocking noise that continued for a while, and when I stepped out of the van I could smell the heat coming from the engine compartment. I figured I should give it a chance to cool down a little, and luckily it was a lovely spot to wander around, particularly as there was a wrecked ship on the beach to go and gawp at. When I got back to the van everything seemed calm again, and I found myself patting it on the bonnet, as if trying to reassure a distressed horse. If I'd had any Polos on me I'd have probably popped a few through the radiator grill.

Once again I'd pretty much run out of road, so I drove back the way I'd come. The climb out of Lower Diabaig and up above the loch seemed steeper on the way up than it had on the way down, but from there it was mostly downhill back to Torridon, sweeping gracefully around the hairpins and luckily encountering very few vehicles along the way. I parked in the same spot and went back into the cafe for a cold drink and some cake, which I'd promised myself and the owner if I made it back in one piece. The wedding guests had also kept their word and had been back in for cake, apparently they were all staying nearby for a week.

With a certain sense of satisfaction I drove back along

the valley to the campsite at Kinlochewe, arriving just in time to settle down and listen to England fail to set the world alight, as usual, but at least they didn't lose.

Shieldaig to Lochcarron
Tuesday, 12th June

I followed the road from Kinlochewe to Torridon this morning for the second time, continuing on along the southern side of Upper Loch Torridon until I crossed a small headland and reached Shieldaig (a different Shieldaig to the one I passed through yesterday). I stopped above the village, overlooking Loch Shieldaig, before driving down to a row of houses along the banks of the loch.

Leaving the village I turned off the main road to the coastal road that would take me most of the way around the Applecross peninsula. The road twisted, rose and fell past several small Crofts that had all been fairly isolated until the road was built in the 1970s. I drove northwest along the sides of Loch Shieldaig, Loch a' Chracaich and Loch Torridon before reaching the western edge of the peninsula and turning to the south, along the Inner Sound, where the peaks of Skye behind the Island of Raasay dominated the view out to sea. I stopped at a viewpoint just beyond Cuaig for a while before I moved further south and stopped at Sand Bay.

A beautiful golden sand beach at Sand Bay had a superb view of the peaks across the sound. I didn't realise it at the time, but having now researched a little and looked at my photos there was a bothy on a grassy area on the northern side of the beach, which was used by Monty Halls to film a BBC series about him renovating it and living there for some time. I didn't see the series, but it would seem from what I've read that he didn't actually spend all of his time living there, and apparently there was no mention of the fenced off MOD facility very close to the beach. It also seems that the residents of Applecross were not particularly happy about the whole affair, or the number of people that have since come to visit the area but not spent much money in Applecross.

Applecross was a few miles south of Sand bay, set in the large Applecross Bay. The bay was mostly taken up by a sand and pebble beach at the mouth of the Applecross River, with the village on the southern side of the bay, the centrepiece of which was the Applecross Inn. I was going to stop at the Inn but the road in front of it was quite busy with parked cars, so I decided to carry on to the furthest point I could reach to the south, before coming back.

On the way I stopped above a small bay at Culduie and watched around a dozen seals playing in the water, before continuing on until I ran out of road at a pier at Toscaig. On the way back I stopped at Culduie again, at a lower point than I had been before, and realised that not only were there some seals in the water, there were more of them basking on rocks in the middle of the bay. I drove back up to the higher point and looked down on the rocks, where the colour of the seals had completely hidden them from me first time around.

I drove back to Applecross and found a space in front of the Inn, intending to get some lunch, but I didn't see anything on the menu that I fancied. So, it was time to travel a stretch of road that I had been aware of for a while now, and I admit had been playing on my mind the last few days.

To get back to the main road from Applecross I could either go back along the coast, or I could head east via Bealach na Ba, the 'Pass of the Cattle', which rose to around 2,000ft. Not having much of a head for heights, and having heard other people's descriptions of the route, I wasn't particularly looking forward to it, but that wasn't going to stop me from trying it rather than taking the 'cowards route' back along the coast.

After passing big red signs at the start of the road, warning caravans not to bother and that the road could be impassable during winter, I started climbing, and climbing, and climbing, and the landscape became more barren. While negotiating a steep hairpin there was a crash from the back of the van as the drawer with the bowls and small plates gave in to centrifugal force and ended up on the floor again (no breakages). I reached a viewpoint and stopped, thinking that I'd been through the worst of it, and that it wasn't that bad really. There were half a dozen cars at the viewpoint, all of them empty, and with no one in sight. No doubt they had all gone walking around the area, but it was kind of eerie. I set off again and waited at the top of a stretch of road with crash barriers on one side, as a guy on a bicycle cycled up towards me. A bicycle! Was he mad?! As I carried on down that stretch of road I saw a tight hairpin bend in front of me and the road disappeared into a valley below me to my left. Oh my word! I rounded the first hairpin and saw some cars coming up below, so I stopped on the next hairpin to let them pass, and again on the third hairpin to let a campervan pass. One more hairpin and it was a fairly steady downhill run-out to the head of Loch Kishorn. I'm glad I did it, and I wish I could have stopped somewhere below the hairpins to take a photo of them, but I won't lie, I'm in no particular hurry to do it again.

I followed the southern edge of Loch Kishorn as far as I could to Achintraid, a pretty small village with several galleries, which I passed through before turning around and stopping on the way back. From there I rejoined the main road and cut across the headland, emerging onto the northern side of Loch Carron at Lochcarron. My map showed a campsite just beyond there, so I thought I would go and see if they had space before coming back to look at Lochcarron, but after a few miles I didn't see anything so I stopped and looked up the postcode, only to find that it was back in Lochcarron. I followed the SatNav back into the village and along a road up a hill behind it, where I found the Wee Campsite, a small terraced site next to a house, where the owner came out and showed me around.

I parked up and followed a path opposite the campsite that took me straight back down the hill and into the village, which ran along the length of the road, which in turn ran along the side of the loch. I wandered up and down the road before sitting in a cafe for a late afternoon milkshake and some kind of cream/toffee/sponge/chocolate cake thing, which I thoroughly deserved for driving up and down a mountain on an empty stomach.

Stromemore to Loch Greshornish
Wednesday, 13th June

I headed southwest to Stromemore first thing this morning, where I found the ruins of a small castle overlooking a bay, and a slipway sliding into Loch Carron, presumably where a ferry used to run across the loch to Stromeferry on the opposite bank. I then returned to Lochcarron and continued northeast along Loch Carron, around the end of the loch through Strathcarron and back down the other side of the loch to Stromeferry, where the road dropped fairly steeply around a hairpin bend down to the slipway that I'd seen from the other side.

From Stromeferry I left the main road, which cut across the headland, and continued along the coast towards Plockton. For the most part the road passed through trees and pink rhododendrons, and was the cleanest, blackest, neatest strip of tarmac that I'd seen for a long time. When I arrived at Plockton I found one of the prettiest places I'd seen for a long time. Surrounded by low peaks and forest, the houses of the village curved around a bay with a pebbly seaweed covered beach that reached out to a grass covered rocky outcrop that was almost certainly an island at high tide. Row boats and catamarans lay on the beach and yachts lay at anchor out in the bay. I followed the houses around the bay to a pier that looked across the bay to a large house at the edge of the forest. It would have been rude not to have stayed for some brunch, so I sat in the cool of a restaurant, out of the glare of the sun.

I returned to the van and set off to cross the remains of the headland to the south towards Loch Alsh. After about 10 minutes I suddenly realised I'd left the restaurant without paying. I'd come close a few times, but this was the first time I'd actually done it. I pulled over thinking that I could pay over the phone, but I didn't have a signal and couldn't remember the name of the place, so there was nothing else to do but head back again. I couldn't visit one of the prettiest places I'd been to and then thieve it of a bacon roll and an orange juice. When I walked back in the waitress recognised me and gave me a knowing smile. She said there hadn't been any drama, at first they thought I'd maybe gone for a walk, and thanked me for coming back.

Setting off again I managed to reach the banks of Loch Alsh without committing any further crimes. I was going to end up on the Island of Skye today, but I first wanted to take a quick detour to the east to Dornie, where Loch Alsh, Loch Long and Loch Duich all converged. Just beyond the village, on a small islet reached by a stone bridge, was the magnificent sight of Eilean Donan Castle. The thirteenth century castle was built for the Scottish kings and witnessed plenty of clan warfare. In 1719 it was destroyed by British forces during the Jacobite uprising, but the ruins were restored to their present glory in the early nineteenth century.

Heading back west again I stopped first at Kyle of Lochalsh, just short of the bridge over to Skye, where a ferry used to run across to Kyleakin, and home to a public toilet that was decorated with pot plants and plastered with posters and postcards of all things Scottish. After crossing the bridge onto the island I doubled back to take a look at Kyleakin. The campsite I'd booked as a base for spending a few days on Skye was just over an hour away at Loch Greshornish, and it was getting late in the afternoon, so I made my way there along dual track roads, stopping briefly at Broadford before driving around the northern side of the Cuillin Hills and stopping again briefly at Portree, the island's capital.

The campsite is on the banks of Loch Greshornish and the owners also run a small croft next to the site. It has a dog called Tara sat by a kennel with a sign asking you to make a fuss of her but not to feed her. I made a fuss of her but didn't feed her.

Uig to Old Man of Storr
Thursday, 14th June

I felt like an easier day today, so I set out to follow the main road in a loop around the northern part of Skye, down to Portree and back to the campsite, thinking that I'd be back early afternoon for some relaxation time.

I made my first stop at Uig, where a Caledonian MacBrayne ferry was just departing, bound for the Outer Hebrides. I ended up staying a while, first in the van uploading the last few days entries when I found a WiFi signal, before decamping myself to a nearby cafe for some tea and a bacon roll, until the uploads had finished.

From Uig the road wound up the side of a hill and continued north above and behind the coast, until I came off it and down to a bay with a small slipway at Bornesketaig. It was a pleasant day with a mix of blue sky and clouds, but when I stopped at Duntulm and walked onto a little headland to the ruins of Duntulm Castle a seemingly localised wind picked up and did its best to blow me off the top. The castle, which was home to the MacDonalds of the Isles, was apparently haunted by a small child that was dropped onto the rocks below, accidentally, by its nurse. I suspect the baby was blown from her hands.

I followed the road along a short section at the top of Skye and came off again to another bay near Kilmaluag. Heading south along the west coast of Skye I was passing through Digg when I noticed a sign for the Small & Cosy Teahouse. The little car park was full and more cars were parked along the verges, which I took to be a good sign, so I parked and went in, taking the last free table. And what a pretty little place it was too, with a tempting selection of cakes on display, a log fire on the go (not really necessary, it wasn't exactly cold, but it was still quite welcoming), and a selection of over 20 different loose leaf Chinese and Indian teas. The cream tea was unfortunately off, they'd run out of scones, so instead I went for some Victoria sponge and some raw pu-erh tea (it's supposed to be good for you). It also had the Amelie soundtrack playing, so all in all a very relaxing place to spend an hour.

Now is probably as good a time as any to mention midges. Specifically, Scottish midges. I doubt there is another creature on this earth that engenders as much hate by weight, or is more despised by size. If you put a Scottish midge under a microscope you'll see that it is approximately 40% wings, 8% body and head, 2% ginger hair, and 50% teeth. Now, I haven't actually come across that many so far, no big swarms of them, but they're around, and only a couple are required to inflict the dozen or so bites that I've picked up over the last two or three days. The mere thought of them causes your skin to crawl, even if there aren't any within a mile, you suddenly start scratching and pawing at yourself. Every little bit of dust drifting through your periphery causes you to snap your head around and scan the air. The biggest problem so far has been keeping the van midge free. As I say, there haven't been many around so far, but for the last three nights I've gone through a ritual just before turning in of switching on a single light in the van and then swatting anything that flies around it. Even so, I reckon I've been bitten during the night a few times. So as of today I've started taking them a little more seriously and packing protection. A very popular product in these parts is Avon Skin So Soft, which many people, including the SAS, have endorsed as the main weapon in the war on the midge. But there's now a new kid on the block, Smidge, which is being recommended by a lot of people. I bought some in Ullapool, firstly because I couldn't find any Avon SSS, and secondly because I was told the fishermen used it. The campsite I'm in now sells both, but recommends the Smidge. All of the many available deterrents can give different results for different people. I've lost the first few battles, time will tell whether I lose the war.

Just beyond Digg, I drove down to a beach at Staffin Bay, before continuing south and stopping at a viewpoint by Kilt Rock. The rocks of Kilt Rock had a base of horizontal layers, or 'sills', of volcanic rock, sandwiched between sedimentary sandstone, and were topped by pillars of volcanic rock that forced its way up through the sandstone layers and slowly cooled, about 55 million years ago, give or take a week.

Moving on again, I stopped at another viewpoint to see the Lealt Falls. I don't know much about the falls, except that they drop about 90m, and I don't have t'internet access to research them, but I expect they're rather old too. From there I was going to make one last quick stop, to see the Old Man of Storr, before heading back to the campsite, already much later than I had intended.

I drove south until I could see the jagged tooth of the Old Man of Storr in front of me, and after passing it pulled in to a car park, expecting a short walk to a viewpoint that would look up towards it. I followed a path that skirted around a forest before plunging into it for a while. There were a fair few midges around wherever the breeze didn't reach them, which was not what I wanted to see, but I supposed it was time to find out whether the Smidge that I'd been rocking throughout the day would make any difference. The path kept going, forever rising, and I was wondering how much further the viewpoint was when I emerged from the trees to see a bunch of jagged rocks way up above me, with the path disappearing up towards them. I hadn't signed up for this, but my stupid brain overruled the rest of me and I kept on going. As I climbed the path I saw a guy in front of me on crutches. On crutches!

What is it with people around here that compels them to ride bicycles or hobble on crutches towards the high ground? As I caught him up I tripped and nearly pitched over forwards. I'm following a guy on crutches and I'm the one that nearly falls over. Not too far from the base of the Old Man the path got steeper and became dirt and scree. It didn't look particularly nice, and would be worse coming down, but again I foolishly carried on. As I climbed up, trying not to slip back down again, I passed a girl coming down. We exchanged glances and laughed, wondering what we were both doing there. The top of the scree became rock again and I was able to clamber up and lie below the 48m pinnacle to look up at it and take a photo. Not far away and a little below was another pinnacle that rose to a point.

The time came to head back down again. As I reached the first part of the scree my feet nearly slid from underneath me, making me crouch and grab hold of any rocks that I could find. It looked like I was going to have to go down on either my backside or my face. I figured that I should probably try to protect the least unattractive of the two, which I decided was my face (it was a close call), so I got as low as I could, with my feet in front and my hands behind me, and tried to look like I was executing a graceful glissade with a very low centre of gravity. I don't think that grace played any part in the end, but I made it down to the rockier path and returned to nonchalant uprightedness for the rest of the journey back to the van, arriving an hour after I'd departed.

When I got back to the campsite I showered off the combination of Smidge, sweat and dirt, then applied some fresh Smidge, just as a precaution.

Stein to Neist Point
Friday, 15th June

I was aiming to take a look at some of western Skye today, so I drove around the head of Loch Greshornish and across and then up the western side of the Waternish peninsula to Stein. A row of whitewashed buildings, including some holiday houses, galleries and an inn, stood above a pebble beach with a slipway disappearing into Loch Bay.

I continued up the peninsula to a small car park next to the ruins of Trumpan Church, scene of a bloody massacre in 1578. In the winter of 1577, 395 MacDonalds were trapped and suffocated in St Francis Cave on Eigg by the MacLeods of Dunvegan, who lit a fire in the cave entrance. The following May, in an act of revenge, the MacDonalds of Uist took advantage of fog to moor their galleys in nearby Ardmore Bay and surround Trumpan Church, while the MacLeods from the surrounding area were congregated inside. The church was set ablaze and all within perished, apart from a young girl that managed to escape through a window. The girl ran to the castle at Dunvegan and raised the alert. An army of MacLeods caught up with the MacDonalds, whose boats had been beached by the ebbing tide, and slaughtered them. Think about that next time you're sat in a branch of the 'Golden Arches'.

I headed across the peninsula to Geary on the eastern side, where houses were scattered along the road above Loch Snizort, looking across the small Ascrib islands towards Uig. From there I returned along the road south and into Dunvegan. I stopped briefly but didn't see much around so decided to head north to Claigan and maybe come back later. I passed the entrance to Dunvegan Castle on the way but couldn't see it through the trees. At Claigan I found a car park and walked further north to the tip of the peninsula, where a couple of white beaches were made up of finely ground coral. From the top of a small hill above the larger of the two beaches I could see north towards Trumpan, across a collection of small islands, including Isay and Mingay.

Driving back south towards Dunvegan, I could see the castle on the edge of a forest behind the banks of Loch Dunvegan. The castle has been home to the MacLeod family for over 800 years, making it the oldest house in Britain to have been continuously occupied by the same family. Among the treasures in the castle was the Fairy Flag, the sacred banner of the MacLeod Clan that was flying when they chased down the MacDonalds near Trumpan. To the south were flat topped basalt mountains known as MacLeod's Tables.

Passing through Dunvegan I headed west again, first to a small harbour at Lower Milovaig and then to the most westerly point on Skye at Neist Point. There was a lighthouse at the point, hidden behind a rock headland that rose high on one side and sloped down to the other side. A path led around the lower side but it was blowing a gale and had started raining, so I really couldn't be bothered to go and have a look on this occasion.

The rain didn't last long but I decided I was going to call

it a day and make my way back to the campsite, but not before stopping in Dunvegan for a coffee and cake at Janns Cakes. I could have spent a lonnng time in that place, if I had unlimited funds and a stomach pump. When I got back to the campsite I sorted out my washing and other chores to give myself a free evening to concentrate on the England match against Sweden. I have a bottle of Crabbie's and an orange Calippo for the occasion. Oh yeah, I'm livin' the high life.

Struan to Arisaig
Saturday, 16th June

I was booked on the 2:30pm ferry from Armadale back to the mainland at Mallaig, so I set off a little earlier than usual to try and see a bit more of Skye before leaving it behind.

I drove down the western side of the middle of the island, stopping at Struan and at viewpoints either side of it, then came off the main road at the bottom of Loch Harport and followed it back up the other side to Portnalong, where various craft were moored in the bay and against a pontoon. I then backtracked to Carbost and took a track across the headland to Talisker, dropping down into a valley and parking near one of a handful of buildings there. I followed a path for about a mile to Talisker Bay, where I found a beach of grey sand.

You may have heard of Talisker, and you may know it from the whisky that bears its name. I backtracked to Carbost again, where the Talisker Distillery - the only distillery on Skye - stood on the shores of Loch Harport. I parked and went into the visitor centre to find a tour was just about to start, which I signed up for. Talisker whisky is made exclusively from the local water, if the supply from the Carbost Burn dries up, production stops. It recently stopped for five days, which was almost unheard of. The tour was well worth the reasonable entry fee, giving an insight into the romantic world of the renowned Scotch Whiskies, and finishing with a taster of the 10 year old single malt. I'm not a huge fan of whisky, and I was driving, so I didn't finish mine, but after an initial roughness and burn it had a pretty smooth finish, which stuck with me for a good few miles down the road. If I'd wanted to take a bottle of the 25 year home with me I'd have had to have parted with £225. The price of Scotch Whisky is not necessarily related to the quality, more to how rare the variety is. The tour guide recommended their 57 Degrees North as his favourite, near perfect whisky, at 57 percent and £57 a bottle.

I had an hour's drive to get to Armadale, and about two hours before I needed to be there for the ferry, so I got going and headed for the Sleat peninsula at the south of Skye, passing once again around the Cuillin Hills along the way. When I got to Armadale I had a quick look around the ferry terminal before heading just down the road to a small bay at Ardvasar. Back at the ferry terminal I picked up my ticket and found a tiny cafe next to it where I got a coffee and a bacon roll. The cafe was so small that I had to sit outside, in the spitting rain, with a Blue Tit to keep me company, hopping around on my table picking up crumbs that I put down for it, just a little too wary to take anything directly from my hand. The bacon roll was so nice that I bought another one (I don't think I've ever done that before) and sat in the van to eat it, before joining a small queue of cars awaiting the ferry.

A lot more cars rolled off the ferry as it docked, followed by a group of bikers, followed by a group of cyclists, followed by two elderly ladies with walking sticks and a member of the crew helping them up the slipway. With all of the waiting vehicles aboard, and everyone on the upper decks, we slid out of port for the thirty minute crossing of the Sound of Sleat.

When we rolled off again in Mallaig I found somewhere to park and walked around the busy harbour village. The harbour and marina were pretty much rammed with yachts and fishing boats. I reluctantly passed up the various cafes in favour of moving off to the south in search of somewhere to stay for the night. But first I stopped at Morar, where some stunning white sandy beaches ran along the sides of the Morar estuary. I walked along one of the beaches and found that several people had pitched tents either on the beach itself or amongst the wooded banks behind it. A little further south I found more scattered white beaches near a golf course at Traigh, and again at Bunacaimb, where there were several campsites stretched along the length of the beaches. I stopped at the first one, the Sunnyside Croft, and selected one of the free pitches. The campsite has been going for about a year and has some of the most modern, cleanest facilities I've come across.

Rather than settle down straight away I decided to carry on just down the road to Arisaig, to get a few things from the store there and take a look around. Arisaig was quite a pretty place, with a bunch of yachts moored out in Loch nan Ceall, away from the rocky bays. As with the other places on this stretch of coast, it looked out to hills on the islands of Rum, Eigg and Muck, particularly the 393m peak of An Sgurr on Eigg.

Back at Sunnyside Croft I went for a walk along the beaches in front of the various campsites, with the rain still spitting sporadically.

Glenuig to Strontian
Sunday, 17th June

It started raining just as I set off this morning, but not heavily and not for particularly long. I followed the main road until I reached the northern banks of Loch nan Uamh and continued until I was at the head of Loch Ailort, where I turned off to the south and followed the loch to Glenuig, where I stopped and had a wander around the bay.

The road cut across the headland to Loch Moidart, then across land again towards Loch Shiel before turning to the west. I came off onto a narrow track heading north, lined with trees and initially following a stream. The track ended on the shores of Loch Moidart, opposite Castle Tioram, stood on a rocky outcrop and linked to the wooded mainland by a spit of sand that is sometimes covered by high tides. Built in the fourteenth century, possibly earlier, the castle was home to the chieftains of Clanranald. In 1715 the castle was burnt down by its occupant, the fourteenth chieftain, before he departed for a battle that he correctly believed he would not return from alive. After walking out to the castle I set off back the way I had come and came across a largish brown bird of prey in front of me, which landed in a tree not far from my driver's side window. Just as I thought it might stay there long enough for me to grab my camera, it flew off. I pulled over and scanned the trees but couldn't see it. There are Golden Eagles and Sea Eagles in this area, so in hindsight I wish I'd stayed there a little longer to see if it returned.

After retracing my tracks I left the road again a little further on to head towards Ardtoe, passing Kentra Bay along the way. A small car park at Ardtoe had an honesty box asking for 50p. I have rarely come across any paid parking in Scotland, and if this had been a pay and display I probably would have had a quick look around and left again without paying, but it seemed wrong to dodge an honesty box, so I paid up. Next to the car park was the cutest little beach with a narrow opening in the rocks at the waters edge. There were several other little beaches in the same bay, and a short distance away over some rocks was a larger beach in front of a few static caravans.

Once again I retraced my tracks, passing a rock by the side of the road for the second time, with eyes and a huge mouth full of teeth painted on it, next to a sign saying 'The Monster Midge'. There's been a Phoney War going on between myself and the midges since I last mentioned them, with very few of them around and none attracted to my 'light trap' the last few nights. I'm expecting them to invade France any day now.

The road headed south to Salen, on Loch Sunart, where I turned off to the west to follow the road all the way to the end of the Ardnamurchan peninsula. For a while the road stuck to the banks of the loch, lined with trees and rhododendrons, passing the occasional bay, until it came to a viewpoint just beyond Ardslignish. The viewpoint overlooked a bay and beach beneath the gaze of Ben Hiant, the flank of a volcano that was formed 60 million years ago. Out across the Sound of Mull was the northern tip of the island of Mull, most of which was formed from lava from another volcano 25km south of there. The viewpoint itself stood on lava from the Mull volcano.

From there the road turned inland, across barren moors, to skirt around Ben Hiant and return to the coast at Kilchoan. As I passed around Ben Hiant I got a view north across the peninsula to Eigg, Rum and Skye. I drove down to a slipway at Kilchoan, from where you could catch a ferry to Mull. Across the bay were the remains of Mingary Castle. Continuing to the west, the road turned into a track that covered the remaining few miles to a lighthouse at the Point of Ardnamurchan, where I ticked off the remaining point on the compass, the most westerly point on the British mainland. It had become a nice day by then, with clear views of the various surrounding islands, such as Coll and Tiree to the west as well as Skye and the Cuillin Hills etc to the north. I stopped for some coffee and cake in a cafe before starting off on the long journey back along the peninsula. I played hop scotch with a group of German bikers that had passed me on the way there and left just before me. I would pass them as they stopped to talk or look at something, then further down the road I would pull over to let them all by. I must admit, on a nice day like today, with some good tunes on the stereo, it was a very pleasant drive along the Ardnamurchan peninsula.

When I got back to Salen I stopped for a quick look around before I carried on to the west along the top of Loch Sunart, until I came to Strontian and located the Sunart campsite. I don't have a view of water tonight, I have the back of some houses instead, so I went for a short walk down to the edge of the loch. The campsite is a nice enough place though, and even has a room you can use with a wood burning stove and free tea and coffee.

Lochaline to Fort William
Monday, 18th June

The Phoney War came to an abrupt end last night, the little s.o.b's went and snuck up on me through the Ardenne. I noticed a few midges flying around in the van mid evening, then noticed a whole load more outside the van. It suddenly occurred to me that the van wasn't airtight, the top of one of the rear doors doesn't close flush with the other one, causing the wind to whistle through it now and again. I checked the back doors and, sure enough, there were quite a few midges between the rear windows and the curtains. After a few moments of mild panic, wondering how I was going to keep them out, or whether I would have to just drive through the night until I ran out of petrol or reached the English border, I started using kitchen towel to plug the gap. There were too many already in the back to deal with, so I started setting up lines of defence, first pulling the shower curtain across the back, then closing the screen between the rear section and the main section, then using Sellotape to cover the gaps at the top and bottom of the screen. Over the next few hours I squidged any that had made it into the main section. Before going to bed I covered myself in Smidge. I'm surprised I didn't just slip straight out of the bed and into the cab.

This morning, with no new bites that I could find, I went on the offensive. I untaped the top and bottom of the screen and squidged a few that were on the shower curtain. Then I pulled back the shower curtain and went to town on those behind the rear curtains, mostly by just pushing the curtains flat against the windows. Shock and awe, baby, shock and awe. Don't get me wrong, I took little pleasure in the whole affair, but the one rule I have developed on this trip, other than going anti-clockwise, is that anything alive in the van that hasn't been invited in gets squidged, zero tolerance.

Anyhoo, Loch Sunart was like a millpond this morning, under a blue sky scattered with clouds. I drove along a road around the head of the loch and west along the southern shore before the road turned south across a lush green landscape of forests, hills and meadows. I rejoined the coast along the side of Loch Aline. A ferry must have just come in, as I had to pull over several times for cars and bikers. When I reached Lochaline the ferry was just departing again, bound for Mull, just across the Sound of Mull. I headed off again on a road that followed the Sound of Mull along the coast to the west. The road pretty much ran through the trees, above the coast, all of the way to Drimnin, where I parked in a lane and wandered down towards the water to get a glimpse across towards Tobermory, the main town on Mull, but I couldn't see the colourful houses for which it was famous. I returned along the road to Lochaline, where I stopped again as another ferry was coming in and indulged my new habit of buying bacon rolls from ferry terminal cafes (just the one this time).

With nowhere else to go on this part of the coast I started back along the road towards Strontian, until I was able to come off it and head east towards Loch Linnhe. Pretty much the entire stretch of this single track B road, until it rejoined the A road at Inversanda, was one of the most enjoyable roads that I've travelled. It wound and bumped its way down through a green valley, passing Loch Uisge and joining the side of Loch a'Choire before reaching the side of Loch Linnhe at Camasnacroise, where I drove down to a handful of houses and a small church behind a large beach. From there the road ran northeast along the western shores of Loch Linnhe, with the Grampian Mountains in full view ahead.

I stopped at Sallachan to look at an area of pebble and sand that stretched out to Sallachan Point, then continued to Ardgour. When I arrived at Ardgour I drove straight onto a waiting ferry, almost without thinking about it, otherwise I'd have stopped to have a look around and caught the next one. Instead I looked back to a pretty little village as the ferry made the five minute crossing of the Corran Narrows to Nether Lochaber. I drove off the ferry and parked, but on this side there wasn't much more than the slipway.

Rather than continuing my route to the south, I headed north on a detour to give me a day off the driving. I passed through Fort William and just up the road to Glen Nevis, where I paid for two nights at the Glen Nevis Caravan and Camping Park, before heading back to Fort William for a wander around, a late lunch, a coffee and to stock up on some provisions for tomorrow. I then returned to the campsite. Last time I was here I was in a popup tent, with no thought towards the life of the campervanner. Apparently the midges have been pretty bad here.

Ben Nevis
Tuesday, 19th June

I'd been looking forward to today for ages. I do like to walk up a mountain now and again, and at 1,344m Ben Nevis is as high as you're going to get in the British Isles.

It was raining earlier this morning, but had stopped by the time I got myself sorted and set off for a short walk down the road to the Glen Nevis Visitor Centre. From there I crossed a delightfully bouncy bridge over a stream, turned right, and started the 10 mile round trip to the summit. The path started climbing along the side of the valley above Glen Nevis, where I could look down to the campsite, before getting steeper as it curved around and up the flank of a ravine called Red Burn. It then zig zagged back on itself and brought me up to a relatively flat area next to a smallish loch called Lochan Meall An T-suidhe.

Just above the loch, I turned right and continued the long, relentless trudge, crossing Red Burn and reaching the first corner in a series of zig zags that took me higher and higher. The clouds started drifting around once I was above the loch, sometimes I could see below, sometimes I couldn't see much at all, and could see very little above. As I worked my way up the zig zags the landscape became increasingly barren, just rocks and loose stone.

Well and truly up in the clouds, I finally reached the first cairn near the end of the zig zags, with a false memory that it started levelling out pretty soon, but there was still plenty of climbing to be done through the cairns and I was getting pretty weary. Eventually I got to a point where the path was covered by a large patch of snow and worked my way up it, slipping back again occasionally. As I joined the path again it started to level off as it led towards a plateau at the top. There was more snow to cross as I reached the edge of the North East Face, which plummeted 2,000ft beneath me. It's easy to be oblivious to this drop when the cloud is down. At last, the rock wall ruins of an old observatory loomed into view, followed by a survival hut, followed by the raised trig point of the summit.

I had planned to stuff my face full of banana loaf, golden syrup cake and lemon cake when I reached the top, but it was cold and the heat that I'd built up while climbing soon left me. So I had a quick bite to eat before setting off down again. It never fails to amaze me how unprepared, or possibly just blasé, some people can be when they climb mountains like Ben Nevis. A group of Scottish lads arrived at the top wearing mostly jeans and trainers, and one of them was just wearing shorts and a t-shirt. Fair play to them, they'd made it up and didn't seem bothered about the cold, but there have been plenty of deaths on this mountain over the years. Apart from being in cloud, the weather on the way up was nice enough, but as I started down it was turning unpleasant, with a bitter wind rising and the cloud thicker than it had been. I can see why there was a small survival hut on the summit with a sturdy metal door, it would be a nasty place to be caught in bad weather.

I had to put my gloves on to try and warm my hands up a bit as the cairns came back into view, one by one, and I felt for the people that I passed still on their way up. I never know whether to lie or tell the truth when people ask how far it is to the top, particularly when they're still asking as you get closer to half way down. I somehow managed to end up coming down the final stretch on a different track to the one I'd gone up, which actually saved me about half a mile as it came out onto the road above the campsite.

It was just before 2:00pm, so I had a lonnng shower and settled down in the van for the rest of the afternoon before driving into Fort William in the evening to reward my efforts with a curry. The weather had brightened up when I got back to the campsite, just in time for the England match against Ukraine, the clouds had lifted above Ben Nevis and the zig zag track was clearly visible.

South Ballachulish to Oban
Wednesday, 20th June

The summit of Ben Nevis was still clear this morning, a nice day to go climbing. Oh well, such is life, I considered climbing it again, but only briefly.

I set off to the south, returning the way I had come until I passed the Corran ferry and continued to a bridge over Loch Leven, stopping briefly when I got to the other side at South Ballachulish. I carried on along the coast and crossed from Highland into Argyll and Bute. It seems like I've been in Highland forever, but it's only been about three weeks. I stopped again at a viewpoint just before Portnacroish, looking out to the island of Lismore and overlooking the small but perfectly formed Castle Stalker, on a little islet, which was used as a hunting lodge by James IV.

Moving on again I stopped at Creagan, just before crossing a bridge over Loch Creran and continuing along the main road. As I drove along the road a little way back from the shores of Ardmucknish Bay I looked for a way to get to the water's edge, firstly ending up at a small airport, then going back on myself a little and stopping at a Caravan Club site. Seeing as I was a member I didn't see any reason why I shouldn't walk through the site and down to the water. I had considered staying a night there, but had booked somewhere closer to Oban instead, which was a shame as it was a very pleasant site that ran along the shores of the bay, behind a sand and shingle beach. The bay itself seemed very serene.

Just below Ardmucknish Bay I crossed a narrow cantilever bridge over the mouth of Loch Etive and into Connel, where I stopped for a quick look around. Below the bridge were the Falls of Lora, rapids that swirled around a submerged ridge at ebb tide. Just outside Connel I topped up with half a tank of diesel. Fortunately the prices seemed to have returned to the merely extortionate every day prices, rather than the ludicrously extortionate prices of the more remote northwest Scotland.

After passing a marina I took my only detour off the main road today to take a look at Dunstaffnage Castle. The castle was literally built on top of a large rock, pretty much following its shape, in the thirteenth century by the MacDougalls. In 1309 it was captured by Robert the Bruce and was later granted to the Earls of Argyll. I walked through a small wood behind the castle until I could see out along the Firth or Lorn and back to the bridge at Connel.

From there I made the fairly short journey to Oban, on the Sound of Kerrera, where the view out to sea was pretty much filled by the island of Kerrera. Oban is a great place, busy with ferries to and from the Hebridean islands, and busy with people today. I parked at a pay and display at the northern end of the town and walked south along the waterfront towards the ferry terminal. The town rose fairly steeply up from the waterfront and was crowned by an out of place looking structure called McCaig's Tower, built to resemble the Colosseum of Rome by a local banker at the end of the nineteenth century. It was intended to be a museum and art gallery, but was never completed beyond the outer shell. The Oban Distillery stood just off the main street.

If any of my family ever visit Oban they are under instruction from my sister to buy copious amounts of haggis and sausage meat or fruit pudding, from the Jackson Brothers Butchers on George Street. This time I was to buy six haggis and two full lengths (about a metre) of square sausage. Disaster, they had sold out of haggis, and the square sausage was now round, but it was essentially the same thing. So I left with 6.6kg of sausage and hauled it to the post office, where I found a box that would just about fit it all in and left it in the (hopefully) capable hands of the Royal Mail, then retired to a nearby cafe for a milkshake.

After walking back to the van I went to find my campsite for the next two nights, Roseview, about two miles out of town, surrounded by forest and green hills.

Oban, Mull, Staffa and Iona
Thursday, 21st June

I got up a little earlier this morning and walked the two miles into the centre of Oban, where I climbed up the streets to McCaig's Tower.

The tower was operating on the open door cat guide system. As you approach the entry archway you're greeted by a cat, who will show you around. My guide was particularly clingy, it would run across the front of me as I walked, then wrap itself around my legs. After tripping over it a few times I worked out that as it crossed my path to the left I could jink right and miss it, then it would cross to the right and I would jink left, so that we zig zagged our way through the gardens within the circular walls, until we reached an exit to a viewpoint. The viewpoint commanded a great view of the town, the island of Kererra, and of Mull beyond it.

I tipped my cat guide and walked back down through the town to the ferry terminal, where I waited for the ferry to Mull. The crossing took about 45 minutes, passing the impressive Duart Castle shortly before arriving in Craignure, the island's main port. As the vehicles drove off the ferry, the foot passengers sought out their coaches, some of which were heading for the castle, most of which, including mine, were heading for Fionnphort at the southwestern tip of the island.

The journey to Fionnphort took about an hour and a quarter, through green valleys and a mountain pass, past wooded areas and lochs. I finally got to see a few stags, having seen only road signs warning of them at various places up until then. No sign of any Golden or Sea Eagles though, of which there were quite a few on the island. One pair of Sea Eagles hatched in a nest on the golf course have been named Pitch and Putt. We did pass a bus shelter in the middle of nowhere, with solar panels on the roof that allowed it to light up at night, and a no smoking sign inside.

When we arrived at Fionnphort it was just starting to spot with rain, for the first time in ages according to the driver. We waited a few minutes before a small ferry to Staffa arrived. I decided to sit inside, which was just as well as the waves occasionally sprayed the few people sat outside. As we approached Staffa we could see the basalt columns in the cliffs, and the hexagonal blocks of stone beneath them. The ferry backed towards Fingal's Cave, the largest of several caves, so that we could get a look, before it moved around the corner to let us ashore. I walked along the side of the cliffs, following a marked path, to get to the entrance to the cave and take a look inside.

I then climbed up some steps to the top of the cliffs, in search of puffins. I walked up to the highest point, just beyond which were five puffins on a little outcrop, but I knew there would probably be more, further along the island. Sure enough, one particular area had loads of the little guys, sitting on the slopes or flying around, trying to land with as much grace as they could manage. Some of them would go in or out of the burrows that they used. Apparently there can be the odd turf war with rabbits that haven't finished using them, with the puffins trying to move in before they've exchanged contracts. They weren't particularly bothered about people being around and I could get quite close in amongst them.

After just over an hour on Staffa the ferry returned to pick us up. The seats inside were all taken by the time I got on, so I sat outside with one of the provided Sou'westers over my legs, but the journey to Iona, apart from a bit of rain, was a dry one. The main feature on Iona was the monastery, originally built of wattle and daub by St Columba in AD563. I used my English Heritage card to get entry to the Historic Scotland site. Iona is the burial place of sixty Scottish Kings, including Duncan and MacBeth, on whom Shakespeare based his play. Not far from the monastery was Dun I, the highest point on the island at 100m, and worth a walk up to the top to get views in all directions, taking in a few sandy beaches along the coastline. I could also see the surrounding Treshnish Isles and the islands of Coll and Tiree.

Seeing as it was raining I decided I may as well spend the rest of my time on Iona indoors, so I went back to a hotel I'd passed earlier, enquired about a coffee, and had an out of body experience. Somebody that looked like me, and sounded like me, was offered a slice of cake, and declined. I think it may have been something to do with already having had some of the banana loaf, golden syrup cake and lemon cake that I'd brought with me, left over from Ben Nevis, but that's never happened before so the results of a full investigation are pending. Once I'd sat in the lounge, along with a bunch of other people from the coach, and my coffee had been delivered, I snapped out of it and went back to ask for a slice. But three women (evil through and through) had beaten me to it and taken the last of it. It was chocolate and strawberry gateau too! Luckily a member of staff went looking for more and came back with some freshly made fig, brandy and hazelnut cake. Crisis avoided.

I walked back to the ferry terminal in the rain, it seemed that summer had passed, along with the solstice. The ferry took us back to Fionnphort where the coach was waiting to drive us back to Craignure. The driver kept those of us still awake entertained with his knowledge of the island and wry sense of humour. When we came across another stag he pulled over and honked his horn (the driver, not the stag) to try and get it to turn back towards us, but the stag ignored him.

After a short wait at Craignure we boarded the ferry for the return trip to Oban. I found the nearest reclining seat and fell asleep, waking as we sailed into the bay at Oban, where the rain was coming down fairly heavily. Rather than head straight back to the campsite I ducked into a fish and chip restaurant for a late supper, before putting on all my waterproofs and walking the two miles back home, tired but satisfied after a good day.

Clachan to Lochgilphead
Friday, 22nd June

It rained heavily early this morning, but stopped before I hauled myself out of bed, and to my surprise pretty much held off for most of the day.

From the campsite I drove back through Oban to join the main road to the south, then came off again towards the Island of Seil. To get onto the island I crossed a 46m long stone humpback bridge at Clachan, called 'The Bridge over the Atlantic'. It may not have been as grand as its title suggested, but it was set in pretty surroundings. I crossed the bridge and had a look around before heading to Ellenabeich at the western tip. A couple of groups of school kids, fully kitted out in waterproofs and life jackets, were setting off from the small harbour in orange ribs. The village had several craft shops and a small brewery, and a ferry that ran the short distance across to the small island of Easdale, which provided slate for several centuries. I drove to the southern tip of the island at Cuan Ferry, which was little more than a slipway for a ferry to the island of Luing.

Crossing back over the 'Atlantic', I rejoined the main road and followed it along the southern shores of Loch Melfort to Arduaine Garden, a National Trust for Scotland site. A path from the Loch Melfort Hotel, with views across the loch to a marina at Craobh Haven, took me to the large gardens, home to plants from six continents, and the odd otter if you're lucky enough to see one.

Continuing south and inland I stopped to look at the ruins of Carnasserie Castle, built in the late sixteenth century and partly blown up in 1685. For a while the clouds parted and the sun beat down. Moving on again I crossed the Crinan Canal and turned west to Crinan. The village stood at one end of the canal, opened in 1801, which travels nine miles to Ardrishaig and links the Sound of Jura to Loch Fyne. The alternative is a 120 mile journey around the Kintyre peninsula. Across the Sound of Jura were the islands of Jura and Scarba. While I was there, a Clyde Puffer sailed into the first lock. The puffers were specially built for the Forth and Clyde and Crinan canals. Just around the corner was Crinan Harbour, where loads of small craft were moored between the shore and a small island.

From Crinan I drove part way down a peninsula separated from the mainland by Loch Sween, to Tayvallich, where a pretty natural harbour ringed by houses and static caravans was full of yachts and small craft. I sat in a cafe on the waterfront for a while with a hot chocolate, but nothing else, I'd already finished off the banana loaf, golden syrup cake and lemon cake by then. I decided not to carry on to Keillmore at the end of the peninsula, but instead headed off to find a campsite at Lochgilphead. The road followed the Crinan Canal, passing several locks along the way, which a handful of boats were working their way up or down.

The campsite at Lochgilphead was just off a road along the head of Loch Gilp, so I found a pitch before going to take a look at the loch and the village. Just as I was about to leave the site the heavens opened with a heavy shower, so I sheltered in the laundry until it reduced to light rain. There have been several more short heavy showers this evening.

Ardrishaig to Carradale Bay
Saturday, 23rd June

It was raining again this morning, but it didn't ease off before I got going this time. I headed down the western side of Loch Gilp to Ardrishaig, where the Crinan Canal emerged through the last few locks and under a swinging road bridge. Not far south of Ardrishaig I turned off the main road to follow the western coast in a large U shape that would take about an hour and bring me out 20 minutes down the main road.

Covering as much of the coast as possible is all very well, but to be honest this was a stretch of coast that I could probably have avoided, the road largely ran through trees and for a while I wondered whether I would just end up reaching a flooded part of the road that would force me to turn back. When I did get to see the coast I could see the islands of Jura and Islay. When I got to Kilberry I drove down a side road to find some sculptured stones, but there was nowhere nearby to park, apart from in the middle of the road, and I didn't fancy parking elsewhere and walking back in the rain, so I carried on to the base of the U where I could see south to the fairly small Gigha Island, before the coast curved back to the northeast and I stopped at Tarbert.

Tarbert was quite nice, at the head of Loch Tarbert, with a horseshoe of shops and hotels running around the harbour and plenty of boats moored in a marina. A passing woman saw me with my camera and commented that it was a lovely place when the sun was out. I could believe her, but at the time it was wet and dreary, so I moved on. Shortly after I'd left Tarbert the rain stopped for most of the rest of the day.

I continued along the western coast of the Kintyre peninsula, initially following the southern side of Loch Tarbert. I stopped at a campsite just north of Tayinloan, where I had a quick look at a beach in front of it, looking across the Sound of Gigha to Gigha Island. You could catch a ferry to the island from Tayinloan. A little further down the coast I stopped on the road next to a cemetery near Cleongart to look at another sandy beach, before stopping once again at Westport to walk onto a larger beach where several surfers were getting ready in the car park.

The road turned to the southeast and crossed the peninsula to Campbeltown at the head of Campbeltown Loch. The town wasn't the most attractive I had seen, but was larger than I expected given how remote it would seem to be near the end of such a long peninsula. I found myself a bakery and bought a chicken, ham and leek pie to take with me on the remains of the journey to the south, to Southend, where I found several sandy beaches, one of them in front of another campsite. From there I turned to the west again and joined a fairly unpleasant seven mile stretch of road that started at a gate. As I approached the gate a young boy that had been stood in the road outside a house opened the gate for me, which was nice of him. The track rose, twisted and fell as I bumped my way along it and eventually came to a small car park and turning area by another gate. I was about a mile from the end of the road so I got out to walk a little further. Beyond the gate I could see the Mull of Kintyre lighthouse below me, and the road falling and winding before me. I could also fairly clearly see the coast of Antrim in Northern Ireland, only 12 miles away across the North Channel, the shortest distance between Ireland and mainland Britain. I wasn't going to walk all the way down to the lighthouse, but I went as far as a corner in the road that allowed me to look down to it. Paul McCartney's desire was always to be here, but I didn't see him, maybe he was in the lighthouse.

I just about managed to get back to the van before some dark clouds rolled in from the sea and briefly rained on me while I drove back along the road towards Southend. The young boy was nowhere to be seen, so I had to get out in the rain and open and close the gate myself, would you believe. I continued past Southend and around the southeastern coast of the peninsula, stopping briefly at Feochaig, with probably the largest gathering of houses along the road (maybe four or five), and again at Kildalloig where the high cliffs of Davaar Island stood just offshore, until I was back at Campbeltown. As I left Campbeltown to join the road up the eastern side of the peninsula I could see a lighthouse on the northern tip of Davaar Island. There are seven caves on Davaar, one of which has a life size cave painting of the crucifixion, painted by a local artist in 1887.

I drove part way up the eastern coast, along the Kilbrannan Sound, with the Isle of Arran filling the view to the east, until I reached a small harbour at Carradale. I backtracked slightly and down to a campsite on Carradale Bay, where I was given a pitch just behind the beach. Apparently it rained here early this morning for the first time in about three weeks, and has rained a little this evening, but has otherwise been quite warm and pleasant, albeit cloudy.

Grogport to Clachan
Sunday, 24th June

I had a fairly easy day planned for today, and it started with a bit of blue sky and some warmth.

I continued my journey up the eastern side of the Kintyre peninsula, stopping at a picnic spot at Grogport that looked across to the Isle of Arran. Further north I took a side road out to Skipness, a quiet little village hidden away behind a beach. Just beyond the village was a short walk to Skipness Castle. Returning to the main road I passed the 5,000 mile mark before stopping for the second time in Tarbert. It still wasn't sunny, but at least it wasn't raining this time, so I had a wander around before finding a cafe for a coffee.

I followed the road back up to Lochgilphead and through it to the east, moving around the top of Loch Gilp and back down the other side for a short distance until the coast turned to the northeast along the shores of Loch Fyne, probably best known for the seafood restaurants of the same name. My first stop on Loch Fyne was at Crarae Glen Gardens. The 50 acres of gardens were centred around the Crarae Burn, with various walks that you could follow. I took a path that climbed along the side of the burn, through an area that had been planted to resemble a Himalayan valley. Along the route I bumped into an elderly Scottish gentleman and his dog, who made my day by using the phrase 'och aye' (the elderly Scottish gentleman, not the dog). A viewpoint at the top of the gardens gave me a bit of a view of the loch, across the tops of the trees.

Next I dropped into the Argyll Caravan Park, the only campsite I had found in the area, to secure a pitch. The woman at the reception seemed quite cheerful about the large number of midges they had there. I haven't had any trouble from them for a while, but I replaced all the kitchen towel that was plugging the gap in the back doors, just in case. Leaving the campsite again I drove on up the coast and through Inveraray, for another seven miles, until I reached Clachan, where I found the original Loch Fyne Oyster Bar. I booked myself a table for early evening and headed back to Inveraray.

Inveraray was quite a striking town, particularly when approached from the northeast, where I crossed a stone bridge that was steeper than it looked and could see part of the town laid out before me. I parked at the far end and walked back through the town, past a museum housed in the old jail, along the main street, with a small but busy whisky shop, and around to a pier. One thing that I noticed about Inveraray, which I really liked, was that all of the buildings, the shops and their signs, were black and white. So the Co-operative, for example, had monochrome signage rather than the usual green. I walked out of the town to the bridge, where I could not only look back to the town but also up river to Inveraray Castle. Both the town and the castle were built in the eighteenth century, the castle as the home to the chief of the Campbells, the third Duke of Argyll. A group of pipers and drummers were rehearsing as I wandered around, and I could still hear them once I'd settled myself in a cafe for the rest of the afternoon.

I returned to the Loch Fyne Oyster Bar for 5:30pm.

There'd been no need to book a table, it was a pretty quiet Sunday evening. Now, oysters are the food of the devil as far as I'm concerned, along with mushrooms and gherkins, so I was having none of that nonsense, thank you very much. Instead I went for a Cajun spiced whole sea bream, with creme fraiche and steamed new potatoes with parsley butter, and a pint of Jarl, followed by sticky toffee pudding with cream. And it was well worth blowing my food budget for the next few days, even if the sea bream did spend most of the time staring back at me. A piece of Scottish fudge with the bill was a nice touch too.

I got back to the campsite, slightly bloated, just in time for a shower and a shave before tucking myself into the van to listen to England exit yet another quarter final on penalties, this time to Italy.

Cairndow to Toward
Monday, 25th June

I set off this morning and retraced the route through Inveraray and Clachan, rounding the end of Loch Fyne and stopping for a quick look at Cairndow before following the southern shores of the loch and stopping again at St Catherine's, where I could see across the loch to Inveraray.

I left the main road in order to stay by the side of the loch and came to a car park next to Inver Cottage, a craft shop and cafe with a view of Lachlan Castle, once a home to the Clan Lachlan but now largely covered by green foliage. Remaining by the side of the loch I came to Otter Ferry, a picturesque little place with a couple of houses, a harbour, a beach and the Oystercatcher public house.

Moving inland I followed the road until I could take a side road back to the coast at Portavadie, where a ferry ran back and forth across Loch Fyne to East Tarbert on the Kintyre peninsula. It also had a pretty modern looking marina complex and several chalets. I returned along the road and took another side road towards Craig Lodge, which showed a large beach on my map. When I got to the road down towards the beach it was barred by a gate with a no entry sign on it. I could just about see the sandy beach through the trees, but I have no idea why it was inaccessible to the public. I continued along the road until I could see the Isle of Arran to the south and the road turned to the north along the side of the western Kyle of Bute, across which was the Island of Bute.

I passed through Blair's Ferry and into Kames, Auchenlochan and Tighnabruaich, which pretty much ran into each other along the shore. I stopped to walk through Tighnabruaich, then drove on a little to a marina, before turning back and rejoining the main road up to a couple of view points that looked down the eastern Kyle of Bute. I followed the road to the north, around the top of what I think was Loch Riddon and back down the other side to Colintraive on the eastern Kyle of Bute, where a ferry ran the short distance to the Island of Bute.

Retracing my steps north again, I took a road inland to the east, through low forested hills, around the top of Loch Striven, past the Tarsan Dam at one end of Loch Tarsan, and across a peninsula to Holy Loch, where I stopped briefly at Sandbank, found a purveyor of steak and gravy pies, and followed the coast south to Dunoon. All of a sudden I was back in civilisation again, the coast was far more built up than I'd been used to for the last month or so. As I followed the coast between Sandbank and Dunoon I found myself with Holy Loch behind me, Loch Long to the north, the River Clyde to the east, and the Firth of Clyde to the south. Between the river and the Firth was the coast of Inverclyde. Pretty much wherever I looked along these stretches of coast I saw houses and other buildings.

From Dunoon I continued south to Toward and a lighthouse at Toward Point at the bottom of the peninsula. Just around the point was a shingle beach with another view of the Island of Bute and also the coast of North Ayrshire south of Inverclyde. I returned to Dunoon for half an hour of unsuccessfully wandering around looking for an ice cream (how can that be allowed to happen?), then I set off to find the Invereck Caravan Park just north of Sandbank.

Last night's threat of a major midge attack failed to materialise, but there are certainly a few of them around this evening, so I'm remaining on high alert for the time being.

Strone to Helenburgh
Tuesday, 26th June

I believe I'm approaching the end of my time in the wilderness of northwest Scotland, but there was still plenty of it to see today.

I drove along the northern shore of Holy Loch and rounded a headland at Strone, where I had a similar view as from Sandbank yesterday, along the River Clyde and down the Firth of Clyde. I then started up the western side of Loch Long until I reached the very picturesque little village of Ardentinny. I pulled over and walked a short distance through the village and back, past cottages with well kept gardens. On the opposite banks of the loch was an imposing naval base, RNAD (Armaments Depot) Coulport, where submarines are armed with various weapons, including Trident nuclear missiles.

Just north of Ardentinny the road turned inland to the northwest, through trees and hills, until it reached Loch Eck and turned north. A conveniently located picnic table gave me a slightly higher viewpoint from which to look up and down the loch and the surrounding scenery. Following the road to the north I returned to the southern banks of Loch Fyne and retraced part of yesterday's route, passing back through St Catherine's, opposite Inveraray, but coming off the main road before Cairndow to head southeast. After driving through some lush forest and meadows I came to the beautiful setting of Lochgoilhead, at the head of Loch Goil (the clue is in the name). A number of people were setting up small dinghies for some leisure time on the water.

I left Lochgoilhead to the northeast, through the same kind of scenery as on the way in, until I came to a point in the road just above the 'Rest and be Thankful' viewpoint, with a breathtaking view along Glen Croe to the southeast, the summit of Beinn Ime ahead, and the road towards Cairndow winding away through the hills to the north. I took the road through Glen Croe to Loch Long and stopped just around the top of it at Arrochar, but failed to find a nice looking cafe or any of the groceries I was looking for. Continuing down the eastern side of Loch Long I drove onto the Rosneath peninsula and onto an MOD road that took me high onto the middle of the peninsula, with Loch Long to my right and Gare Loch to my left, where I could see another large naval base, HMNB Clyde, more commonly known as Faslane.

The road took me down to the entrance to RNAD Coulport, where I turned left to carry on down the eastern side of Loch Long. Looking back I couldn't see the large warehouse-like building that was visible from Ardentinny. When I got to the bottom of the peninsula I stopped at Kilcreggan for a while in a cafe for some coffee and cake. A passenger ferry ran from Kilcreggan to Gourock on the Inverclyde coast, or around the corner to Helensburgh. I carried on around the peninsula and back up the other side, along the western side of Gare Loch, where the large complex at Faslane was clear to see on the other side of the loch, particularly the blocks of flats that housed some of the 6,500 personnel that worked there. The base was the Royal Navy's main presence in Scotland, and home to most of the

Submarine Service.

I stopped at Garelochhead and found the groceries I was after, then drove around the barbwire fences of Faslane and stopped briefly at Rhu before carrying on to Helensburgh. I stopped for a while and wandered around the waterfront and grid-pattern streets of the largish, fairly unattractive town.

I'm going to take tomorrow off, so I've taken a detour inland to Luss, on the banks of Loch Lomond. It's largely been raining since I arrived here, and it looks set to continue tomorrow, but my plans for the day don't really extend beyond a long lie in, followed by chores and relaxation.

Luss

Wednesday, 27th June

My day off at Luss hasn't exactly been everything I had hoped it would be (not that I was hoping for much).

The midges were playing silly buggers again last night, each time I turned on the light a few more would appear. I couldn't see anywhere that they could be getting into the van, so I could only assume that they had all come in on the handful of occasions that I had opened the door to get in or out. In the end I decided to just leave the light off and take the approach that what I didn't know about couldn't hurt me (flawed, I know, but welcome to my world). I haven't actually had any new bites since the first few days of entering the west Scotland midge zone, maybe I've absorbed so much Smidge by now that I'm no longer tasty to them.

I got up slowly this morning, had some breakfast, shaved and showered. It was a pretty miserable day; grey and rainy. The midges were everywhere, flying around the campsite, in the toilet blocks, in the showers etc. The pitch that I was on was pretty much in the trees, which made it quite dark and even when it wasn't raining the trees were dripping water onto the roof of the van. I'm at the first site for a while to have WiFi, but it didn't reach the van, so I spent a while last night, and again this morning, sat outside the reception trying to upload the last week of entries, while absent mindedly swatting at the midges. I think the diary entries uploaded okay but it was so slow that the photos didn't. A family of ducks came to say hello, which was nice.

Rather than spend the day sat in a dark van, or on a bench outside reception with no plug to keep the laptop charged, I decided to head into nearby Alexandria to see if I could find somewhere nice to spend the day. I think it's fair to say that Alexandria was not the greatest place in the world, so I failed. I ended up sat in a well known high street fast food chain (yes, that one) for lunch and then found that I couldn't get the free WiFi to work, so that was kind of a waste of time.

I forlornly returned to the campsite, seeing as I had some laundry to do, but I'd already decided to skip emptying the toilet, otherwise I'd end up with the van filling up with midges while I had the rear doors open. When I got back to the campsite I noticed that one of the pitches near the reception was empty, so I went to see whether it was free tonight, and indeed it was. So I moved the van to an altogether brighter spot (relatively speaking, it was still cloudy and mostly raining) within range of the WiFi, and kicked off the upload. Things were looking up.

Apart from doing the laundry and getting the entries uploaded, I've managed to achieve very little today. I had intended to spend some time learning a bit more about editing photos, but that hasn't really happened. So not the greatest day all in all, but hey, with this being the least memorable day since starting out (if there has been a less memorable day, I've forgotten it), I can't really complain. And the ducks seem happy, which is nice.

Dumbarton to Prestwick
Thursday, 28th June

I appeared to be well and truly back in civilisation today, which was a shame. I have travelled along major roads, with traffic and everything, through industrial towns and seaside resorts. It was all a bit of a shock to the system, and on a mostly grey and sometimes rainy day it brought back unwelcome memories of the Thames Estuary at times.

The early rain eased off a little just before I got going this morning. I drove back to the coast at Helensburgh and continued along the River Clyde, into West Dunbartonshire and the town of Dumbarton. I didn't find much in the way of a seafront, apart from a park next to the fortified twin peaks of Dumbarton Rock and Castle Rock, the latter being the higher of the two. Along the river to the east were the twin towers of the Erskine Bridge.

No sooner than I had entered West Dunbartonshire I was leaving it again, over the bridge into Renfrewshire, which I passed through even quicker without so much as stopping, into Inverclyde. Port Glasgow used to be a port that served the city of Glasgow, until the Clyde was deepened in the 1800s, after which it became a centre of shipbuilding. Today only one ship yard still remained,

Ferguson Shipbuilders, situated next to Newark Castle.

Not far from Port Glasgow, Greenock was also a port and shipbuilding centre. I stopped at one of the docks, redeveloped with apartment buildings, but with a huge crane still standing proud over the water. The rest of the town behind the waterfront largely seemed to be supermarkets and retail parks, overlooked by the domed towers of the council buildings. To the west of the town a long esplanade ran part of the way to Gourock, where I stopped at Gourock Bay and at least got a view of some boats moored in the bay, with a similar view on the other side of the town at West Bay.

Moving on again, I took a quick look at a pebbly beach at Lunderston Bay before carrying on to Inverkip, where a marina was surrounded by new build houses in a development called Kip Village. Passing beyond the tall tower of the oil fired Inverkip power station, I stopped behind a concrete skirted beach at Wemyss Bay, in site of a pier that housed a ferry terminal and part of a railway station. Wemyss Bay used to be Glasgow's gateway to the resorts along the Firth of Clyde, and you could still catch a ferry to Rothesay on the Island of Bute.

Just below Wemyss Bay I crossed into North Ayrshire and on to Largs, which had a slightly nicer feel to it than anything I'd seen up until then. A pebble beach and promenade ran in front of a park and large church, to a ferry terminal and breakwater. The buildings on the seafront helped to conceal the shops and the rest of the town that opened out behind them. Further south, just beyond Seamill, I managed to park in a lay-by, rather than the height restricted car parks, and walk onto a long sandy beach, scattered with rocks. The beach ran all the way to a harbour and headland at Ardrossan. Beyond the headland was the large and sandy South Bay, and at the other side of the bay was Saltcoats, with its own fairly unattractive smaller bay.

As I drove into South Ayrshire I had high hopes for Troon, where the Open has been held at the Royal Troon Golf Club, one of six courses there. I had images of the beauty of St Andrews, but ultimately I was disappointed. The harbour on a headland was quite industrial, but there were large sandy beaches either side of it. The town and high street were functional with none of the romance of St Andrews. I drove along one edge of the Royal Troon Golf Club on my way to Prestwick, where I stopped between another golf course and sandy beach, with a concrete kids play area.

I was pretty much ready to give up by then, it hadn't been the greatest day, being brought back down to earth with a bump after the weeks of beautiful beaches, islands, lochs and mountains, dampened down with the occasional shower of rain. So I headed straight for the Craigie Gardens campsite in the middle of Ayr. On the plus side, it's a Club Site so it's pretty good, as most of them are, there's been a bit of blue sky this evening, and best of all, there are no midges!

Ayr
Friday, 29th June

Seeing as I was back in civilisation, I figured I may as well make the most of it and take another shot at a day off. So I had a lie in, breakfast etc and eventually left the campsite late in the morning to walk a fairly short distance to the centre of Ayr.

The walk took me across the River Ayr to the high street, running parallel to the river. I wandered along the high street, making note of the places I would come back to, then along the side of the river, past some remains of an old fort and several riverside and seafront apartments, until I reached the beach and a view along it to the south.

With the sightseeing portion of the day completed, I headed back to the high street and was unsuccessful in trying to find a few things I was looking for. So with the shopping portion of the day completed I settled myself into a cafe for several hours for some lunch and some quality time with the iPad. Outside I could see umbrellas going up and down as showers came and went.

After a while I went to find a cinema, but had a bit of time before the next showing so I found a different cafe serving chocolate cake. I didn't order a drink, but the Italian owner kindly brought over a glass of water "for the sugar". A wise precaution. I noticed a bunch of photos on the wall opposite me, as you tend to see in some well established restaurants, of the owner with various famous people. They were mostly of the guy that had served me on a cruise ship (I don't mean he had served me on a cruise ship, I mean the guy that had served me was on a cruise ship in the photos, capiche?), with Sandra Bullock and Jason Patrick in some of them, and a double page spread from a local newspaper telling how Nino had been afloat with movie stars. This kind of photographic self promotion amuses me, I have to say, but Nino seemed like a nice chap and was chatting to several customers that clearly knew him well, so why not.

Having narrowly avoided a dry throat full of sugary (and exceedingly nice) chocolate cake, I made my way back to the cinema, unfortunately ending up with a 3D showing (I'm with Mark Kermode, 3D largely sucks) on a screen so small I doubted it would make much difference.

Movie Review No 5: Men In Black 3 in 3D - Men In Black was a decent film, Men In Black 2 was, uhhh, I can't even remember if I've seen it, which isn't a good sign, and it had Johnny Knoxville in it, which isn't a good sign. Men In Black 3 wasn't bad at all, but wow, Tommy Lee Jones went and got old! I'm not Will Smith's biggest fan, but I have to admit he's pretty versatile, and he pretty much pulls off the comedy here, and Emma Thompson seems to be a reassuring presence these days (she used to annoy me). I just about managed to follow the 'plot', which is pretty good for me, despite not being able to stop myself thinking 'that would never have happened' several times (in a film about a secret organisation policing alien species and wiping the memories of those that see them, which clearly could happen), I enjoyed it, apart from the 3D, which was annoyingly distracting at first and barely noticeable by the end. I don't see the point of 3D, we live in 3D, so the human brain just starts to filter it out after a while. At least mine does, but then there's a growing list of things that my brain filters out.

The high street and the rest of Ayr had pretty much shut up and gone home by the time I came out of the cinema. I couldn't be bothered to cook tonight, and didn't feel like a full meal, so after a quick 'sandwich' in a well known high street fast food chain (not that one… yup, that one), I walked the short distance back to the campsite.

...nure to Stranraer
...turday, 30th June

The coastline took a turn for the better today, and despite the odd heavy shower, so did the weather.

I drove along the seafront through southern Ayr, where I could see the cliffs to the south known as the Heads of Ayr, and the striking ruins of a castle or building perched right on the edge of a low cliff. My first stop was at Dunure, a lovely little village set next to a harbour and a small bay and beach. On a headland at one end of the bay were a dovecote and the remains of a castle. Out to sea to the south was the island of Ailsa Craig. It's said that in 1307 Robert the Bruce sailed from Ireland and landed at Dunure, to begin his fight to free Scotland from the rule of the English.

Driving along the coast towards Culzean, I came to a stretch of road called Croy Brae, also known as Electric Brae. Supposedly the road gives drivers the false impression that they are going uphill when they are in fact going downhill, and vice versa in the other direction, due to an optical illusion caused by the configuration of the land on either side of the road. The road was dubbed Electric Brae as it was originally thought that the phenomenon was caused by magnetic fields. Whatever the explanation, I didn't notice anything unusual while driving along it.

I stopped at Culzean Castle (pronounced 'Cullain') to take a look around the National Trust for Scotland property, sat atop the cliffs. The immaculate building was set in the equally immaculate grounds of a country park and included an apartment that was given to General Eisenhower in recognition of his achievements during WWII. When visiting many of the English Heritage properties I've been given an audio guide to take around with me, which I usually accept and just end up carrying around my neck without really using. At Culzean Castle I was given an iPod Touch, with videos and all sorts of information about the castle. Very progressive. However, as there was only myself and one couple wandering around I decided it would be rude to use it and ignore the guides that gave up their time to sit in some of the rooms waiting to be asked questions. I've spoken before about the guides at these places, and their overwhelming desire to impart all of the information they have to offer. Sure enough, in the entrance hall I asked the guide whether Culzean was actually a castle, or more of a stately home, which he answered (it was the latter) and then continued to seamlessly reel off his knowledge of the entrance hall. Most of the other guides were happy to just ask me where I was from and what I was doing, which I obliged by telling them all about my trip. I'm thinking of preparing an audio guide of my own to hand out in the future.

I stopped briefly at a harbour at Maidens before continuing to Turnberry, another of Scotland's finest golfing centres, and another distant runner-up compared to St Andrews. There was a beach rugby tournament due to start on the beach (the best place for beach rugby), but I had no desire to hang around to see the boys and girls play a few games before drinking a gallon of McKewan's and farting the national anthem. It's said that in 1307 Robert the Bruce sailed from Ireland and landed at Turnberry, to begin his fight to free Scotland from the rule of the English. Hang on a minute, that sounds familiar.

I moved on and stopped again to wander around the seafront at Girvan, with a long sandy beach and harbour, and a stretch of grassy park. Girvan claims to be the home of Ailsa Craig, which seems a bit odd to me, surely Ailsa Craig is the home of Ailsa Craig? Boats from the harbour could take you the 10 miles out to the island, a 335m high plug of a long extinct volcano and home to guillemots, kittiwakes and thousands of gannets.

As I drove into Lendalfoot the heavens opened with a heavy shower, which had pretty much stopped again by the time I drove out the other side of the small village and stopped by a monument to a Russian cruiser that had presumably sunk nearby. On the hillside above the village was the ruined tower of Carleton Castle. A tale tells of one of the castle's owners, Sir John Cathcart, whose hobby was to marry heiresses and push them off the cliff at nearby Games Loup. It seems that he found his soul mate in the eighth heiress, however, who had the same idea and pushed him off the very same cliff.

At Ballantrae I found a small harbour with beaches either side of it, and a garden centre with a coffee shop, an ideal place to stop for some lunch. When I crossed into Dumfries and Galloway and reached Cairnryan on the side of Loch Ryan I was into ferry country. A Stena Line ferry was docked to the north of the small town, although my map didn't show a route from that point, and a sleek looking P&O ferry was docked to the south, which sailed a route to Larne in Northern Ireland. Not much further along the coast, at the head of Loch Ryan at Stranraer, was an empty ferry terminal that serviced ferries to and from Belfast. I caught a ferry from Belfast to Stranraer last year with a couple of friends, on our way to Fort William while climbing the five peaks. It took us about four hours to get from Stranraer to Fort William. It's taken me 11 days to make the return trip.

I've travelled a little ahead of myself this afternoon, to a campsite at New England Bay on the southern arm of a hammerhead peninsula, which I'll explore more closely tomorrow. As with many of the campsites, there are plenty of rabbits roaming around and grazing on the grass.

Corsewall Point to New England Bay
Sunday, 1st July

I set off this morning aiming to do a loop around the peninsula, then make a start to the east if there was time.

After driving back through Stranraer I followed the road up the western side of Loch Ryan, then across to the northwest towards Corsewall Point. I stopped near the end of a single track road, just short of a lighthouse, now being run as a hotel. The lighthouse was opened in 1816 and was designed by Robert Louis Stevenson's grandfather, Robert Stevenson.

From there I headed to the south, following a road a little way inland from the coast until I came to a signpost for another lighthouse, which I followed until I reached the coast again at Black Head. The Killantringan lighthouse cottage and light keepers house had become self catering accommodation. It seems everybody wants to stay in a lighthouse these days. There was a little bay and beach to one side of the lighthouse, with a house just above it, and a larger beach off to the other side, with some kind of platform not far out from shore.

Not far south of Killantringan I came to the pleasant town of Portpatrick, set out around a sheltered bay with a harbour at one end and its own little lighthouse at the other end, no doubt with somebody spending a holiday in it. Behind the harbour, almost tucked out of sight, was a sculpture in honour of 'the Portpatrick Lifeboatmen, who fought bravely to rescue the Princess Victoria' on the 31st January 1953. The current lifeboat was moored in the harbour. I walked from one end of the bay to the other before stopping in a cafe for a bacon roll and a can of Vimto, the late breakfast of kings. Heading further south, I arrived at Port Logan, a small village at one end of Port Logan Bay. A handful of boats were moored by the breakwater, from which several people were fishing.

Feeling like I should be looking at another lighthouse, I drove south until I could drive south no further, reaching the Mull of Galloway, the most southerly point in Scotland. It was also a perfect spot for a lighthouse, which was open to the public, or you could rent the light keepers cottage, surprise surprise. From the Mull I could see across to Northern Ireland, the Isle of Man, and Cumbria. By then I'd decided that I wouldn't get off the peninsula today and may as well return to the same campsite as last night, so I had plenty of time to take advantage of a cafe not far from the lighthouse. Coffee and cake, obviously. They say the first step to recovery is to admit you have a problem. If I saw cakes as being a problem I suppose I would be admitting to it. But what's the problem?

Heading north again, I stopped on the eastern coast of the peninsula at Drummore, the most southerly village in Scotland. A few rows of whitewashed cottages stood above a beach, next to a large harbour that appeared to be a final resting place for several run down old boats. Another stretch of beach and some more houses lay on the other side of the harbour.

It was only mid afternoon but I figured I would head back to the campsite, where I returned to the same pitch as last night, and the same family of rabbits, to spend the rest of the day mooching around.

Sandhead to Graplin
Monday, 2ⁿᵈ July

I'll be honest, my heart wasn't really in it today. It was a dull dreary day, foggy and often drizzling with rain, so I didn't really feel inclined to spend long in places or stray far from the beaten track.

I started off with one last stop on the peninsula, at Sandhead, which stood at one end of the eight miles of Luce Sands. Most of the beach was used as a bombing range and was therefore out of bounds to the public. Travelling to the east, I crossed the Water of Luce and followed the coast to Stairhaven, where I found a beach and a small number of houses. I got the impression that a white cottage that stood on its own used to be the only building there and that the other houses, all in a uniform style, may have been built far more recently. A little further on I came to Auchenmalg Bay and another stretch of beach, this time largely overlooked by static caravans.

I stopped to wander around a harbour at Port William, next to rows of houses behind a sea wall. A park area above the harbour had several sculptures, including a man leaning on a railing, looking out to sea. From there the road moved away from the coast for a while until I reached Isle of

Whithorn, which wasn't actually an isle. I parked on one side of a large bay and walked along a road through the village, past some colourful houses to a harbour. Beyond the harbour was a narrow headland that rose up a small hill to a whitewashed tower, from where I could look back to the harbour and bay.

Moving on again, the coast turned to the north along the side of Wigtown Bay and brought me to Garlieston. Several damp looking bowling greens lay between a row of cottages and the bay, at the far end of which were a harbour and several apartment buildings, separated from the main village by a Caravan Club Site. Garlieston was used to build and trial sections of the Mulberry Harbours, portable harbours that were towed across the channel in sections as a crucial part of the D-Day landings in WWII.

The road moved inland again to Wigtown, where I stopped to have a walk around the town square, with another bowling green at its centre and a noticeably high number of book shops around it. I found a butchers and purchased a steak pie, which I took with me as I drove a short distance out of the town to a harbour on the River Bladnoch. The harbour was given a new lease of life after it had long been silted up from the early twentieth century, but a lot of the boardwalk was overgrown with grass. I consumed my pie while surveying the mud flats. If anybody asks who ate all the pies, I put my hand up to a fair percentage of them, but it's just a phase, like the tea cakes.

From Wigtown I worked my way up and across the River Cree before coming back down the other side, through Creetown, to stop at the rather petite Carsluith Castle. The castle was built in the 1560s, in a style favoured by the Scottish gentry at those times, stacking rooms on top of each other in a lofty tower. It even had a balcony, allowing the owners to sneer at any peasants passing below. Further along the coast road I turned off and squeezed the van along a narrow tree lined road until I came to the Cairnholy Cairns. I didn't realise at the time that there were two chambered tombs, the second was about 150m away in the fog. The tomb that I looked at was apparently the more elaborate of the two, with a facade of standing stones and a forecourt, most likely used for ceremonies, and around 4,000-5,000 years old.

Just beyond the head of Fleet Bay, overlooking the Water of Fleet, I had a look around Cardoness Castle, built by the notoriously badly behaved MacCullochs in the late fifteenth century. I then drove into Gatehouse of Fleet but did nothing more than sit in the van in the rain, trying to figure out where I could stay tonight. Apparently a Scottish historian and essayist by the name of Thomas Carlyle once told Queen Victoria that the only road finer than that between Gatehouse of Fleet and Creetown was that between Creetown and Gatehouse of Fleet. That may well still be the case on a clear sunny day, but I would beg to differ on a foggy day like today.

I had a few possibilities for campsites tonight, but first I drove back to the coast at Sandgreen, where I parked in a static caravan park so that I could take a quick look at the nearby beach. I then came back inland and passed through Borgue on my way to Graplin, where I pulled into the Brighouse Bay Holiday Park and came face to face with a stationary Meteor jet plane. Random. I paid for a pitch and parked up, then went for a quick walk in the drizzle to a private slipway within the grounds of the large holiday park.

Today, I have had no cake. What the hell?!

Kirkcudbright to Powfoot
Tuesday, 3rd July

Today pretty much started as yesterday had finished, grey and cloudy. But at least it wasn't raining.

I got going a little earlier than usual, to continue my journey along the Solway Firth, and made my first stop in the town of Kirkcudbright (pronounced 'Kirkoobree'), at the mouth of the River Dee. I walked through the town, past the ruins of MacClellan's Castle, to a marina. I noticed that the door to a bakery was open, early though it was, so I went in in search of pies, and came out with a chicken curry pie and a cream doughnut. I may be completely wrong about this, but I've only noticed these little round pies since I've been in Scotland, and I also don't remember seeing ring doughnuts cut in half and filled with cream elsewhere. I may have been pleased with myself for sorting out lunch so early in the day, but I then had to go through the mental torture of trying to resist eating it for the next four hours.

Following the main road to the east, some way inland from the coast, I stopped briefly to take a look at the remains of Dundrennan Abbey through locked gates, before reaching the coast again along the side of Auchencairn Bay and heading towards Balcary Point. Not far from the point, just past a B&B, I drove around a couple of tight corners and found myself at the beginning of a private road to Balcary House, so with nowhere to turn around I carefully reversed around the corners, parked by the B&B and took a look at a beach in front of it. The house and point were concealed by trees to the south and Heston Island was about a mile offshore.

Heading north again I came to a tiny harbour at Palnackie, on the Urr estuary, where two of the vessels present were lying in the mud and a third was up on the quayside, undergoing maintenance. After crossing the Urr further to the north and coming back down the other side I dropped into the villages of Kippford or Scaur and Rockcliffe. At Kippford or Scaur a yacht club lay amongst the mudflats, a short distance from cottages and houses above a small beach. At Rockcliffe the houses were spread out behind a rocky beach, looking out to Rough Island.

Back on the main road I came inland a little again until I got to Southerness, where an eighteenth century lighthouse stood on the beach, then turned to the north and stopped at a viewpoint just outside Drumburn that looked out across the Nith Estuary. Further north again I stopped at the Sweetheart Abbey in New Abbey. The abbey was established in 1273 by Lady Dervorgilla of Galloway, four years after the death of her husband, John Balliol, whom she was so devoted to that she had his heart embalmed (after he died) and kept it in a specially made casket, her 'sweet, silent companion'. When she too died in 1289 she was buried in the abbey with the casket and the monks named the abbey in her memory. I guess it sounded better than Stinkyheart Abbey.

My journey to the north ended at Dumfries, where I whiled away a couple of hours by walking along the side of the River Nith, eating the pie at long last (chicken curry, the tastiest one yet), finding a book I'd been looking for, sitting in a cafe (just coffee, no cake) trying to find somewhere to stay tonight, and stocking up on groceries. When I was done with all that I followed the other side of the river down towards Caerlaverock Castle. The castle, surrounded by a moat, was built in the late thirteenth century and was impressive from the front, but somewhat drafty at the back, like a fortified equivalent of a hospital gown. Modified several times over its life, the interior walls were in a completely different style to the outer walls. This was actually the second castle to be built there, 200m away were the remaining foundations of the first castle, built in the early twentieth century but in an area so wet that it started to collapse.

Heading east I stopped by the roadside at Brow Well, where the poet Robert Burns (a.k.a Rabbie Burns) came in ill health to drink of its water, which contained salts of iron. Within a month he was dead. Judging by the state of the 'water' that I saw there today I'm amazed he didn't die on the spot.

For my last night in Scotland I had selected the Queensberry Bay Holiday Park, at Powfoot. The pitches on the shores of Solway Firth were all taken so I was given a pitch in the field behind, separated by a fence from another field populated with sheep, horses, ponies, donkeys, llamas, alpacas, cows and who knows what else, all part of a very good family run campsite, half the price and twice as good as some of the campsites I've stayed at. The gents has a sofa in it, I may go and sit on it for a bit, just for the hell of it.

Annan to Allonby
Wednesday, 4th July

It was another grey day as I set off from the campsite this morning, on my way to Annan, a market town on the banks of the River Annan. I parked in the town, beneath blue and yellow bunting that snaked back and forth across the central street. After walking back to take a look at the bridge over the river I walked through the town and couldn't stop myself from stepping into a bakers, for one last Scottish pie. But disaster, they didn't have any steak or chicken curry pies, only scotch pies and haggis pies. The scotch pies scare me, quite frankly, I have no idea what was in the two that I've had, and I wasn't sure about haggis pie either, although I don't mind a bit for breakfast now and again. I carried on along the high street, hoping this was a two bakers kind of town, but alas not. My hopes rested on Gretna.

When I arrived in Gretna I was expecting to see the streets full of brides and bridegrooms, queuing up to be wed by Elvis impersonators. Then I realised I was in the wrong place. Gretna did, however, have a bakers, and they did, rather splendidly, have steak pies. I considered buying every last one that they had, but sense and the thought of my expanding waistline prevailed and I exited with just the one. I have nothing else I can tell you about Gretna.

When I arrived in Gretna Green I was expecting to see the streets full of brides and bridegrooms, queuing up to be wed by Elvis impersonators. To be honest I didn't know what to expect, I just possessed the basic knowledge that Gretna Green was where people could elope across the border to be married without parental consent. In 1753 a marriage act was passed in England stating that anyone wishing to be married under the age of 21 required parental consent, but in Scotland boys of 14 and girls of 12 could marry without consent. Gretna Green was the first village in Scotland along the coaching route from London to Edinburgh, and so became the destination of choice among elopers, and because Scottish law allowed weddings to be conducted in front of two witnesses by almost anyone, the local blacksmiths became known as 'anvil priests'. Nowadays there are several venues in Gretna Green, all conducting weddings 'over the anvil', but I found that the touristy side of the village centred around the 'World famous Old Blacksmiths Shop', which fronted a fairly small area of black and white buildings housing shops, restaurants and food halls, with a coach park at the back to accommodate the many visitors. There were also various romantic sculptures, the largest of which was by Ray Lonsdale, who also created the fisherman at Filey and Freddie Gilroy, sat on the park bench at Scarborough.

Alas, it was time to leave Scotland, so it was with no small amount of sadness that I joined the M6, and at 10:28am I crossed the border back into England, and Cumbria. Scotland is the gift that keeps on giving (maybe not quite so much when you get south of Glasgow), a beautiful country of lochs and mountains, beaches and harbours, forests and islands. For much of the six or so weeks that I spent there I forgot that I was in Scotland, it wasn't exactly the wall to wall kilts, haggis and highland cattle that you may have been led to believe, I didn't see a single caber being tossed (although that obviously does happen), and the Scottish accents were probably in a minority among the voices that I heard, but nonetheless it was uniquely Scottish. I'm sure I shall return one day.

Back in the motherland, I made my first stop in Carlisle, where I decided to spend an hour or so, firstly wandering past the castle and through and around the town centre and cathedral, then sat in a cafe with a coffee (no cake again, I do hope I'm not cured) to think about where else to go today and where to stop for the night. There wasn't a hell of a lot to see on the southern banks of the Solway Firth (or the northern banks, for that matter), but I stopped at Burgh by Sands, where King Edward I died in 1307 while leading a campaign against Robert the Bruce. A statue of said king stood between the Greyhound Inn and a footy field, just as he would have wanted it.

I stopped again just beyond Bowness-on-Solway, to look across the Solway Firth, having driven along a road that followed the course of Hadrian's Wall to its western end. Not far to the west was the promontory of Herdhill Scar, where the Solway Viaduct used to run a mile across the Firth to Scotland from 1868 until 1935, allowing trains to transport iron ore from the Cumbria mines to the Lanarkshire smelting furnaces. I drove around the headland and stopped again to the south of Cardunock, where huge antennae belonging to a NATO radio station at nearby Anthorn shot up into the sky, and I could see across the Channel of River Wampool. Crossing the River Wampool I turned to the west again to Newton Arlosh and stopped at the fourteenth century St John's Church, where cattle were often hidden in the nave through centuries of raids from Scottish marauders.

At Skinburness I reached the coast again and drove

through a row of houses to a pebble beach and a promenade that I followed a mile to the south to Silloth, where I started to feel a little like I was back at the seaside again, with fishing trawlers chugging along the coast. Large areas of green, fringed with pine trees and flower beds made it quite a pleasant place. Further south again I made my final coastal stop of the day at Allonby, where the houses sat behind a sand and pebble beach and a stretch of fairly wild grass. The coastline to the south disappeared into the mist.

I'm meeting a friend of mine, Lisa, in the Lake District tomorrow for a few days, so I decided I may as well extend the booking forward by one night and take the morning off there while she was driving up from Hampshire. So I drove the 50 odd minutes from the coast into the Lake District, and into the mountains, just beyond Keswick to the Troutbeck Camping and Caravanning Club Site. I love the Lake District, it's a beautiful place, to rival parts of Scotland. Lisa has never been here, or this far north, so she jumped at the chance to meet me up here, and judging by the forecast and the occasional downpours this evening, she's going to see the place in its natural state. Wet.

Keswick

Thursday, 5th July

It was a beautiful morning today, and one that I could enjoy by not doing much at all.

Lisa wasn't due to arrive until mid afternoon, so I gave the van a much needed clean, then loafed around reading my book and snoozing. I was expecting the weather to turn at any moment, but it held off, and even got brighter and warmer when Lisa turned up at about 2:30pm.

After putting up her tent and sitting down for a cup of tea we drove (Lisa drove, I get to be chauffeured around for the next few days) the 10 minutes or so into Keswick to take a look around. Keswick's a nice place, with a central square where a market was going on in front of a clock tower, which housed a tourist information centre.

Once we had wandered up and down the main part of the town, taking a look in a few of the many outdoor clothing shops, and getting some groceries, we stopped for a coffee in one of the cafe bars on the square, staffed mostly by Aussies, before heading back to the campsite for the rest of the evening.

I had originally booked us into one of the two Camping and Caravanning Club Sites in Keswick, situated right on the banks of Derwentwater, but they called me earlier in the week to cancel my booking because the recent heavy rain had made the site too wet for a campervan.

Lake Windermere and Haverthwaite
Friday, 6th July

No sooner had we sat down to some breakfast this morning than the rain started coming down.

Fortunately, the plan was to spend the day pottering around in boats on Lake Windermere, rather than out in the open. So we drove to Waterhead, just south of Ambleside, at the northern end of Lake Windermere, and bought a day ticket for the boats that cruised up and down the lake. Lake Windermere is the largest natural lake in England, just over 11 miles long, nearly a mile at its widest point and about 65m at its deepest.

The first leg of the journey, aboard the Swan, took about 30 minutes, to Bowness-on-Windermere, the main town on the lake. We stayed onboard and took the next leg of about 40 minutes to Lakeside, near the southern end of the lake. From there we boarded an old carriage belonging to the Lakeside & Haverthwaite Railway, for an 18 minute steam train journey to Haverthwaite to the southwest, ending with a short passage through a pitch black tunnel. At the pretty Haverthwaite station we waited a few minutes for the return journey back to Lakeside. It's not the destination that matters, but the journey, when it comes to old steam trains.

When we got back to Lakeside we waited to board the Tern to take us back to Bowness-on-Windermere, where we got off to have some lunch and a look around. Bowness was another nice place with the usual outdoor clothing shops, as well as cafes, restaurants, confectionery shops etc. The quayside area was full of swans, wandering around between the tourists, and row boats or motor boats could be hired and taken out onto the lake. There was also a golf course and a park nearby.

We boarded one of the 'Cumbria Class' boats to take us back to Waterhead, with a brief pickup and drop-off at Brockdale. There were various impressive buildings on the banks of Lake Windermere, including Wray Castle, country houses and hotels, plus many boathouses, some of them older stone structures. One of the boathouses on the eastern shore, north of Bowness, was recently sold for £1.4million, and was having an extension built.

The rain came and went today, for the most part we were sat on deck under an awning. The trip from Lakeside to Bowness was fairly breezy and quite cold, but from Bowness to Waterhead we were able to sit up top without an awning. We headed back to the campsite, stopping briefly at a viewpoint above Thirlmere. The ground was a little damp but Lisa's tent had remained watertight, which was just as well as it rained heavily again during the evening.

Helm Crag and Easdale Tarn
Saturday, 7th July

It was time to do a bit of walking today, and the forecast and start to the day was looking good, so we drove down to Grasmere and parked up, once we'd got past a herd of cows being driven through the village.

Grasmere was a lovely little place, full of outdoor clothing shops (naturally), cafes, restaurants and independent shops. It was quite busy today with tourists and walkers, and quite a few groups of school kids, some of them asking people to complete questionnaires for their GCSE's. Just the other side of the village green we took a road away from the village, past a youth hostel, to a track that led towards a climb up the side of Helm Crag.

Part of the Central Fells, at 405m Helm Crag was not particularly high, but it was a nice climb in a beautiful location. At the top were a couple of rock formations known as the 'Lion and the Lamb', which when seen from certain angles are supposed to look like a lion standing over a lamb. We sweated our way to the top on a day that was a little hotter than you'd like for this kind of activity, but which provided excellent views all around, down to the village and to Easdale Tarn, a small lake with a stream and waterfalls running from it that had been swelled with the recent rain. We spent a bit of time on the ridge at the top, trying to avoid several squadrons of flying ants, before walking from the rocky formations at one end to the base of the true summit at the other end, a steeper, craggier formation. There were quite a few people up there but not many of them attempted the scramble to the precarious top of the rocks.

The plan had been to climb Helm Crag and then make our way to Easdale Tarn, but I hadn't put enough time on the car parking, so as we would have to come most of the way back to the village before heading for the tarn anyway, we came all the way back down to have some lunch. After lunch we extended the parking and set off again past the youth hostel, but took a different track that climbed fairly gently along the stream and up to the waterfalls. Beyond the waterfalls the tarn had moved several hundred yards further away than last time I was there, or so it seemed, but we eventually came over a rise to find it in front of us. By then the day was pretty much perfect, warm but not hot, breezy at times but not windy, making for a very pleasant walk back to the village and a much needed ice lolly.

Before heading back to the campsite we drove a little further to the south to take a look at Ambleside. Yet another nice place, outdoor clothing shops, etc, etc. A friend of Lisa's had recommended a cafe called Lucy's, which we went to sit in for a drink. Over time Lucy's has grown from a specialist grocers to a cafe, restaurant, and wine bar, and also offers outside catering and a cookery school. It seemed almost criminal as I looked at but didn't touch the mouth watering display of cakes. It was a very laid back kind of place, next time I come to the Lake District I shall make a point of spending some more time there. Just as we were about to pay up and leave a heavy shower started up, so we waited a few minutes but ultimately got a little wet walking back to the car.

After returning to the campsite, which seemed to have missed the rain, and a quick shower and a change of clothes, we went into Keswick for a very nice Thai meal, then walked down to the campsite that we would have been staying at if the weather had been better. The location on the lake was perfect, and the ground seemed dry enough, but I guess it would have been a different story a couple of days ago.

Maryport to St Bees
Sunday, 8th July

It was time to get the van moving again today, after it had been stationary for the last three days.

Once we had packed up the tent and sat down for a bit of breakfast, Lisa set off at about 9:40am to spend most of the day driving back to Hampshire, and I got going just after 10:00am, to head back to the coast at Maryport. On a pretty nice Sunday morning, Maryport was a good place to get back into the swing of things. I spent a while walking around a multi sectioned harbour and marina until I reached the sea and wide beaches either side of the harbour entrance. Out in the Irish Sea was the Isle of Man and to the northeast was the coast of Dumfries and Galloway.

Heading south, I drove past wind turbines through the industrial outskirts of Workington, where collieries used to mine deep under the sea. I stopped initially on the side of the River Derwent before moving to a car park at the end of a point of land at the mouth of the river, with a view of a large wind farm and a pebble beach that ran to some cliffs to the south.

Moving south again I stopped at Whitehaven, next to a large area of harbours and marinas. I wandered around the area, which has seen a fair amount of rejuvenation since the millennium, including a 40m high crow's nest and a wave like structure that supposedly changes colour with the changing of the tide. A C2C marker identified the western end of the coast to coast cycle route and various sculptures and statues around the harbour celebrated times and industries gone by. I had some lunch in a cafe in one of the newer buildings before returning to the van just as the Wimbledon men's final was beginning. I wanted to listen to see if Andy Murray could overcome Roger Federer, and I had four days worth of blog entries to write, so I decided to head to a campsite at St Bees and call it a day.

I arrived at Seacote Park at one end of St Bees and parked on a pitch overlooking the beach, at the base of some cliffs that rose to the north. St Bees was the western end of Wainwright's Coast to Coast walk, 190 miles from Robin Hood's Bay, but I didn't notice any signs similar to those I had seen at the other end. Rather than just sitting in the van listening to the tennis, I grabbed my radio and headphones and set off to walk to the other end of a shingle beach, where I could see a few houses that presumably marked the far end of St Bees. When I got there I had a chat with a horse in a field behind the beach, before turning around and walking back again, then continued past the campsite and up onto the cliffs, where I got a good view back across St Bees and further down the coast to a nuclear processing plant at Sellafield. I continued along the coast path until I could see a lighthouse ahead of me at St Bees Head. Black guillemots were flying around overhead and below me, and I watched a kestrel hovering, almost stationary over the cliffs.

The tennis was still going on when I got back to the beach, so I bought an ice cream from a nearby cafe and sat just above the beach for a while, where a dog surprised me when it snuck up on me and licked my ear, before returning to the van just before the disappointing but increasingly inevitable conclusion to the match.

Braystones to South End
Monday, 9th July

I got going a little earlier today, on a warm and muggy morning.

Almost immediately, I had to wait five minutes for a train to pass through St Bees and the barriers to lift, before I joined a narrow single track road, with very few passing places, to keep as close to the coast as possible. When I reached Braystones I parked in a lay-by and went in search of the sea. Once I'd been turned back by a few private roads I followed a sign to a railway station, where I could cross the coastal rail tracks to see up and down a large beach. Walking back to the van I could see the somewhat ugly towers and chimneys of Sellafield.

I joined the main road to drive around Sellafield and rejoin the coast at Seascale, first of all behind rail tracks above a beach, then passing under the tracks to a car park behind the beach. I then came inland a little to Ravenglass, a little village on the banks of the River Esk. With the tide out the area in front of the village was mostly sand, with boats lying high and dry. I walked through the short main street, lined with cottages, and out the other side, to find a similar view of sand and boats. Ravenglass was at one end of the seven mile Ravenglass and Eskdale Railway, a narrow gauge track with small trains and carriages.

Not far from Ravenglass was Muncaster Castle, where I stopped for a while to walk through gardens to the castle, which was originally built in the fourteenth century but mostly rebuilt in the middle of the nineteenth century. The grounds were also home to the World Owl Centre and the headquarters of the World Owl Trust. The centre had one of the largest collections of owls in the world. The inhabitants, ranging from small pygmy owls to large eagle owls, sat on branches and watched me suspiciously. The centre also had a red kite and a common buzzard called Mortimer. I wasn't sure where or when I was going to stop for lunch, so I had a tea cake at the cafe (yup, first in a while) to keep me going.

From Muncaster I continued south and left the main road to reach the coast at Stub Place, in the middle of the MOD Eskmeals test firing ranges. When I arrived the red flags were flying and there was some smoke drifting not far to the north. The large beach stretched away in both directions and I could see north to Sellafield and beyond to the cliffs at St Bees, west to the Isle of Man and south to an offshore wind farm. About five minutes after I arrived I noticed another puff of smoke to the north, followed a couple of seconds later by a loud boom and a low fizzing sound that continued for several seconds. Looking out to sea I eventually saw what looked like a flare slowly arcing through the sky. The same happened about five minutes later, but I stuck around for another 10 minutes after that with no further firing. The Eskmeals range has 14 firing locations that can be used for proving weapons up to 1km over land, or up to 49km out to sea, at up to 80,000ft.

Further south at Silecroft I found another stretch of beach with the 600m Black Combe as a backdrop, before passing through 6,000 miles and continuing to Haverigg and an even larger area of sand and mud flats, in front of dunes and rows of cottages along the side of a small inlet. Pretty much next door to Haverigg, but reached by driving through Millom to avoid a caravan park, some old iron mines at Hodbarrow were flooded after the last mine closed in 1968, creating a large area of water that has become an RSPB nature reserve.

After leaving Hodbarrow I drove north along the Duddon Channel. With little chance to get down to the shore, I carried on around the top of the channel and into heavy rain as I came back down the other side. By the time I found somewhere to briefly stop, up above the channel near Ireleth, the rain had stopped again and there was a pretty impressive view across the channel and Duddon Sands, back to Hodbarrow and Haverigg. At low tide Duddon Sands can stretch for two miles at its widest point and it can be dangerous to attempt crossing it without local guidance.

By the time I had dropped down into Askam in Furness and found a route to the sands it was a scorching hot afternoon. The grassy sands, scattered with beached boats, the channel and the hills behind all made for a pretty nice view. I walked a little way until I was standing on a long spit of rock that jutted out into the sands, beyond which was more sand and the headland of Lowsy Point.

I returned to the van and drove further south to Barrow-in-Furness, where I stopped and walked through one of the wide main streets, past an impressive red sandstone town hall, then down to a bridge across a large harbour. At one end of the harbour were three naval vessels, and at the other end the imposing BAE Systems hanger-like building, where Trident nuclear submarines have been built. A submarine lay at anchor to one side of it. Barrow's past lay in iron ore and shipbuilding, and by 1870 the steelworks were the largest in the world, but are no longer in production.

I set off to find a campsite for the night by crossing a bridge onto the Isle of Walney, a 12 mile strip of land that provides a natural shelter to Barrow. After initially passing through houses, the road emerged into the open and I could see across to Barrow. As I moved further south I could see a castle on Piel Island and a lighthouse near the southern tip of Walney. Shortly after that I reached the campsite at South End, where it's been a glorious evening in a superb location.

Vickerstown to Grange-over-Sands
Tuesday, 10th July

Before leaving the Isle of Walney this morning I stopped by the bridge in Vickerstown, opposite the huge BAE Systems building, to take a look up and down the Walney Channel. The tide was low and the sky was overcast, in complete contrast to when I crossed the bridge yesterday afternoon. I drove through Barrow-in-Furness to the south, until I reached and crossed a narrow causeway to Roa Island, where a number of houses were clustered around the main street. The street came to an abrupt end with a view over to Piel Island and a raised walkway to a lifeboat station.

Starting the journey up the western side of Morecambe Bay, I stopped briefly at Roosebeck, Newbiggin and Aldingham to see the coast unfold in front of me and the miles of endless wet sand in the South and Ulverston Channels. At Aldingham the Church of St Cuthbert and Aldingham Hall were the last remnants of the original village, the rest of which had been taken by the sea over many centuries. Just outside Baycliff the higher elevation gave me a view out across Morecambe Bay.

Coming a little inland I stopped for a while in Ulverston, birthplace of Arthur Stanley Jefferson, better known as Stan

Laurel. Behind the town, on Hoad Hill, stood a 30m monument in the shape of a lighthouse, to commemorate another local hero, Sir John Barrows, an explorer and Secretary to the Admiralty. Ulverston was linked to the coast by a near arrow straight canal, which allowed it to prosper as a port in the late nineteenth century. The somewhat unimpressive head of the canal was almost hidden behind a timber merchant and scrap yard. I wandered up and down quaint cobbled streets at the centre of the town and had a quick search for the Laurel and Hardy museum before finding a cafe to sit down for a coffee. A footpath could be followed for just over a mile along the canal to Canal Foot, but I took the road option to the now decommissioned lock gates. To the north, the 49 span Leven Viaduct crossed the Leven Estuary.

Further up the estuary I stopped by the road outside Greenodd, near a road bridge that crossed the River Crake, which flowed from Coniston Water in the Lake District, and walked out onto a footbridge across the estuary, which was fed by the River Leven flowing from Lake Windermere. After crossing the River Leven I stopped at the railway station at Haverthwaite that myself and Lisa visited on the train from Lakeside a few days ago. Four little owls were sitting on perches inside the station, or were carefully placed by their handler onto the hands or shoulders of children. I hadn't planned to stop there for lunch, but I couldn't resist the smell of bacon sandwiches coming from the station restaurant.

Heading south again I drove to Old Park Wood, one of the few parts of this stretch of coast accessible by road. I followed a path a short distance around the outside of the wood, along the edge of the mud flats and sand, a little to the north of the Leven Viaduct. I then crossed the headland and followed a narrow track to a car park of sorts at Humphrey Head, where a peninsula of limestone cliffs jutted out into Morecambe Bay. With no obvious route up onto the 50m cliffs, I started walking along their base as it started to drizzle, over the mud flats until I began to run out of the muddy bank between the cliffs and a stream. With the mud getting softer and the drizzle getting harder I abandoned the idea of reaching the end of the cliffs and returned to the van to move northeast to Grange-over-Sands.

I parked on the street and walked through a little park with a bandstand in search of the promenade, which I didn't find at that point but as I walked along the road I could see it below me, on the other side of train tracks. Further through the town I dropped down the hillside and under the tracks to the promenade. I could have been forgiven for thinking the sea had turned green, as the water was actually 100m or so away across grass covered mud flats, making Grange-over-Sands a kind of seaside-wannabe resort. I walked back up to the main street and settled myself in a cafe with a pot of tea while it started to rain outside.

Tonight I am staying inland at Meathop Fell, a Caravan Club Site, where I've been able to complete all of my occasional chores once again.

Sandside to Fleetwood
Wednesday, 11th July

I set off this morning and took the main roads up and around the Kent Estuary, arriving on its eastern banks at Sandside. I stopped briefly by the road and then moved on to Arnside, just past the Kent Viaduct, where I walked along the waterfront to a little pier in front of some shops.

Driving inland, I crossed into Lancashire and stopped to stroll through the small village of Silverdale, which used to be on the banks of the River Kent until it changed its course to the north. The place had a friendly feel to it and I got the impression that most of the residents, some of which were queuing at a van selling fresh fish, probably knew each other. From a field at the edge of the village I could see out to Morecambe Bay. Working my way back to the main road I drove into Carnforth and took a look around, but didn't find much other than the Lancaster Canal running through it. I got back to the coast again at Hest Bank, where I waited a while for one of many trains to pass before I could cross the tracks and park just behind a shore of grass covered sand. To the south was Morecambe, which was where I headed next.

Morecambe was a pleasant surprise, I was expecting it to

be a lot tackier and rundown for some reason, but the four miles of promenade were quite nice, with a series of gardens, sculptures, and beaches between breakwaters. Morecambe's favourite son, Eric Morecambe, has been immortalised in statue form, skipping along the promenade with many of his jokes and the lyrics to 'bring me sunshine' etched in the ground in front of him. It was fairly quiet as I walked part way along the promenade, to a deserted stone jetty. From the west facing side of the town I could see right across Morecambe Bay to Piel Island and the lighthouse at the end of the Isle of Walney.

Not far from Morecambe was the pretty little village of Heysham, where a narrow street led to the Church of St Peter and, just above it on a headland, the remains of St Patrick's Chapel. In front of the chapel were a set of graves carved out of solid rock, thought to date from the eleventh century. From the headland I could see Heysham nuclear power station to the south and a port from which ferries ran to the Isle of Man. Back in the village I grabbed some lunch in a small cafe restaurant.

Cutting across the remains of the larger headland, I followed the River Lune to Lancaster and parked in the centre. Walking back down to the river I took a look at the Millennium Bridge, then walked up the streets to Lancaster Castle and Priory, built next door to each other, the current incarnations of which date from the twelfth and fifteenth centuries respectively. Next I headed south down the other side of the Lune and came to Glasson, a combination of working docks, canal and yacht basin. Moving on again I stopped at a picnic site just outside Dam Side and found myself looking out across a vast area of grassy sand. I could only really tell that there was water further out because I could see Heysham power station and the BAE Systems building at Barrow-in-Furness.

At Knott End-on-Sea there was more sand and grass, but

also the mouth of the River Wyre and a ferry running the short distance across it to Fleetwood. On my way around the Wyre, which took me some distance to the south before I could cross it and head north again, I stopped briefly at Stanah for a view of the river, albeit once again across an area of grassy mud, before continuing to Fleetwood. I stepped out onto a sand and shingle beach, on a day that had been pretty warm and sunny at times, and could see clearly across Morecambe Bay to many of the places that I had visited in the previous 48 hours, plus of course back across the Wyre to Knott End-on-Sea. Before leaving I bought an ice cream from a little kiosk above the beach, where the owner said that he'd seen me wandering around with my camera and asked me whether I had taken a picture of the kiosk, as it was quite famous. I had no idea if it was indeed famous, but I took a picture of it anyway.

I've travelled a little ahead of myself again this evening, to a Caravan Club Site at Blackpool South.

Cleveleys to Crosby
Thursday, 12th July

It was a lovely summer's day today, and I saw enough sand to keep me going for a lifetime.

I started off by heading back up the coast to Cleveleys, where I walked along a pristine promenade of flowing lines, clean shapes and sculptures, running behind a golden sandy beach beneath a deep blue sky. There were very few people around, just a few cyclists, runners and dog walkers.

Turning around and heading south again I drove back to Blackpool and parked one street back from the promenade, having briefly driven the wrong way up a one way street. Luckily there was no traffic coming the other way at the time. I walked out just to the side of Madame Tussauds (I've never understood the appeal myself) and just behind Central Pier. Far to my left was South Pier and the roller coasters and thrill rides of Pleasure Beach, to my right was North Pier and Blackpool Tower (with a big bandage around the top), and in front of me was a wide sandy beach. Love it or hate it, Blackpool is an incredible place, the ultimate British seaside resort, but I was glad to be there in the morning, rather than among the stag and hen parties that roam the place in the evenings. Blackpool has around

3,500 hotels, 120,000 beds, and during the Blackpool Illuminations season has around 500,000 extra lights. It had been a few years since I was last there, when I used to work in Warrington I would occasionally come up with some friends to ride the Big One, sometimes over and over again if it was a quiet night. I don't remember the promenade being anything special, but today it looked pretty impressive, scattered with huge pebbles, curved lamp poles, angular buildings and a large section of pavement that had been covered with quotes from comedians and television shows. Several massive black poles topped with 'buds' were swaying around in the breeze. Today, this morning, I was prepared to like Blackpool, quite a lot.

On my way south again I stopped briefly by the Pleasure Beach to stand below the Big One and watch some empty carriages plummet over the initial steep drop, before moving on to St Annes. An altogether quieter place, St Annes had sand dunes leading up to a modest pier that ended an awful long way from the sea, barely making an impression on the huge golden beach. At Fairhaven Lake you could watch the migrant birds or get out on the water in boats or wind surfers and try to avoid, or not, several large clear plastic inflatable balls that were just floating around.

At Lytham, a windmill built in 1805 stood on the large expanse of Lytham Green, behind the grass and sand shores of the River Ribble. To the south I could see the beach and buildings of Southport. The Royal Lytham & St Annes golf course will once again be hosting The Open this year, next week in fact. I followed the Ribble to the east, crossed it in the outskirts of Preston and turned west again to come back to the coast and into Merseyside at Southport, where the road ran behind another huge beach. I parked between the road and Marine Lake, which appeared to be a clear blue in the sunshine, and walked towards the pier. The seafront at

Southport (not that the sea was anywhere close) all seemed quite new, the pier and the building at the end of it looked quite modern, and there were retail parks, fast food restaurants and a cinema, plus the modern structure of Marine Way Bridge. I walked out to the end of the pier, set in a sea of sand, trying not to get run over by the trams. The entire length of the pier and tramlines, from the seaward end to the other side of the lake, was about a mile.

On the way to Ainsdale I drove into the Ainsdale Sand Dunes, one of the largest dune systems in Britain, stretching from Southport to Crosby. The dunes were more evident from the road than from where I stopped in Ainsdale, next to a large Pontins, and had a quick look at the beach. I drove back into the dunes on my way to Formby, where I headed for a car park near Formby Point, but turned around when I saw the £5 parking charge at the entrance. I parked further away on the street and walked back to the car park and beyond into the dunes, then out onto yet another large sandy beach. To the south, through a heat haze, was the skyline of Liverpool.

I moved on again to stop at Crosby and walk out onto the beach. Randomly scattered across the two miles of beach were 100 cast-iron figures, an installation called 'Another Place' by Antony Gormley. Some of them were high on the beach, some of them partially submerged in the sea. As modern art goes, from a distance I quite liked it, there was a kind of communal isolation to the figures, loneliness within a crowd, all staring out to sea, to who knows what. Up close, however, they were kind of eerie, covered in rust and barnacles, like malevolent creatures from a Dr Who episode whose facial features gave the impression that they could open their eyes at any moment. A couple of them had donned knitwear and one of them out in the sea had a seagull sat on its head, probably a pet. I decided to move on before more of them became self aware. At the southern end of the beach was Crosby Marine Park, an area of parkland, a boating lake and the larger Marine Lake.

I'm staying with a friend tonight, Jody, in Lymm on the other side of Warrington, so I spent a while on a few motorways, reacquainting myself with some of the moronic things that people do when driving on motorways. We went to Jo's local Mediterranean restaurant in the village, a lively place with friendly owners and a Greek night tonight that meant we just sat down at the table and they brought out mezze dishes throughout the evening, while a guy sat in one corner with a guitar playing Greek music. At one point a Greek conga broke out, with half of the patrons snaking out of one door onto the street and back in through the other door. I didn't take part for fear of pulling a hamstring and bringing the whole trip to a premature end.

Liverpool
Friday, 13th July

It was a miserable day today, weather wise, it barely stopped raining. Fortunately I didn't have much sight seeing planned.

After breakfast I said goodbye to Jo and drove to a Starbucks just off the motorway at Warrington, to meet up with another friend, Lindsay, and baby Caitlin. Linz and I both left work at Christmas, to respectively start our maternity leave and sabbatical, so for most of last year we had the common cause of being excited, albeit for very different reasons, with leaving dates within a day of each other that we could both look forward to. It was nice to have someone to be smug with without fear of annoying them! Caitlin was a model of quiet cuteness.

Not content with seeing just two friends in 24 hours, I drove to West Derby, to friend number three's house, Peter. We set out to drive into Liverpool, to the Albert Dock, with Peter leading and me following in the van, parking near the BT Convention Centre and Echo Arena and finding a cafe to sit down and catch up. Peter also left work shortly after me, but for opportunities elsewhere, so he had to leave after a while to get back to the real world to take a conference call. I took a wander around the large Victorian warehouses of the Albert Dock, now a heritage area since it closed as a working dock in 1972. At one end of the docks was the modern Museum of Liverpool and the Royal Liver Building, built in 1908 and topped by two mythical Liver Birds. At the other end of the docks was a Ferris wheel in front of the Echo Arena. As a Manchester United fan I cannot bring myself to say that I like this part of Liverpool, but I shall go so far as to say that I do not dislike it.

The weather did not encourage me to stick around for long or explore further, and I was pretty tired after a few long days where I've probably crammed in a little too much distance, so I was keen to get to my campsite early and call it a day. My SatNav sold me a dummy on the way to the Birkenhead Tunnel, so I drove in a big circle before I passed under the River Mersey and out into Birkenhead, then continued to Grange Farm at Storeton, roughly in the middle of the Wirral peninsula.

I've gone back to basics tonight, staying on a small farm rather than a club site or caravan park. I just hope I can get off the field tomorrow morning without spinning my wheels into the increasingly wet ground.

Port Sunlight to Thurstaston
Saturday, 14th July

To quote a blog entry not a million miles from here, "I just hope I can get off the field tomorrow morning without spinning my wheels into the increasingly wet ground".

I got about five feet before I slowed to a halt and my wheels started to spin. I couldn't go forward or backward, I was stuck. When I found someone to speak to in the stables they told me I would have to wait for about an hour for the farmer to get up and tow me out with a tractor, he had been on the milk delivery run this morning so had gone back to bed. Ah well, it wasn't as if I had a plane to catch or a meeting to get to. I tried pushing the van, no chance, and had a look around the farm to see if I could find any sacks or anything else useful to put under the wheels. I tried the two doormats that I have in the van, but one of them was just spat out backwards as the wheel spun it underneath. I now had two muddy doormats and a stuck van.

I used the time to look for possible places to stay tonight, then just after 10:00am I tried the farmhouse again and found the farmer's daughter, and her very friendly sheepdog, who went to get her dad out of bed (the farmer's daughter, not the sheepdog, it was friendly but it wasn't

Lassie). Shortly afterwards she drove a tractor (again, not the sheepdog) up to the field and her dad appeared with a piece of rope to pull the van forward the few feet required to unstick it. I made a mental note to make sure I found a campsite with a hardstanding tonight, although the forecast for today was pretty good.

Back in business again, I drove east to Port Sunlight. I'd been wanting to see Port Sunlight since I read 'The King of Sunlight', a funny and heart warming book about a remarkable man, William Hesketh Lever, co-founder of Lever Brothers (his brother James was never much more than a figurehead), a company that made its fortunes in soap and merged with Margerine Unie in 1930 to become Unilever. Lever, born in Bolton, was a businessman, a Liberal MP for Wirral, a Knight, a Lord (of the Western Isles), a Viscount, a tribal chieftain, Mayor of Bolton, High Sheriff of Lancashire and a multi-millionaire. He was also a philanthropist and a social reformer, who believed in a welfare state, votes for women and workers rights. Port Sunlight was built by Lever Brothers as a model village for the workers in its soap factory. Lever employed and personally supervised nearly thirty different architects, each designing and building different blocks of houses. Around 800 houses were built from 1899 to 1914 to house 3,500 people. The village also had a cottage hospital, schools, a concert hall, an open air swimming pool, a church and the Lady Lever Art Gallery. Lever was also just a little bonkers, mostly in a good way, with beliefs such as ballroom dancing could save the soul and the only healthy way to sleep was outdoors (he and his wife slept in a bedroom with no roof). Port Sunlight was declared a Conservation Area in 1978 and is a fascinating example, within the context of the life of William Hesketh Lever, of what could be considered a possibly uneasy mix of philanthropy and social engineering. I can thoroughly recommend reading 'The King of

Sunlight'.

Leaving the varied and eerily quiet buildings of Port Sunlight behind, I drove north to Birkenhead, where I stopped next to a huge ventilation tower above the Birkenhead tunnel that I'd driven through yesterday. I hadn't so much stopped to see Birkenhead as to look back across the Mersey to Liverpool. I moved north again to New Brighton at the northeast corner of the Wirral. A beach started just to the south at Wallasey and ran all around the northern edge of the Wirral and down the west side to beyond Thurstaston. Fort Perch Rock once guarded the mouth of the Mersey, across which were the cranes and dockyards of Bootle and Seaforth. Next to the fort was a lake backed by amusements, casinos, shops and cafes. I stopped at the far end of Kings Parade, by a lifeguard station, to see the beach stretching in both directions, then again about half way along the northern shore at Leasowe Common, where the remains of a lighthouse looked out across a vast expanse of sand.

Towards the northwestern corner of the Wirral I stopped by a lifeboat station and a colourfully graffitied boat at Hoylake, where I got my first glimpse of Wales to the west across the Dee estuary. Just around the corner at West Kirkby I struggled to find somewhere to park near Marine Lake, eventually stopping briefly on a double yellow. The place was heaving with cars and people, some taking part in dragon boat races, others walking around the edge of the large lake to cross the sand, exposed by the low tide, to the islands of Hilbre and Little Hilbre.

Continuing down the west side I came off the main road down to Thurstaston, first stopping above the cliffs to look out across the estuary to Flintshire, then driving parallel to the coast to a sailing club, where yachts and fishing boats were mostly high and dry on the sand, about 200m out. The road to the sailing club took me past the Wirral Country

Park Caravan Club Site, which I had tried to book last night but they had been full. Seeing as I had lost an hour this morning, it was a nice day for relaxing, and I didn't want to rush to get to the next group of campsites near Prestatyn, I dropped in to see if they had a free pitch tonight, which luckily they did, having had a few cancellations. So I parked the van on a pitch and walked up the road to a cafe, for a late lunch and some quality sitting down time to write today's entry. Yeah, yeah, and some cake. I've just been for a stroll down to the sailing club and onto the beach, where the yachts are happily afloat again.

Parkgate to Rhos-on-Sea
Sunday, 15th July

I made one last stop on the Wirral this morning, at Parkgate. The view from the village was of salt marshes, but it used to be a seaside resort and one of the main terminals for ferries to and from Ireland, until the sea decided to part company with it.

I was then on my way towards the mouth of the River Dee, crossing into Wales and Flintshire at 8:49am and crossing the Dee shortly afterwards. I made my first stop in Wales at Flint, to take a look at the remains of a castle, built by Edward I, that stood on the western banks of the Dee. As I walked towards one of the towers I could hear screeching coming from inside, which I figured was probably seagulls, but when I walked in I surprised two kestrels, which took off and flew to one of the other towers. When I walked around to that tower one of them was on the grass just beside it. It stared at me before taking off and landing on the wall behind, then circled overhead for a while before joining the other one in the tower. This time they were both happy to perch in the tower while I stood below them, initially together on the same ledge.

Heading northwest along the fairly industrial banks of

the Dee estuary I came to Llannerch-y-mor and was greeted by the sight of the Duke of Lancaster, a ferry that has been docked there in decline for the past 33 years. I'd been looking out for it as I'd seen some pictures of it taken by a friend. The ship was not far from the main road, near a market run by its owners. I could get close to it on the far side of a narrow inlet of water, but on the other side it was surrounded by fencing and watched over by a security guard. There have been various plans to restore the Duke, or convert it to a hotel, but none have come to anything. Personally I liked it the way it was, streaked with rust and lying empty, it seemed so much more interesting that way. There were reports last year that it would be used for filming scenes from World War Z, a zombie movie starring Brad Pitt (based on an excellent book by Max Brooks), but again nothing came of it. Shame, it would have been perfect for the part.

Leaving the Duke to its uncertain fate, I moved to the end of the estuary at Talacre, where I parked among a few amusements and fish and chip shops and walked out to a large beach that disappeared into a heat haze to the west. There were plenty of people around, and a few horses and riders in front of the dunes. In the middle of the beach was an old lighthouse with paint flaking off the walls and a strange mirrored figure standing on the balcony near the top. To the east I could see back to the docks at Bootle and Seaforth. To the south, just around the Point of Ayr, I could look along the length of the estuary.

Turning to the west I drove into Denbighshire and stopped in Prestatyn near a large Pontins at Barkby Beach, one of three beaches along the length of Prestatyn, then carried on to Rhyl, firstly stopping at the eastern end then driving to just beyond the middle of the promenade and parking up to walk back towards the central street leading away from the sea, where I stopped for some lunch. I've heard some disparaging things about Rhyl, but it wasn't too bad really, the long beach scattered with groynes was quite nice and the amusements and fairgrounds weren't overly offensive.

Just the other side of the River Clwyd, in Conwy, I stopped at Kinmel Bay to see a collection of fishing boats at the mouth of the river and another large beach stretching away to the west. At Towyn, in the midst of acres of static caravans, I walked along a street of amusements and chippies, over a railway bridge, through a fairground and out onto the beach again. To the east were a number of kite surfers, to the west the coast was becoming hilly towards the Great Orme. There were similar scenes at Pensarn but with a car park, amusements and shops just behind the beach, whereas at Llanddulas there was nothing but a small car park behind a pebble beach.

I'd driven the stretch of coastal road from Pensarn to Colwyn Bay several times before, going from Warrington to Snowdonia, so I'd seen Colwyn Bay from the road before, but until today I had never come off the road to take a look at it. Apart from another decent beach, I don't think I'd been missing much to be honest, the pier looked like it had been derelict for some time, but there was a new waterfront project under development. Much nicer than Colwyn Bay, and just along the road, was Rhos-on-Sea, where houses, cafes and restaurants were just behind a quieter road, rather than being separated by the busy A55, as they were at Colwyn Bay. I also got a great view on a nice day all the way back along the coast to the east. I wandered along the seafront, past a bunch of fishing boats on the sand behind a rock breakwater.

Rather than heading straight for my campsite I sat down in a cafe for half an hour before driving inland through some narrow country lanes to Tan-y-Bryn Farm at Bryn Pydew. I'd read some good reviews about this small friendly site, and sure enough I spent a while in the owner's kitchen chatting to him about travelling and the Olympics. One of the reviews had also mentioned a walk to a nearby obelisk, so I got some directions from the owner and set off to find it. When I reached the tall brick pinnacle, on the top of a hill, the views were excellent, I could see along the coast to the Isle of Anglesey in the west, along the River Conwy to the south, and over to the mountains of Snowdonia to the southwest.

When I did the washing up this evening there was a cat dozing on a chair next to the sink, which according to some other people on the site had been there for hours. I might go and see if it's still there before I turn in.

Penrhyn Bay to Bangor
Monday, 16th July

The cat was still there.

It had gone this morning though, so I set off in the rain without getting to tickle it behind the ears. I returned to Rhos-on-Sea and turned left to Penrhyn Bay, where a seawall was made up of large rocks and Little Ormes Head rose above the village to the west. The road moved inland and climbed a little as it passed Little Ormes Head before returning to the coast at Llandudno Bay. A pebble beach and wide promenade ran around the bay into Llandudno, at the foot of the Great Orme. The town looked pretty nice, even in the rain. I drove on into the town, stopping at several points along the seafront as the beach changed from pebbles to sand. At the western end a long pier started from below the Grand Hotel.

If you want to get up to the 207m summit of the Great Orme you can take a tram or a cable car from the town, or you can drive up to it from Marine Drive, a toll road that follows the coast all the way around the base. I paid the £2.50 toll and set off along the one way road until I could turn off it and up some steep hairpin corners. I just about got around the first corner but a car had stopped on its way down on the second corner to take a photo of some sheep, so I had to beep my horn to alert him to my presence. Further up I crossed over the tram tracks and carried on to a car park at the summit, next to a visitor centre and the tram station. The view from the top to Llandudno and Snowdonia was somewhat misty. I sat down in the Summit Complex for a while with a pot of tea and a Danish pastry.

On the way back down to Marine Drive I had to stop and reverse on both hairpin bends to get around them, and the same again at the bottom to get around the corner back onto the one way road. Further around the road I came to a lighthouse, now a B&B, below the Rest & Be Thankful cafe. Even I didn't consider stopping again so soon for more tea and cake. At the end of Marine Drive I dropped down into the western side of Llandudno, where I stopped in the rain and walked onto the sandy beach.

A little further on, at the head of the Conwy estuary, I stopped briefly at Deganwy to look at a beach and the many small craft out in the estuary. To the south, across the estuary, was the mightily impressive sight of the circular towers and turrets of Conwy Castle. I parked just before a bridge over the estuary and considered my options for the rest of the day, the persistent rain was somewhat annoying and I was already somewhat wet, so I abandoned my plans to get onto Anglesey today and booked a campsite in Bangor, giving me a more relaxed afternoon. I also remembered a recent invention called the 'umbrella' (my brain is in a different time zone sometimes), so I grabbed mine and went for a walk around Conwy, a town enclosed by the castle and fortified walls, before finding somewhere to stop for lunch.

The rain had pretty much stopped when I got back to the van and moved on to Penmaenmawr and walked under a railway to get to a pebble and sand beach. The village was hemmed in on both sides by hills with road tunnels through them. Travelling to the west, the two lane carriageway passed through the tunnels, but in the other direction another two lanes passed around the base of the hills, above the sea. At Llanfairfechan I drove under the railway to another beach of pebbles, sand and groynes, in front of a stretch of grass with the local small boats stored on it.

After passing into Gwynedd I stopped to take a look around Penrhyn Castle. The castle was built for the Pennant family between 1820 and 1837 by Thomas Hopper, in a neo-Norman style, apparently. Inside was a maze of opulent rooms, many of them with decorations and furniture designed by Hopper. The castle also contained one of the largest collections of art in North Wales, including pieces by Rembrandt and Canaletto, and a one ton slate bed made for Queen Victoria. There were quite a few people wandering around, out of the rain, so I didn't get collared by any guides bursting with unspoken information.

My last stop today was in Bangor, on the Menai Strait. I think maybe I didn't see the best of Bangor today, but it was raining again and I couldn't really be bothered to explore very far, other than walking out along a pier that reached so far across the Strait that you could throw stones at Anglesey and have a decent chance of hitting it. Maybe.

My campsite is just about in Bangor, at Treborth Hall Farm. It's not the most inspiring campsite, it tends to work out that the more you pay the worse the site is, but at least I'm on a hard standing and hopefully won't get stuck in the narrow strip of grass between the gravel and the track. I've just seen a three legged cat hopping past. I don't even get a complete cat for my money!

Beaumaris to Trearddur
Tuesday, 17th July

I got going early this morning, as the forecast for this afternoon wasn't good, and was soon crossing the Menai Bridge onto the Isle of Anglesey, where I started up the Menai Strait to Beaumaris. I parked on the seafront and walked around the bay, full of small craft, to a small pier, then into the town and along the high street. At one end of the high street was Beaumaris Castle, a thirteenth century castle built by Edward I, surrounded by a moat.

Turning to the west I stopped at Red Wharf Bay as it started to drizzle. A number of yachts were afloat out in the bay, but would most likely be beached at low tide, on about 10 square miles of sand. At Benllech I found a beach of golden sand in front of a sea wall and a large static caravan site up above the sea to the west. At Moelfre there was a small pebble beach in the middle of the village, with small boats hauled up onto it and clear water lapping against it. At Lligwy Bay was another sandy beach, backed by dunes, and out in the sea was a small rocky islet, Ynys Dulas, with a tower on it that acts as a landmark for sailors.

I stopped for a while at Llaneilian, where I used to come for family holidays when I was a kid. To be honest none of the scenery really rang any bells, neither the little bay and beach nor the lighthouse out on the headland of Point Lynas, but that's not unusual for me, I find it hard to remember two days ago. However, when I walked a short distance around the coast path I confirmed my memory of a little rocky hill overlooking the field that we used to camp in. The field had become overgrown. Back at the beach, a group from Plas y Brenin, an outdoor pursuits centre based in Snowdonia, were getting ready to set off in sea kayaks.

I also didn't remember Amlwch Port, which we used to visit to buy bait for fishing from the rocks near the campsite, but I parked in the village and walked along to a harbour. A little further along the coast I drove into Porthllechog (also known as Bull Bay), passing the Bull Bay golf course on the way. I vaguely remember spending a day on the golf course watching a tournament, and getting so sunburnt that my face blistered. I'm pretty sure I played a round there one year too. The village was based around a small rocky cove.

Next I moved on to Cemaes Bay, a picturesque little place where I wandered around a harbour and beach on one side of the bay, with a crescent of beach on the other side. A bit of blue sky was showing through by then, rather than showing signs of the rain that was forecast, and it was still there when I emerged from a cafe after having some lunch.

On my way to Cemlyn Bay I came across a farmer stood in the middle of the road with a gate opened half way across it. After a while a herd of cows appeared from the other direction, being shepherded by a small car along the road and into the gate. At Cemlyn Bay I parked at one of two RSPB car parks either end of a sweep of shingle that sheltered a salt water lagoon. The shingle ridge was dramatically changed by a huge storm in the nineteenth century and continues to move inland and change shape, sculpted by the sea.

Moving on to the western coast of Anglesey I stopped at

a sandy beach, strewn with rocks and seaweed, at Church Bay, before moving further south and crossing a bridge onto the much smaller Holy Island that lay just off the western coast of Anglesey. I stopped at the main town and port of Holyhead. I don't really know where the good parts of Holyhead were, if indeed it had any, I couldn't find them last time I was there and I didn't find them this time, other than a marina that lay within two lengthy breakwaters. A friend of mine was stranded there for two days after missing a ferry to Ireland, and still holds a grudge. I walked through a park and gave a goalpost a kick on his behalf, but not hard enough to stub my toe in a John Cleese kind of way.

From Holyhead I continued west and drove into fog on my way to South Stack, the most westerly point of Holy Island/Anglesey. I parked at a visitor centre and started walking in the direction of a lighthouse. At first I couldn't see a thing, which made South Stack uncannily similar to Cape Wrath, but eventually I started walking down several flights of stone steps until I could see a metal bridge below me and the outline of a rocky island at the other side of it, with some buildings on top. I went as far as the bridge but didn't much fancy shelling out nearly £5 for the privilege of crossing to the island and seeing very little. Instead I walked back to the visitor centre cafe, for the usual. While I was there I got a text from O2 welcoming me to Ireland. I know it was foggy, but I'm sure I would have noticed driving onto a ferry or a very long bridge.

On my way to the Bagnol Caravan Park in Trearddur I stopped at a large beach before driving around a bay, past a couple of smaller beaches, to the campsite. Once I'd found a pitch I walked through the campsite back to the two smaller beaches, next door to each other in little bays full of pleasure craft, sheltered by rocky outcrops. The rain has just unleashed itself for five minutes, but it's been a much better day than I had expected.

Borthwen Bay to Caernarfon
Wednesday, 18th July

I made my way down a narrow winding road from the village of Rhoscolyn to Borthwen Bay, parked in a small car park at the end and stepped out onto a sandy beach in a pleasant little bay. There were several houses dotted around the bay, a small island at one end and a few boats pulled up to the dunes behind the beach.

I left Holy Island behind me as I crossed one of the three bridges back to Anglesey, then headed for the south coast at Rhosneigr. First I stopped at the southern edge of the town and had a look at a beach with a couple of people body boarding in the surf, then moved around the corner to a large bay with several little islets and a beach running around it. In the distance I could see the 220m summit of Holyhead Mountain, which had been hidden in the fog yesterday. The air was filled with the roar of jets taxiing and taking off from RAF Valley, just above the beach to the north. I believe HRH William Wales has been stationed there flying Sea King helicopters.

A little further along the coast I stopped just off the road in a car park behind Porth Trecastell, a small bay and sandy beach that was also known as Cable Bay due to the transatlantic telegraph cable that came ashore there. At Aberffraw, a little eighteenth century stone bridge crossed the narrow River Ffraw just before it passed some grassy dunes on its way to the sea at Traeth Mawr. Small boats were moored on the river or resting on the grassy banks. The little village used to be the capital of Gwynedd, the kingdom of North Wales, between 870 and 1282. At the head of the Cefni estuary I stopped at Malltraeth, where floodgates and an embankment called the Cob, built by Thomas Telford in 1818, prevented flooding of the river.

When I reached Newborough I turned to the south and drove through a toll gate into Newborough Forest, continuing through the forest until I came to a car park just behind Llanddwyn Bay, where I walked through dunes onto a beach. The sand stretched in both directions, backed by dunes to the east and forest to the west. Also to the west was Llanddwyn Island, which was actually more of a peninsula than an island, where I could see a couple of white towers and a cross. I hadn't really intended to go very far, but as I walked a little along the beach to the west I figured I may as well keep going until I got to the end of the island, but in the hope that no rain clouds came in as I hadn't taken any waterproofs with me. I needn't have worried, by the time I got onto the island the clouds were breaking and the sun was shining through, so instead I started worrying about not having any sun cream. As well as a couple of crosses, which commemorated St Dwynwen, the patron saint of Welsh lovers after whom the island was named, and the two towers, one of which was a disused nineteenth century lighthouse, the island also had a ruined Tudor church and a row of cottages that were home to pilots that guided ships around the sandbars at the entrance to the Menai Strait. The whole place was a beautiful area, with several small beaches along both sides of the island. I managed to get back to the van without getting wet or sunburnt.

My last stop on Anglesey was at a place that many people have heard of but few can pronounce. I parked on the street near a train station with several coaches parked near it, outside a building that sold all sorts of tacky souvenirs as well as various household goods and food. The only reason the building and the coaches were there was because the village was called Llanfairpwllgwyngyllgogerychwyrndrobwllllantysiliogogogoch, which translates as 'The church of Mary in the hollow of the white hazel near the fierce whirlpool and the church of Tysilio by the red cave'. It's more commonly known to its mates and signposts as Llanfair P.G. The train station was the focal point of the village, where you could still buy tickets with the full name printed on them. To be honest I felt a bit embarrassed wandering around taking pictures of the signs, but so was everybody else, and I felt even more embarrassed about contributing to the whole touristy nonsense by having lunch at a cafe in the souvenir building. I really should have asked somebody to direct me to the church, white hazel, fierce whirlpool or red cave.

I departed Anglesey over the Britannia Bridge and turned south to Caernarfon, site of another mightily impressive Welsh castle, or should I say mightily impressive castle built by Edward I to keep the Welsh in check. After getting a bit lost in some roadwork diversions among the narrow streets I parked next to an Asda and worked my way back towards the castle, emerging at a large square with cafe seating at one end. I walked around the castle to a river and quayside, lined with yachts. The fortified walls continued from the castle around the maze of streets in the old town.

I'm back in the mountains tonight, I've come to a forestry commission site just outside Beddgelert, one of my favourite places in Snowdonia. Once I'd found myself a pitch among the trees I set off for a 15 minute walk into Beddgelert, where several rivers came together, surrounded by hills. Behind the village were open fields and a short walk to two trees surrounded by a fence in the middle of one of the fields. There lay the thirteenth century grave of Gelert, the faithful hound of Llywelyn, Prince of North Wales. One day, unable to find Gelert, Llywelyn went hunting without him. When he returned he was greeted by Gelert, who was covered with blood. The prince rushed to find his son, but found an empty cot surrounded by bloodstained bedclothes. Believing Gelert had killed his son, Llywelyn plunged his sword into the hound's side. Gelert's dying yell was answered by a child's cry. Llywelyn searched and found his son unharmed, but nearby lay the body of a mighty wolf that Gelert had slain. Filled with remorse, the prince is said to have never smiled again. He buried Gelert on the spot that is now called Beddgelert. That story still brings a lump to my throat.

The campsite has a bakery, so I ordered a pizza for tonight, some chocolate croissants for breakfast and some white rolls to take away for lunch. Approximately five minutes before I was due to pick up the pizza it started raining so hard that it was getting difficult to see anything outside the van. I waited five minutes before getting my golf umbrella out from under the sofa, by which time the rain was lighter. By the time I'd picked up the pizza and was heading back to the van it had stopped. There were a few loud thunder cracks and that was it, back to blue sky again.

I had noticed a fly buzzing around the van just before I left Llanddwyn Bay, and have just found it sat in the corner of one of the windows, so I let it out. I wonder if flies care where they are, or whether that one was wondering where the hell it was and how it was going to find its way home?

Llanberis and Betwys-y-Coed
Thursday, 19th July

The forecast today was for showers in the morning, clearing up in the afternoon, so I had a lie in before collecting my croissants and rolls and having some breakfast.

Just before 11:00am I set off towards Pen-y-Pass, from where I was intending to climb Snowdon. As I followed the final winding stretch up the side of a valley I drove into cloud, then into horizontal rain as I parked in the car park. I sat in the van for about half an hour, trying to decide what to do, before getting out and going into the main building to look for a weather forecast, which was pretty much the same as the one I'd seen yesterday. The short walk from the van and back was wet enough, so I decided to head into Llanberis and come back in a couple of hours.

Llanberis sat along the banks of Llyn Padarn, a lake that you could take rowing boats onto or travel along one side and back on a little train. You could also take the Snowdon Mountain Railway from there to the summit of Snowdon. There were a few people waiting for the next train, and others milling around the shop and restaurant. I ate my lunch while walking back to the van, intending to head back to Pen-y-Pass. I had driven back out of the cloud and rain when I left Pen-y-Pass, but when I got back into the van it started to rain. So much for clearing up in the afternoon. Another Timberland van beeped its horn as it drove past me out of the car park, you don't see many of them around.

When I got back to Pen-y-Pass there hadn't been much change in the weather, so I decided to abandon the climb and instead carry on to Betws-y-Coed, another of my favourite places in this area, and have a relaxing afternoon. I drove back into Conwy and parked just outside the village, so that I could walk in past a little stone road bridge with the River Conwy running rapidly below it. When I used to come up here with my family as a kid, Betws-y-Coed was always a sign that we were nearly there. The journey would usually start early in the morning, with myself and my sister getting into the car in our pyjamas and falling asleep again surrounded by pillows. North Wales is a lonnng way from Bristol when you're a kid, time doesn't pass as quickly as when you're older. When we reached Betws-y-Coed we would often play around on the tree lined rocks below the bridge. Further down the village was a large green, the other side of which was a train station and a row of shops and cafes.

I wandered around the village for a bit before finding a cafe with WiFi to sit myself in for an hour or so, while the rain started up again outside. I only got so far with uploading the last few days of entries before the laptop battery ran out again, it seems to take longer and longer to upload all the photos. I didn't even have a phone signal back at the campsite, so I'd just have to wait until I found another campsite with WiFi to get everything up to date again.

On the way back to the campsite the clouds had lifted a little, but the summit of Snowdon was still covered. It's not been unusual to have rabbits running around the campsites in the evenings, but on this one, in the forest, they seem to be out and about all day long, you can't move without startling a few of them, or the occasional squirrel.

Dinas Dinlle to Abersoch
Friday, 20ᵗʰ July

It was looking like a nice day as I left Snowdonia and headed back to the coast at Dinas Dinlle. From a pebble beach I could see Llandwyn Island to the northwest and the three peaks of Yr Eifl to the southwest. Just behind the beach was a hill with an Iron Age fort on top, but no public right of way since erosion had made the summit dangerous. I continued a little way north to Morfa Dinlle, where the beach became sandy and the rest of the headland was taken up by Caernarfon Airport, a small airfield used primarily for pleasure flights.

Turning south again I began my journey onto the Lleyn Peninsula, stopping first on a pebble beach at Aberdesach. I could clearly see terraces on one of the peaks of Yr Eifl, where granite had been quarried. I stopped again below the peak at Gwydir, where I found a small harbour. From there the road moved inland and rose up around the flanks of Yr Eifl, then returned to the coast as it dropped down towards Nefyn. I drove through Nefyn along a road that wound steeply down to a beach along a crescent shaped bay, ending at a headland to the west. On the other side of the headland I parked in a National Trust car park and walked down to a beach at Morfa Nefyn, in a larger crescent bay. Both bays were very attractive in the sunshine.

Continuing along the peninsula to the west, I followed signposts that I thought would take me to a beach at Porth Towyn, but I never found it, either the signposts disappeared or I missed one of them. Passing through the country lanes, I passed a field where I startled two birds of prey into the air, and just around the corner I found one of them, or possibly a third, in the middle of the road, which again took off as I drove towards it. I pulled over next to a gate to see if I could spot the birds and eventually spotted one of them, quite large, sitting on a fence some distance away. I climbed over the gate to get a little closer to it before it took off and circled around for a while. I was hoping it was a golden eagle, and the photos I took of it looked similar to the profile of an eagle in the bird book that I had, but having sent a copy of one of the photos to my mum and sister later in the day it looks like it was a buzzard. Golden eagles are generally found further north in Scotland.

The road suddenly dropped steeply down to a small car park, where I stopped and followed a stream a short distance to a sandy beach at Porth Colmon. More narrow country lanes took me to another National Trust car park at Porth Oer, where I walked down a steepish road to a beach, then realised I'd forgotten my camera and walked back up again to get it. Porth Oer is also known as Whistling Sands, a name I remembered from my childhood, because walking on the dry sand can cause the grains to make a whistling or squeaking noise. A very convenient beachside cafe gave me somewhere to sit down and have some lunch outside as the sun beat down.

After lunch I drove up onto the 160m summit of Mynydd Mawr, the most westerly point of the peninsula. The views were spectacular, all the way back along the peninsula and south along the Welsh coast. Two miles off the mainland, across the strong currents of the Bardsey Sound, was Bardsey Island. The island was low lying on one side, but rose to 167m on the other side. In 516 St Cadfan built a monastery on the island, and in the Middle Ages it became a place of pilgrimage. So many pilgrims were buried there that it became known as the 'Island of Twenty Thousand Saints'. Pilgrimages are still made to the island today.

Starting back along the peninsula to the east I drove down into Aberdaron and walked onto a beach, overlooked by the Church of St Hywyn, which was protected by a seawall from the erosion that had brought it dangerously close to the beach. I stopped again at a National Trust property called Plas yn Rhiw, a small seventeenth century manor house set in a woodland garden. I didn't really have any interest in the house, although I had a quick look around it, quick enough so as not to give the guides time to speak. I was more interested in the view that it was supposed to have across Porth Neigwl, a four mile stretch of low cliffs and beach. Driving through Llanengan brought me down to a car park from where I could walk out to the beach. Porth Neigwl is also known as Hell's Mouth due to the threat that it posed to ships being blown inshore there, but it's a popular spot for surfing.

Moving across a headland I made my last stop of the day at Abersoch, where two beaches were separated by a rocky outcrop. I parked in the village and walked to the southern beach, which was covered with boats and quite a few people. The dunes behind the beach had a row of beach huts in front of them and there was a fairly tired looking concrete structure of huts rising up the cliff towards the rocky outcrop. The number of people and kids running around the beach were probably a sign of things to come, with the schools having broken up for the summer and the weather looking to improve from the months of rain that

I'd heard about while I'd been up north. Quieter and much nicer was the northern beach, a vast expanse of almost empty sand.

Tonight I'm staying at the Willows, in Mynytho. When I phoned this afternoon and the owner said he could give me a pitch for £25 I decided to look elsewhere, but the reviews of the place were good and it sounded nice, so I thought I'd give it a go. When I arrived his wife was at reception and let me in for £20, which is still quite expensive, but it's certainly a nice place, well kept, very clean and tidy, with free WiFi (always welcome), and in a beautiful location. I could see a tower up on a hill outside the site, so I walked along the road towards it. I could hear the same bird call that I had heard around the buzzards this morning, and sure enough as I walked along the road I saw a buzzard to my right just as it dropped off a fence post and swooped across a field. I watched it circle for a while then carried on to the tower on the hill, where the views were excellent, before coming back to the van to get my zoom lens and returning to the field. After searching for a while I saw the buzzard swoop across the field again and sit on a fence post the other side. It didn't seem like it was going to go anywhere so I eventually started back towards the campsite, at which point it took off, dropped below the hedge between me and the field, then flew directly over my head, so close that I couldn't find it in the viewfinder on full zoom, typical! It then flew to a tree where two other buzzards took off and started circling around. Given that I was only just to the south of where I had seen two, possibly three buzzards this morning, they may well have been the same three.

Llanbedrog to Harlech
Saturday, 21ˢᵗ July

It was a beautiful day today, on the equally beautiful Lleyn Peninsula, which I've grown rather fond of.

I started the day at Llanbedrog, where I found yet another National Trust car park and walked out onto a sand and shingle beach, near a wooded rocky headland at one end of a bay. Along the back of the beach, in front of a tree lined bank, was a row of colourful beach huts. Moving along to the next bay I stopped above South Beach at Pwllheli, backed by dunes, a road and terraced houses. I walked a little way to the east but realised I was further away from the marina area than I had thought, so I returned to the van and drove as far as I could along a narrow peninsula that sheltered the marina and harbours, stopping at the entrance to a holiday park that covered the neck of the peninsula. I then drove around to the landward side of the harbour and attempted to find somewhere to park from where I could look around the marina and the beach that ran to the east from the harbour entrance. But I got caught up in traffic and controlled parking for some kind of event that was going on, so in the end I gave up and drove out of Pwllheli to the east.

In all I spent about an hour driving up and down, being turned around at private roads and large holiday parks, trying to get to see the beach, but I was thwarted until I found a road that I thought would take me down to the next bay along, at Afon Wen. The road ended at a path that led to a beach, so I carefully turned the van around in a tight space and parked on the side of the road behind another car. When I walked onto the beach a dog came over to stand next to me while it shook itself dry, and its owner told me that it was a shame I hadn't been there 10 minutes ago to see the dolphins. I didn't know whether to believe him or not, but either way I didn't see any myself.

I was expecting hordes of people to descend on the coast today, it being a sunny Saturday during the school holidays, but overall it was pretty quiet. I guess one of the drawbacks of not working for a period of time is that weekends and weekdays swap over, the weekdays are nice and quiet and the weekends can bring out the annoying cars and crowds. Not a huge drawback, admittedly, particularly as half the time I don't know what day it is, most of the time I only realise it's the weekend because the DJs change on Radio 1.

Next I stopped at the very pleasant Criccieth. Overlooking the town from a rocky headland was Criccieth Castle, built in the thirteenth century. I parked to the west of the castle and walked past Victorian terraced houses above a pebble beach, then around the corner and below the castle to a larger bay. The Blue China tea rooms had a few tables outside with a view across the bay, and it would have been wrong to pass up the opportunity of sitting in the sunshine with a cup of tea and a tea cake (I'm back on the tea cakes with a vengeance recently).

Continuing on again, I drove into Morfa Bychan and found a road that headed south towards the beach of Black Rock Sand, where I found somewhere to park not far short of the beach, rather than having to pay to drive onto the beach, where I would no doubt have spun my wheels into the sand (even though it wasn't soft) and passed the rest of the day watching the tide coming in. Other cars were scattered around the large beach, with most people trying to stake a claim to their own acre or two. Not far from there, at the end of a road that could easily be missed, was Borth-y-Gest, a little gem of a place set around a sheltered bay. Almost hidden from the surrounding land by trees, the little village had a quiet charm to it, with small craft resting on the sand at low tide and a sign on one of several grassy patches that proclaimed 'The best kept village of the year in Caernarvonshire'.

Porthmadog was an altogether larger and busier affair, with waterfront apartments and yachts moored in the harbour. The town was also a terminus for two narrow gauge railways, the Welsh Highland Railway, which travelled to Caernarfon, past the back of the campsite that I stayed in at Beddgelert (right behind the pitch that I stayed on, in fact), and the Ffestiniog Railway, which was originally built to transport stone from the quarries at Blaenau Ffestiniog, 13 miles away through the mountains, to the harbour at Porthmadog.

I left Porthmadog along a mile long embankment called The Cob, built across the Glaslyn estuary in the early nineteenth century, and made my way to the incredible village of Portmeirion. If you're old enough to remember a television show called The Prisoner (before my time), you'll have seen Portmeirion. It was built between 1925 and 1975 by Clough Williams-Ellis, inspired by a visit to Portofino in Italy. His motto was 'cherish the past, adorn the present, construct for the future'. Set on a wooded hillside, there were approximately 50 buildings around a central plaza, a bell tower, a small harbour, a lighthouse and a beach, plus various architectural oddities from around Britain, including an eighteenth century colonnade salvaged from Bristol.

Every which way I looked was a photograph, I've rarely been to a prettier or more visually interesting place. A wedding had recently taken place and the official photographs were being taken around the plaza, they couldn't have asked for a nicer day, but unfortunately it meant that the hotel grounds that led down to the harbour, lighthouse and beach were off limits for the reception. Once again it would have been irresponsible, possibly dangerously so, to not sit down outside a cafe with some coffee and cake.

You could probably spend an entire day at Portmeirion, but I had booked a campsite at Harlech, so I crossed the River Dwyryd, pretty much leaving the peninsula at that point, turned to the south and parked on the street below Harlech Castle, 61m above me on a large rock platform. I walked along a road towards the coast, through a golf course and dunes, onto a beach at the southern end of Morfa Harlech, a nature reserve of dunes and salt marshes. Once again it was surprisingly quiet on the beach. My campsite was at Merthyr Farm, which was up above the small town. The route that I took was pretty much straight up, past the castle and onto a stretch of road through the town that was one in four steep, narrow and through several hairpin bends. I prayed that nothing was coming in the other direction as there was literally nowhere to pass and reversing would have been a nightmare. But boy was it worth it for the views from the farm, looking back along the length of the Lleyn Peninsula on a lovely afternoon and evening. At the entrance to the farm I had to coax some cows out of the road by inching the van towards them until they moved. When I commented to the owner about the road up to here she apologised and said that they usually warn people to come a different route, apparently a coach tried going down that way and ended up stuck.

There were a couple of large birds of prey circling around in the distance, I'm guessing buzzards.

Llandanwg to Borth

Sunday, 22nd July

It was toooo hot today, at times. I left my iPhone on the dashboard while I got out briefly at a viewpoint, when I got back a few minutes later it was displaying a warning saying that it was too hot and wouldn't function until it cooled down.

I didn't have to drive back down the steep roads into Harlech, but instead followed a shallower road, with great views to the south, until I had dropped back down to the coast at Llandanwg. I walked along a sandy beach until I reached the mouth of the Artro estuary, which opened out behind the narrow strip of beach and gave a sheltered area of water and beach for mooring small craft. I walked back to the van across a meadow, past a small church nestled in the dunes behind a stone seawall.

At Dyffryn Ardudwy I walked onto a stretch of sand and pebble beach, backed by sand dunes. At Llanaber I walked over a footbridge across a railway line that ran right next to the sea, behind a seawall. I stopped for a while at Barmouth to have a good look around, starting at a palm tree lined promenade and a large sandy beach, then walking into and through the town, part of which rose up on a hillside. At one end of the town was the wide mouth of the Mawddach estuary, although it had a breakwater jutting out into it on the Barmouth side and a long spit of land on the Fairbourne side. A railway bridge with a pedestrian walkway crossed the estuary, as did a passenger ferry that linked with the Fairbourne and Barmouth Steam Railway on the other side. I saw a sculpture related to protecting the dolphins that inhabit this stretch of coast, so it seems that I did indeed miss some yesterday off the beach at Afon Wen. Barmouth was a nice place, fairly busy today but not crowded, with a good mix of old town, beach, harbour and a sprinkling of amusements along the seafront.

I had to come inland quite a long way to cross the Mawddach, but to begin with it was like being back in Scotland, driving along a loch surrounded by wooded hills. After crossing just to the west of Dolgellau I turned back to the west and stopped at Penmaenpool, a lovely little place where an old toll bridge (which the van was probably too heavy for) crossed the Mawddach next to a whitewashed railway station and hotel, where a number of cyclists were stopping for a break.

I rejoined the coast at Fairbourne, where I drove all the way along the spit of land until I was looking back across the estuary to Barmouth. A little steam train ran back and forth through the dunes behind a narrow beach, passing through a short tunnel. I then drove back into Fairbourne and stopped above the beach just before it came to an end at a large hill, which I was soon driving along the side of. As I drove above the coast past Llwyngwril I couldn't find any way to get down to the pebble beach below, or anywhere to stop on the road until I got to a viewpoint before reaching Rhoslefain, where the coast disappeared around the hill ahead. I then followed the road inland for a while, returning to the coast at Tywyn. The wide promenade at Tywyn ran behind another long stretch of beach, punctuated by groynes and a few rock breakwaters.

The crowds were out in force at Aberdyfi, also known as Aberdovey, on the beach and dunes and in the town. There were so many cars around that I ended up having to stop briefly on double yellows in the town, but as I was also blocking a slipway I couldn't really leave the van and take much of a look around. As I moved on I got more and more frustrated by the continuous double yellows on both sides of the fairly narrow road that ran through the town, along the side of the mouth of the Dyfi estuary. Eventually I drove out of the other side, muttering to myself and annoyed about not having seen much, but in general I don't regret the places I don't get to see, they just remain on my list of places to see some time in the future. Besides, I'd get to see it from the other side of the river.

Again I had to drive quite a long way inland before I could cross the Dyfi, where I drove into Powys and then into Ceredigion as I worked my way back to the coast at Ynyslas. I turned north and followed the road to a car park on acres of sand on the opposite side of the estuary to Aberdyfi. I walked along the sand and around the tip of the dunes to the seaward side of the beach. I figured I would cut across the dunes to get back to the van, so I clambered up into them and found myself in a sea of sand covered in grassy tufts. It seemed like days passed as I climbed each rise under the beating sun, finding nothing ahead but more dunes. I felt like a Bristolian Beau Geste, in Wales, trying to forget... uhhh... something.

Not far from Ynyslas I stopped at Borth and stood on a seawall that protected the mile or so of houses behind the road. To the south, at the end of the beach, the land rose up again onto green hills edged by cliffs. I found my campsite, Brynrodyn Park, somewhere up on those hills, in Upper Borth. It's not the greatest campsite, and I've gone and parked myself next to a path that seems to act as the central thoroughfare through the site. I'm looking forward to when the onsite bar empties out after this evening's karaoke.

Clarach Bay to New Quay
Monday, 23rd July

It was nice and cool this morning when I got to Clarach Bay and walked along the beach. The small bay, split in two by the River Clarach, was surrounded by caravan parks and wooded hillsides, with an almost cute little amusements park behind the beach.

On a completely different scale was Aberystwyth, a Victorian seaside resort and university town. At the north of the town was Constitution Hill, which you could climb on foot or on Britain's longest electrically powered cliff railway. The promenade curved around the bay, backed by pastel guest houses and hotels, past a pier to a headland on which stood the ruins of a castle built by Edward I in the late thirteenth century. Just before the headland was an impressive Gothic-revival grand hotel, which became part of Aberystwyth University. Beyond the headland the beach and promenade continued on around another curved bay, past more colourful houses, to a harbour and marina. The town stood at the mouths of the Rivers Ystwyth and Rheidol.

The main road came a little way back from the coast for a while until I could drive down past a holiday park to a pebble beach at Llanrhystud, where a couple of cars were parked at the top of a terraced beach and a fisherman was casting his rods into the sea. I stopped again on the main road at Llannon and walked along a side road into the small village of Llansantffraed, to the slate clad St Bride's Church and beyond to another pebble beach in front of low eroded cliffs.

As I passed through Aberarth I didn't like the look of the two steep narrow roads that disappeared into the village, so with nowhere else to stop on the main road I had to sail on through and continue just down the road to Aberaeron, where I stopped for a while. I started off at yet another pebble beach at the southern end of the town then worked my way north to breakwaters at the mouth of the River Aeron, where I started to see how nice the town was. On the northern banks of the river were colourful buildings, including the largest of them, the Harbourmaster Hotel. On the other side was a grassy bank backed by more colourful houses, and between the two banks were rows of moored yachts and smaller craft. The houses continued around a small sheltered harbour, beyond which a wooden footbridge gracefully arched over the river, which continued under a brick road bridge, beneath the main road. All in all, quite a pretty town.

After sitting down for some lunch I moved on to stop for a while again at New Quay, where I parked at the top of the town and walked through yet more colourful houses down to a small sandy beach where the sunshine and heat was bringing people out again. Next to the beach was a curved harbour wall, ending in a small jetty from which boat trips were departing. The harbour wall sheltered a slightly larger sandy beach with more people packed onto it. Yachts and pleasure craft were moored in the shallow water just off the beach. Another nice little place.

I've come inland a little for tonight, to the Cardigan Bay

Camping and Caravanning Club Site at Cross Inn, which is pretty quiet, maybe because it's not right on the coast. I got a text from some friends today, who happen to be staying about 20 minutes from here, so I'm going to meet up with them tomorrow.

Cwmtydu to Penbryn
Tuesday, 24th July

An excellent day today, I even went in the sea after four and a half months of looking at it.

I started off with a narrow, steep and winding descent into Cwmtydu, a small bay with a pebble beach, set in one of the few breaks in the cliffs along this stretch of coast. The rock strata at either side of the beach curved and folded over on itself.

Climbing back up again I drove through more country lanes to get to Llangrannog, where I parked just outside the village and walked through it down to a beach, also set between high cliffs. It was a nice looking place in the morning sunshine, just starting to wake up as the air was already getting hot. I walked up the road to the west of the beach to where a statue of Saint Carannog overlooked the bay. Apparently Saint Carannog came to Llangrannog by sea during the sixth century, intending to meditate and spread the word of Christ. But before long he changed his mind and spent the rest of his days surfing and hanging out in one of the cafes, eating cake. Cake can do that to you.

More country lanes brought me to Penbryn, and a lovely cottage where the friends that texted me yesterday were staying for the week, quite by chance. I last saw Ian, Jane and their kids Tom, Joe and Emma, when we camped near Glastonbury last year, and I hadn't seen Jennie for ages, possibly since another camping trip a few years ago. Once they had all had a tour around the van, and I had had a tour around the cottage, we had a cup of tea and started a game of Kubb in the garden. Kubb is a Scandinavian game that involves a pitch, or court, where you stand up several wooden blocks at either end, with a King block in the middle. You then have to throw wooden sticks, like relay batons, and try to knock over the blocks, while trying to avoid hitting Jennie's car on the driveway. As far as I can tell, there is no way to end a game, which probably explains the Scandinavians insistence on staying outdoors in all weather, as long as they're wearing the right clothing.

We called a break in play to have some lunch and head off to the nearby beach, hauling body boards, an inflatable dinghy, wet suits, flippers, sun cream, books, rugs and spades with us, on a glorious afternoon. After a quick wade into the sea to check the temperature (chilly but not life threatening), Ian and the kids got into their wet suits and headed in with the dinghy and body boards, with Jennie following shortly afterwards. I stayed at knee depth until my shorts looked like I'd wet myself, so I figured I may as well change into my swimming shorts and rash vest and get a little more acquainted with an element that has been almost ever present in my life for the last four and a half months. I'd not been that bothered about getting my feet wet up until then, it's not that much fun on your own to be honest, but it's different when you've got people to play with. After the initial shock of the relative cold, I spent a while bobbing around, being laughed at by Emma for not getting out of my depth, and failing miserably to catch any waves on a body board, before my teeth started to chatter and I bolted for the hot sand.

For the rest of the afternoon we buried each other in the sand (up to various different limbs), Emma and I explored an unchartered stream (nearly as long as the Amazon), Jennie 'rested her eyes' for a while, and the kids and I got lost in a sand maze (okay, I got lost) while Ian, Jane and Jennie played boules. A fine afternoon.

Back at the cottage we all showered the sand off and Ian and Jane went to get fish and chips, while I put the van on the driveway to spend the night here in it. After dinner we got in a few more rounds of Kubb without any outcome. I fear they will all still be here, long after I've got home, trying to find a winner.

Tresaith to Newport
Wednesday, 25th July

I joined the others in the cottage for a relaxed breakfast, before saying goodbye and getting underway again, and was missing them all by the time I got to Tresaith.

I parked in the village and walked the short distance down to a fairly small beach between rocky cliffs, where the organised RNLI lifeguards had set out flags to mark out areas for swimming and surfing or kayaking, a common occurrence for the beaches that I saw today. Sailing boats and sea kayaks were lined up at the back of the beach. When the tide is partially out you can walk around the rocks to the beach at Penbryn.

When I got to Aberporth I parked on a headland between two halves of a beach, without noticing the £3 charge for the day until an attendant in a rugby shirt came over as I was getting out. When I said I was only going to be there for 15 minutes or so he said that was fine and there was no point charging me. Very decent of him. A few people had set themselves up on the beach, a couple of them were in the sea under an overcast sky, but the air was pretty warm. The road climbed out of the village as I followed the narrow lanes for a while until I drove into some coastal fog not long before reaching a car park at Mwnt. A flight of steps led down to a small bay where the sea disappeared into the fog.

It was still a little foggy when I got to Gwbert, where the coast had turned to the south towards the mouth of the River Teifi. I stopped at first in the village, just above the cliffs, then moved down to a pebble beach along the side of the road where swans mingled with plenty of yachts and small boats moored amidst the murk. I carried on to the south and stopped at Cardigan to walk a short distance along the river and through the town. Shortly after crossing the river I was heading back up the other side, and into Pembrokeshire, as the fog lifted. I pulled over when I realised that I was on the opposite bank to the beach at Gwbert, where I could now clearly see the mass of boats.

Just up the road I parked near the delightfully named Poppit Sands, a fairly wide stretch of sandy beach in front of low sand dunes. To the north of Gwbert I could see Cardigan Island, a private nature reserve that was home to Soay sheep and the waters around it played host to bottle-nosed dolphin and grey seals. As the sun broke through the clouds I sat down for some lunch outside a cafe behind the beach.

After lunch I plunged into the lanes again, dropping steeply into and back out of Moylegrove on my way to Ceibwr Bay, the only point of the coast touched by a road for an 11 mile stretch between Poppit Sands and Newport Sands. The long bay was flanked by rugged cliffs with the exposed strata twisting in all directions and the occasional cave providing places to explore by kayak, with a pebble beach at the end. From there I drove on through the narrow lanes to Newport Sands. You can usually rely on these lanes being fairly quiet, wherever you are on the coast, as the narrowest lanes are generally in the remotest places, but I came across more than my fair share of cars coming in the opposite direction today. You can usually tell who's in a good mood, who's grumpy, who's used to driving through narrow lanes and who isn't, by the reactions of the drivers, from cheerful waves of thanks, to looks of relief when you pass without scraping anything important, to staring straight ahead and not even acknowledging you.

Newport Sands was a large area of muddy sand, across the Nyfer estuary from the town of Newport, backed by sand dunes, a golf course and low cliffs, with fog drifting across the tops of them. I drove across the Nyfer and into Newport itself, where I went to find one of the campsites in the area. I had pretty much no phone signal today, so I wasn't able to phone anywhere to check if they had space. The first place I tried was at the end of a road near a sailing club and quay, in an area called The Parrog. The campsite reception was in a cafe restaurant, but they had no space tonight. So I moved a little further out from the town, to the Conifers, a couple of fields overlooking the estuary and Newport Sands. There was plenty of space in the fields and a sign with a mobile number to call. Luckily I had a signal there, so I called the number and five minutes later the owner turned up in a car, with her kids in the back, to take payment.

With my spot for the night secured, I drove back to The Parrog to have a look around before returning to the cafe for a coffee. The staff were happy for me to stay there after they had closed, while they were clearing up, and I even got a sneaky slice of cake in before I eventually felt I had outstayed my welcome. I walked along the high street to get some groceries, then headed back to the campsite for the rest of the evening. The sun has come out again and is currently burning a hole in my sweaty forehead through the open side door.

Cwm-yr-Eglwys to St Justinian
Thursday, 26th July

It was overcast again when I set off this morning, making my first stop at Cwm-yr-Eglwys on the eastern side of the neck of Dinas Head. I parked in a car park that was for the residents of a nearby static caravan site, and strictly prohibited campervans, but it was early on a quiet morning and I didn't see the harm, plus there was nowhere else to stop in the tiny village. Overlooking a small shingle beach in a secluded bay were the remains of St Brynach's Church. The church was devastated by a storm in 1859, which also wrecked more than 100 ships in one night.

Next I stopped at the largish town of Fishguard, parking on the road just above Lower Town and walking back down to the mouth of the River Gwaun. A quay was lined with houses and the estuary was covered with small boats. From the end of the quay the view of the open sea was blocked by a long harbour breakwater in the distance at Goodwick. I drove through the main part of the town and stopped at the other end at Goodwick, where a sand and seaweed beach ran through several groynes to the shorter of the two harbour breakwaters. The village and the harbour were intended to host ocean liners to New York, but the transatlantic trade moved to Southampton and the harbour became a departure point for ferries to Rosslare.

Leaving the main roads behind again, I drove to Strumble Head. A short bridge provided access to a working lighthouse on the small island of Ynys Meicel. Part way down the western side of the headland I stopped at Pwllderi to look at a misty view to the west towards St David's Head, then again at the base of the headland at Aber Mawr, where a pebble beach lay at the end of a long bay.

Turning to the west again I dropped down steeply into Abercastle to a small sandy beach in a narrow bay. I struggled a little to turn the van around on the road to the beach, but got going again to Abereiddy, to find a fairly busy car park behind a pebble beach. I walked along the coast path to the right of the beach, which took me to the Blue Lagoon. Formerly a quarry, the lagoon was created in 1910 when the quarrying came to an end and a channel was blasted to the sea, flooding the quarry to an icy depth of about 25m. A group of kids were kitted out in wet suits, life jackets and helmets for some coasteering, throwing themselves off different heights and gradients into the lagoon. Above the lagoon by the channel were the ruins of the engine house, used to haul slate out of the quarry.

There was no real access to the coast again until I reached Whitesands Bay, after passing the 7,000 mile mark, on the western edge of Pembrokeshire. I joined a queue for the car park, but turned around when I found that you couldn't pay for an hour, just for the day, so instead I parked in a lay-by about half a mile up the road and walked back. The clouds of the morning were clearing and the sun was beating down onto a popular sandy beach, pretty much at its smallest while the tide was almost in. I had some lunch in a cafe above the beach before walking onto a little headland between the beach and a small bay.

Moving on again I drove into St David's, one of my

favourite places in Pembrokeshire. St David's is the smallest city in Britain, with a cathedral as impressive as it is unlikely, given the small size of the rest of the place, but understandable given that it was the birthplace of the patron saint of Wales. St David established a monastery there in the sixth century and pilgrims arrived during the Middle Ages. The cathedral was largely built in the twelfth century. Next to the cathedral, the ruins of the Bishop's Palace dated from the fourteenth century. The rest of the city centred around an attractive little green in the middle of a one way system, surrounded by small shops and cafes. After a quick wander around I settled myself in the garden of The Bench, my favourite cafe there, with a delicious coke float (a glass of coke with a scoop of ice cream in it), the first one I'd had since I was last there.

Once I'd finished I stocked up with groceries from a supermarket around the corner and headed west back to the coast at St Justinian, where I was going to spend the night at Rhosson Gannol, a basic campsite that looked across to Ramsay Island, where I'd camped before with friends. I'll be without electricity tonight, and a lot of the other comforts of other sites, but I couldn't help but smile when I drove into the first field to be met by a familiar view, then looked at the small toilet block, still stocked with the boxes of square toilet paper sheets, and was almost disappointed to see that there was no longer a box outside the shower where you used to deposit 20p before running in and washing as quickly as possible. It's a proper campsite, with an excellent view, and the need for a torch when it's dark.

A short walk from the campsite was a lifeboat station at the base of the cliffs, reached by stone steps and serviced by a trolley winched up and down steep tracks. Various boat trips can be taken from there, but the jet boat and dolphin watching trips were fully booked for the next few days, otherwise I would have considered spending tomorrow here too. Above the campsite is a small rocky hill, which I used to run up at least once a day, so I ran up it for old time's sake.

Addendum: I somehow managed to completely miss one of the places that I had intended to visit on this stretch of coast. So when I returned to Pembrokeshire at the end of August, for a weekend's camping at Rhosson Gannol, I went to see Porthgain, between Abercastle and Abereiddy. It was an unusual place in that one side of the harbour was dominated by large brick hoppers, built at the beginning of the twentieth century. The hoppers were used to store crushed granite road stone until it was loaded onto small ships. Prior to shipping road stone, Porthgain received slate from Abereiddy in the second half of the nineteenth century and manufactured bricks around the turn of the century. It was an interesting place to visit, not least for its art galleries, cafe and pub.

Caerfai Bay to Little Haven
Friday, 27th July

The forecast had been for cloud today, but it was another hot and sunny day.

The owner of the campsite drives around in his van at about 9:30am each morning, collecting any fees due, so I had a lie in and paid up when he arrived. My plan was for a relaxed morning, so I drove into St David's and returned to The Bench, to have another coke float for the road and to use their WiFi to upload the last few day's worth of blog entries. I'd only managed to find a parking space with a one hour limit, so just after an hour, with the blog still slowly uploading, I left my laptop in the care of the fellow next to me (he had a small child, so I assumed he was trustworthy, but then again he may have stolen the child and was looking for a laptop to go with it) and went to see if there was a free parking space in the two hour zone, but there wasn't, so I decided to risk it and return to the cafe.

I eventually gave up waiting for the blog to finish uploading and got back on the road, driving a short distance to the south to a small car park above Caerfai Bay. The tide was largely in, so the beach in the small sheltered bay was mostly pebbles and small rocks, but there were several people on the beach and some in the sea. My next stop was at Solva, another of my favourite places in the area. I parked in a busy car park at the end of an inlet, in front of the Harbour Inn and a B&B/cafe (fancy staying in a cafe, I'd be broke within a few days). I had a look at a small sandy beach on one side of the clear River Solva, with old lime kilns a little further on along the river bank, before walking along the path on the other side of the river to a boat club at the end, where most of the yachts and small boats on the river were moored. I stopped for some lunch in the boat club cafe.

Moving on again, as I drove into Newgale I could see the two miles of pebble beach before me. The sand in front of the pebbles was pretty much covered by the tide, and the beach, which is popular among surfers, kite surfers and swimmers, was fairly quiet. With the coast turned to the south I dropped down into the small village of Nolton Haven, circled once around the small, full car park, but luckily found a lay-by as I drove back out again up a hill. The little cove had a stream running through one side of a pebble and sand beach, where a lifeguard sat on his surfboard watching a handful of people in the sea. I drove on through some very narrow lanes until I came to a lay-by at Druidston Haven, with a few cars parked in it, which I assumed must mean the beach was nearby, and indeed it was, down a path leading off the road. One of the more remote beaches, there were very few people there, and no lifeguards. Four large tankers, also visible from Newgale and Nolton Haven, were moored out to sea, towards Skomer Island.

Larger and busier was Broad Haven, a resort with the road running behind a large sandy beach. Once again it was too busy to park so I turned around and parked on another lay-by on a hill on the northern side, then walked down to a small promenade in front of hotels and apartments. I paused by an ice cream van to buy something to help me walk back up the hill. Driving back down behind the seafront, and up a hill on the other side, I passed a sign for Little Haven that said something in smaller letters about '16 feet long' and 'impassable'. I checked my 'dimensions card' that I keep behind the sun visor to see that the van was just over 21 feet with the bike on the back. Ah well, how bad could it be?

Pretty bad, actually. The road ended in a t-junction that turned left up the hill, or tightly to the right, down into Little Haven, between a house on the corner and a wall on the other side. It looked like I might just be able to get through, so I started turning to the right, reversed up a bit, then continued the turn, inching forward as I could see the rear drivers side of the van getting closer to the wall of the house. It looked as though I had enough room on the other side of the van, but just as I thought I was round the bend I came to a stop. I raised the clutch to give gravity some help from the engine, but I wasn't going anywhere. I hadn't heard any nasty scraping sounds so I figured the rear driver's side tyre must have come up against the wall of the house. For a nasty moment I thought I might be wedged stuck, and I knew that the van didn't like reversing uphill, which was my only option. To make things worse a car appeared below me, waiting to come up the road. I grimaced at the driver and shook my head, before putting it in reverse and praying, but without really thinking about what might be behind me. Luckily, nothing was behind me as the van shuddered backwards. I wasn't going to give it another go, so I turned to the left and went up the hill, accompanied by a nasty burning smell. I pulled into a lay-by just up the hill and inspected the van, but couldn't see any scratches or damage. I let the burning smell subside a little before gingerly pulling away again.

The campsite I was going to stay at tonight was on the

other side of Little Haven, so I took a longer route around the village and came to the campsite from the other side. The woman that I had spoken to on the phone came out to meet me and asked me if she had mentioned prices, which she hadn't. She then suggested that as it was £25, and it was just me, I might like to try a different campsite the other side of the village, which would be cheaper. How refreshingly decent of her. I said that I'd go and take a look and maybe come back, so I drove down into Little Haven and back out the other side, up the road that I hadn't been able to turn down, where I found the campsite she was talking about. It was a small field, sloping fairly steeply, with a note saying to phone a number before selecting a pitch. As I had no signal, and the slope was a little too steep, I decided to carry on around the same loop I'd driven before, where I'd passed another site. The other site was £22.95, but I couldn't be bothered looking elsewhere so I paid and found a pitch.

I still hadn't seen much of Little Haven, so I drove into it for the second time and parked in the car park. It was a nice place, where the houses rose up the hill and circled around the bay, up the cliffs on either side. People were lounging on a small green outside one of the pubs and were scattered around the beach. As I walked out onto the beach I realised that it continued around the cliffs to the right and opened out into a larger beach, where there were several caves in the cliff face. I found a cafe with WiFi and sat down for a while to finish uploading the blog. The owner was very accommodating, allowing me to stay while she tidied up post cafe time, pre evening meal time. It was clearly a village with a communal feel, as various people that she knew wandered in and out. Three of the four tables were reserved for people coming in later for meals, so I told her to kick me out if she needed my table, but she said she would have already kicked me out if I had been any bother. A couple of locals assured me that she certainly would have done. As it was early evening by now, and the blog was nearly done, I ordered a pizza to take back to the campsite.

St Brides Haven to Angle
Saturday, 28th July

It was looking like being a nice day again when I arrived at St Brides Haven (there are a lot of Havens in this area). The little Church of St Bride stood not far behind a sandy beach, surrounded by rocks. A fisherman was casting from some rocks jutting out into the sea, while some dogs played around in the surf. Several large tankers, probably some of those I'd seen yesterday, were moored out in the bay. In the fields behind the beach stood St Brides Castle, which belonged to the Holiday Property Bond and could be rented as holiday accommodation, along with its swimming pool, tennis court etc. A diver was getting his gear ready when I got back to the car park in front of the church.

At a small beach at Martin's Head, quite a few divers were getting ready, along with a small queue of people that may have been waiting for ferries to Skomer or Skokholm Island. Day trips to the National Nature Reserve on Skomer didn't get going until mid morning. I walked into a walled area known as the Deer Park, which covered the headland that looked out to Skomer to the west, beyond the much smaller Midland Island, and Skokholm to the southwest. I could see five tankers out in the bay to the north.

I had intended to take a look at Marloes Sands as I travelled to the southeast, but the road that I thought would get me there ended at a fence across a private road, so I continued on and drove into Dale, where a load more divers were kitting up in the car park. Plenty of boats were moored in a large bay in front of a shingle beach, and in the distance were the chimneys of the Milford Haven oil refineries. From Dale I continued to the south until a sign on the road stated that there were no turning places beyond that point, so I parked in a car park at the same spot and walked the remaining mile to St Ann's Head. At the end of the road was a lighthouse, a coastguard station and a few rows of whitewashed cottages. Below the lighthouse a section of rock in the cliff curved around itself in an S shape.

I drove north back through Dale, joined the main B road but came off it again to head south through narrow lanes and into a wood at St Ishmael's, where I parked by the Norman Church of St Ishmael, next to an overgrown graveyard. A path led from the church along the side of high walls, through the wood to Monk Haven, where a gap in another wall acted as an entrance to a pebble beach in a narrow bay. Opposite the bay was Dale Fort, built in 1856 on Dale Point to deter Napoleon III from invading the west coast of Britain and Milford Haven. I carried on to the east to Sandy Haven and the muddy banks of a tidal creek, before moving on to the town of Milford Haven, on the waterway and deep water harbour of the same name. I parked on the road above a large marina and walked down to wander around it. Several tankers were docked on the other side of the harbour, below one of the oil refineries. Milford Haven was developed as a whaling station and naval dockyard, before becoming a major centre for the fishing industry, and later prospering in the 1960s, 70s and early 80s during the oil boom.

I stopped briefly a little further to the east, at Neyland,

where I looked across the River Cleddau to Pembroke Dock, before crossing the Cleddau Toll Bridge to the south and stopping in Pembroke Dock to look back to Neyland. An Irish Ferries ship, bound for Rosslare, was docked not far from a Martello Tower, made from Portland stone and reached by a walkway from the shore. A little further to the south I parked on the high street in Pembroke after crossing a small bridge over the River Pembroke. Standing on the banks of the river was Pembroke Castle, another large Welsh castle, damaged and captured by Cromwell's forces during the Civil War. Inside the main walls the castle was quite open, with a large round keep at the centre. Beneath the Northern Hall, a spiral staircase wound down to a big natural cavern called the Wogan Cavern. The cavern has been used as a shelter during the Middle Stone Age, as a storage area for supplies and boats by the Normans, and as somewhere to keep Terry Wogan in between Eurovision Song Contests.

I turned to the west and drove beyond an oil refinery all the way to Angle, and further beyond to West Angle Bay, where I was surprised to find quite a busy car park in what I had assumed would be a pretty remote location. The owners of the cars were spread across a fairly large sandy beach, and along several attractive smaller beaches and bays along the right hand side. Just off the coast was Thorn Island, home to a large fort built in 1854 as part of the defences of Milford Haven. I drove back into Angle, parked, and walked to the east to Angle Bay, where the view towards the refineries was nowhere near as nice. Within the village was St Mary's Church and a fortified tower, possibly Norman.

I've come back to the east a little way for tonight, to Newton Farm, which has a view of the sea to the west and a view of the oil refinery to the north. Fortunately I'm parked facing the west.

Freshwater West to Tenby
Sunday, 29th July

Again with the hotness. I would quite happily accept a bit of good old British coolness for the next few days, but no rain, thank you very much.

I started the day by heading a little way back to the west, to a large beach at Freshwater West. There were quite a few campervans already there, wild camping in several car parks or along the road. I could see a large tanker emerging from Milford Haven, beneath the buildings on St Ann's Head, and beyond to Skokholm Island. The vast expanse of golden sand, backed by sand dunes, became rocky towards the south, where a small thatched hut looked as if it was half buried in the grass above the beach. The hut was one of around 20 that belonged to the women of Angle during the early part of the twentieth century and were used for drying seaweed. The seaweed was sent to Swansea and used to make laver bread, a delicacy in South Wales, served fried with bacon in the morning.

Heading to the east again, I drove through Castlemartin, around the edge of a firing range that took up the southwestern part of the peninsula, then south again into the firing range and back to the coast to a car park near the

Elegug Stacks. The stacks were a couple of detached limestone pillars, on a rugged stretch of coastline with various holes and gaps in the cliffs. To the east was the Devil's Cauldron, a wide shaft in the cliff that was open to the sea via an arch, and to the west was the Green Bridge of Wales, an arch about 24m high. I had to drive back to the main road to avoid more of the firing range before driving into it again to another car park near St Govan's Chapel. The little chapel was one of the more bizarre things that I'd seen along the cliffs of the British coastline, built half way down the cliff, wedged between the rocks. I had to walk down some steps and through the chapel to continue down the cliff. Supposedly, St Govan was being pursued by pirates when the rocks split open, giving him somewhere to hide, where he stayed to preach and pray until he died in 586. The chapel there now was built in the eleventh century. To the west was a large cleft in the cliff called the Huntsman's Leap. Legend has it that a huntsman jumped his horse across the 55m gap, then died of fright when he looked back.

A little further to the west, on the other side of St Govan's Head, I stopped at a National Trust car park and walked down to a beautiful sandy beach at Broad Haven (far more wild and quieter than the Broad Haven I passed through two days ago). Out in the sheltered bay, adding to the attractiveness of the place, was a jagged rock, silhouetted by the sunshine. Next I moved on to Stackpole Quay, within the Stackpole Estate, and another National Trust car park. A small rocky bay there was dominated by a large disused quay, which was built to bring in fuel for the Stackpole Estate and ship out limestone. I walked a little way along the coast to the south until I could look across another large sandy beach at Barafundle Bay. Back at the car park was a National Trust cafe, selling cream teas, so I figured it was time to try one in Wales. One huge scone, just about enough clotted cream and way too much jam (for me, anyway). Nothing to trouble Pinky Murphy's, but I had that familiar slightly sick feeling afterwards.

Only part way through today's beachfest, I continued to Freshwater East, where a stream ran through the beach and several people were kayaking from it, and then to a smaller beach at Manorbier, also with a stream running through it and looking slightly more crowded. Set some way back from the beach was a pretty sturdy looking Norman castle.

My last stop for the day, still fairly early in the afternoon, was at Tenby, an altogether busier prospect. Tenby was a pretty place, especially in the sunshine. Colourful houses, shops and pubs lined the narrow streets and overlooked a harbour and four beaches. Between the long South Beach and the smaller Castle Beach, gardens and palm trees decorated the sides of a sloping seawall, with paths on several levels, and a rocky outcrop that splits Castle Beach in two when the tide is in. St Catherine's Island stood just off Castle Beach, which could be reached on foot at low tide and was crowned by a fortress that formed part of the Milford Haven defences. The harbour was packed with small boats and was busy with people on Harbour Beach, among the smells and sounds of Caribbean cooking and music during some kind of event. Across the bay was North Beach, with the distinctive Goskar Rock in the middle of it. Tenby had two lifeboat stations, a fairly new one and an older one that had been converted into a home. Lying several miles out from South Beach was Caldey Island, where Cistercian monks inhabit a monastery and make perfume and chocolate.

My campsite tonight is Well Park, not far from Tenby. I'm hoping all the screaming coming from kids on the other side of a hedge will have died out by later in the evening.

Saundersfoot to Llanelli
Monday, 30th July

Saundersfoot (as well as Tenby and Caldey) is held dear in a corner of my heart due to enjoyable times spent there recently with dear and special friends, a man could not ask for better companions.

At least that's what one of my dear and special friends told me to say.

I started today at Saundersfoot, where I did indeed spend a memorable long weekend with friends a few years ago, and from where we also visited Tenby and Caldey. Saundersfoot was not as big, as pretty or as popular as neighbouring Tenby, but it was a nice place, with a large sandy beach and a harbour to wander around, plus sea kayaks for hire that you could paddle across to some more remote beaches, and a nice little pub called The Old Chemist Inn that had a beer garden and a back gate onto the beach. The beach this morning had had so many holes, trenches and castle moats dug in it over the weekend that it looked like a Time Team dig.

Not far from Saundersfoot, I stopped briefly at Wiseman's Bridge, a short stretch of road behind a beach with an inn at one end, before continuing to Amroth, where a row of shops and houses sat behind the road on top of a pebble bank. A couple of horses galloped along a lengthy beach towards the border between Pembrokeshire and Carmarthenshire. After passing into Carmarthenshire I drove down a steep hill into Pendine, parked, and walked out onto Pendine Sands, where I could clearly see back to Tenby and Caldey Island. The sands stretched for six miles along Carmarthen Bay from the village, through a firing range, to the Taf estuary, and the tide can go out for about a mile. In the 1920s the sands were used for land speed record attempts, due to the firm flat surface of the beach, but on the 3rd March 1927 they came to an end with the death of J.G. Parry-Thomas.

I reached the salt flats of the Taf estuary at Laugharne (pronounced 'Larn'), where I walked past the remains of Laugharne Castle, home to the Welsh prince Rhys ap Gruffud in the twelfth century. Laugharne was also home to the writer Dylan Thomas. A stroll along Dylan's Walk, overlooking the estuary, took me to the boathouse where he lived with his wife and children, and the garage where he wrote 'Under Milk Wood', which is believed to be based on Laugharne, and practiced his impression of Richard Burton.

After crossing the rivers Taf, Cynin, Dewi Fawr and Cywyn I drove through country lanes to Llansteffan, near the mouth of the River Tywi. I walked through the village before I found the beach, overlooked by the ruins of a thirteenth century castle on a wooded hill. A drive up the Tywi, crossing it at the outskirts of Carmarthen, and back down the other side, brought me to the opposite bank at Ferryside. I crossed the train tracks that hugged the eastern banks of the river, onto another sandy beach. Hugging the coast myself, I stopped to look south across the Gwendraeth estuary to Pembrey Forest and Cefn Sidan Sands, much of which was used as a firing range, on my way to Kidwelly on the Gwendraeth Fach. I only really stopped at Kidwelly because I'd water skied there, although I couldn't tell you exactly where, somewhere on the estuary I believe. Turns out that it has a twelfth century castle and church, who knew!

Turning to the south I crossed the Gwendraeth Fawr towards Pembrey, where I stopped short of the Pembrey Country Park on the edge of Pembrey Forest. The whole area was made up of woodland, sand dunes and a beach that ran from the Tywi estuary to the Loughor estuary. I walked a little way towards the dunes, but I would have needed most of the day to explore any further so I moved on to a harbour at Burry Port. A little lighthouse stood on a breakwater outside the harbour, from where I could look back to the dunes and beach. To the east I could see Llanelli.

When I got to Llanelli I stopped at North Dock, a former industrial dock, where some interesting looking buildings stood behind a beach and several kite surfers were making the most of the wind. Behind the beach was a boating lake flanked by modern apartments and office buildings. I crossed the Loughor estuary into West Glamorgan to find a Caravan Club Site at Gowerton.

It's been a little cooler today, still getting pretty warm at times, but this evening the rain has appeared for the first time in a while, completely ignoring my weather request from yesterday.

Pen-clawdd to Threecliff Bay
Tuesday, 31ˢᵗ July

I set off to take a look at the Gower peninsula today, stopping first at Pen-clawdd, where a few boats lay in the muddy creeks of the Loughor estuary and a number of horses grazed on the grassy mud flats. The early morning rain had eased off a little to drizzle.

With not much to see along the northern edge of the peninsula, I made my way towards Llanmadoc. I passed through the village and arrived at a car park but was turned away, they didn't accept motorhomes. So I backtracked and took another turn towards another car park, but misread a sign and ended up at a dead end at a locked gate with a Cwm Ivy National Trust sign on it. I turned around again and parked in the village, put on my waterproofs, walked back to the gate and carried on beyond. The road became a track that took me to within sight of Whiteford Sands. The drizzle had stopped and it was pretty muggy, so I ended up carrying my jacket and swishing along in my waterproof trousers, suppressing an urge to just find a tea room and spend the day in it. When I reached the beach I found acres of sand and a view across the estuary to Burry Port.

I had to come back east a bit before I could turn south

and then west to Rhossili, at the southwest corner of the peninsula. The village of Rhossili sat on a cliff above the long sandy beach of Rhossili Bay, a large crescent shaped bay with the small island of Burry Holms at the northern end and the tidal island of Worms Head at the southern end. The cliffs behind the bay provided quite an impressive backdrop and are popular with paragliders and hang-gliders. I walked southwest from the village along the top of a headland, until I was looking out along Worms Head. For several hours either side of low tide you can walk out to the end of the curiously shaped strip of rock. After returning to the village I had some lunch in The Bay, where you could sit on a patio overlooking Rhossili Bay.

After lunch I moved on to Port-Eynon and walked a little way out across a beach that had a large rocky section, where families were searching among the rock pools for crabs and shrimp. I then drove into some more narrow country lanes and did a little more damage to the van when I caught the passenger wing mirror on a wall, while making sure I gave a walker enough room on the other side. The mirror was flipped inwards, as it should do, and I pushed it back out a little further down the road, but when I took a look at it from the outside I found some scratches in the paint. I was very annoyed with myself by that, I've had to scrape against loads of branches and hedges, but up until then I'd managed to avoid hitting anything more solid (while going forwards, at least). When I reached Oxwich I parked in a car park just behind yet another golden sandy beach that swept off into the distance. A few people were dotted around and three sailing dinghies were being made ready to be taken out onto the sea.

I carried on to the east and parked in front of a shop at Parkmill, where I had to pay for the privilege because it was one of the places from where you could walk to Threecliff Bay. I paid more for parking today than on any other day, it seems the Gower expects people to stay everywhere for a day at a time, rather than offering cheaper options for less time. A mile walk took me through a wood then out into a sand and grass valley with a stream running through it. Up on a hill to the left were some castle ruins. At the end of the valley was a beach that was part golden sand, part pebbles and part seaweed, with the stream snaking through it. Just in front of the sea, on the left side of the beach, were the three craggy peaks that gave the bay its name, one of which had a hole pierced through it. I walked towards the peaks and through the hole, where I was surprised to find the beach opening out to the east. The tide was on its way in, so there wasn't a lot of sand on the seaward side of the peaks, but it was a beautiful spot, and must be more so when the tide and the sun are out.

There didn't appear to be many campsites near Threecliff Bay, so before leaving this morning I booked another night at Gowerton, as it's only about 20 minutes away from the southeast corner of the peninsula, so that's where I've returned for this evening.

I've been lucky with the weather today, the forecast was for rain all day, but apart from some early rain followed by a little drizzle it's been dry and overcast, with the sun making an unsuccessful attempt to come out at Threecliff Bay. I haven't been so lucky with catching the van wing mirror, and the software that I use for creating and uploading the blog has somehow corrupted the file that it uses, which is causing me no end of problems. It'll be touch and go as to whether anybody actually gets to read this and the remaining entries.

Caswell Bay to Dunraven Bay
Wednesday, 1st August

The wind was blowing when I got out of the van at Caswell Bay, on an overcast morning. I walked out onto a sandy beach between rocky headlands. Beyond the headland on the right the beach extended a little further to the west, beneath an apartment building and some houses on the hillside. At Langland Bay I found a longer beach, also between rocky headlands, but with a seawall and a row of green and white beach huts behind it, beneath houses along the hillside.

I drove southeast to the tip of The Mumbles, where the small rock islands of Middle Head and Mumble Head lay just beyond a slightly higher headland, looking like a typical image of the Loch Ness monster, a curved back rising out of the water three times. A lighthouse surrounded by scaffolding sat on Mumble Head. On the eastern side of the headland, within Swansea Bay, a long pier branched off to a lifeboat station. From there a promenade ran past the main seafront buildings and beach of The Mumbles.

Following the road along Swansea Bay, I stopped part way along at Black Pill, where the road ran behind a strip of sandy beach just above an expanse of flat, wet sand that surrounded the bay. When I got to Swansea I parked on the street and walked along the beach to a seawall beneath the concrete structure of the Civic Centre building. Beyond this were apartment buildings and high rise flats of a regenerated seafront. Behind the buildings was a large marina. As I reached the furthest point from the van it started to rain, but for once I'd had the forethought to take my jacket with me, and it didn't last long anyway.

From Swansea I skirted along the side of the M4 to get to Aberavon, just short of the industrial harbour of Port Talbot. Aberavon had a nice long stretch of beach, backed by a seawall and promenade. To the east were the Port Talbot cranes, and chimneys from a steelworks belching flame and smoke into the air. Keeping away from the motorway again I carried on, through Port Talbot and past the steelworks into Mid Glamorgan. I parked at a nature reserve at Kenfig and walked about a mile, through seemingly endless low dunes, to another long stretch of beach at Kenfig Sands. If you walk along the beach to the north it becomes Margam Sands as you pass back into West Glamorgan. Both beaches combined were about five miles long.

Once I'd trudged back through the dunes to the van I carried on towards Porthcawl but turned back to the west to Rest Bay, one of the best surfing beaches in Wales by all accounts. The beach was backed by a layer of rocks. When I got to Porthcawl I intended to stop for a while for some lunch and a sit down, but I first walked around the harbour and the promenade. To the east of the harbour were two sandy beaches in neighbouring bays, Sandy Bay and Trecco Bay, and beyond them was a larger beach. The south facing beach in front of the promenade was much rockier. Within about five minutes of sitting down in a cafe it started pouring with rain, but when I left an hour or so later half of the sky was blue and the sun was shining, while the wind drove the waves against the beaches.

The roads took me inland for a while until I crossed into South Glamorgan and followed the Ogmore River back to the coast at Ogmore-by-Sea, where the river swept past grassy dunes and a sandy beach to the west, into the sea. To the east, on the Ogmore-by-Sea side of the river, the beach became more shingle and rock. Further to the east I drove down to a small car park at Dunraven Bay and squeezed the van into one of the remaining spaces. A pebble beach was flanked by cliffs that looked like they were made from bricks, with horizontal layers of limestone and shale. Below the cliffs were ledges of rock that the sea was rolling over.

I'm staying with a friend tonight, so I've come to Bridgend to see Sarah and her son Tom, both of whom I ski with whenever possible. We were joined by another friend, Rachel, who's also skied with us, for a meal at the house, before watching some of the day's Team GB medal wins at the Olympics.

Monknash to Cardiff
Thursday, 2nd August

I spent my time dodging showers today, but nearly all of them occurred while I was driving or indoors.

I started the day by parking near the end of a road next to a farm at Monknash. From there I walked to the end of the road and into a wood, then followed a stream through the wood until I emerged into the open again, misjudged the dismount from a stile, and fell over sideways into a bush. No damage done, except to my pride, I felt so old and infirm. Luckily there was no one around to see it or to patronisingly offer me assistance for the rest of the short walk to a pebble beach. The cliffs either side of the small beach were a continuation of the limestone and shale layers that I'd seen yesterday, with more ledges of rock that had been rubbed smooth by the passage of water over them, from the stream and the sea.

I managed to get back to the van without losing my footing again and set off towards Nash Point, where I walked towards two lighthouses, only one of them still in use, and up to the edge of the cliffs above rocks that looked like thousands of jigsaw pieces stuck together. When I reached St Donat's I was hoping to get a look at St Donat's

Castle, a fourteenth century fortress that was now part of Atlantic College, an international sixth form college. The college grounds were closed to the public, so instead I found a coast path that I thought might take me along in front of it, but I ended up climbing down steep steps to another small rocky beach. For the second time this trip I got to the top of a climb and realised I didn't have my lens cap, which I found back down at the bottom of the climb. Another branch of the coast path took me to a field where I could see the large castle in the distance.

Continuing along B roads and lanes, I drove through the village of Llantwit Major and down a narrow road to a car park at Col-huw Point, where I was pleasantly surprised to find a largish patch of sandy beach in among the rocks. I found a similar rocky, sandy, seaweedy beach at Limpert Bay, in the shadow of Aberthaw power station. The bay was at one end of the Heritage Coast Walk, the other end being 18 miles away at Porthcawl.

For some reason, when I was a kid, I thought of Barry Island as a place of mystery, full of thrilling fun rides and excitement. I'm not even sure if I went there as a kid, but I suspect I did. I was under no illusion that it would be anything like that today, and I wasn't wrong. The beach was nice enough, but the rest of it looked pretty tired and the fun fair wasn't going to trouble Blackpool any time soon. There were plenty of people around though.

Just as I left Barry Island it started to pour with rain, which continued until just after I parked at Lavernock Point. I walked a little way along the coast path until I got a view of the sea. I'd obviously been aware that I had been looking at the Bristol Channel recently, but it still hit me with a certain amount of surprise when I realised that the two islands I was looking at, one flat with a lighthouse, the other a high mound, were Flat Holm and Steep Holm, and just visible across the channel was Weston-super-Mare, which I passed through on my first day, nearly five months ago. It was from Lavernock Point that Guglielmo Marconi transmitted and received the first wireless signals over open sea, between the point and Flat Holm, on May 13th 1897. I found a path that led down to the rocky beach below, and damn near ended up on my backside when I slipped on the final muddy stretch. To the north I could see a pier at Penarth and beyond to Cardiff. Before returning to the van I took another path down to the beach around the corner on the southern side of the point.

Moving on again I stopped at Penarth. It was about this time that my right walking shoe developed a double squeak, it would squeak when I put my foot down and again when I lifted it up. It's hard not to be self conscious when you sound like you're an illegal mouse smuggler. I had intended to spend a few hours there, but once I had squeaked along the pier, with paint peeling off the main building walls, I didn't really get the kind of vibe that suggested I would find a nice relaxing cafe. Instead I decided to head for tonight's campsite. There weren't a lot of campsites in this area, so I had booked one in Cardiff, which turned out to be next to the Swalec Stadium cricket ground. As per the general rule, paying £25 resulted in a less than impressive campsite, the facilities weren't great and the pitches were the closest together that I'd come across, but it would do.

I spent a while bringing the blog up to date with yesterday's entry, which is taking me twice as long since the software went screwy, then just after 6:00pm I drove down to Cardiff Bay to treat myself to a meal. I quite like the bay area, I'd been there plenty of times for various reasons. The centre piece was the Millennium Centre, an arts and theatre centre with a distinctive design that combined bronze coloured copper coated sheet steel cladding with multi coloured layers of Welsh slate. The bronze cladding had large windows in the shape of letters that spelled out, in

Welsh and English, 'In these stones horizons sing'. In front of it was a tall silver tower that water continually cascaded down. Next door was the ornate red brick Pierhead Building, built in 1897 as the headquarters of the Bute Dock Company. Along with restaurants, shops, other interesting shaped buildings and walks around the bay, it's a nice place to spend some time.

Back at the campsite I've been wrestling with the blog again, before I settle down for my last night on the road.

Peterstone Wentlooge to Severn Beach
Friday, 3rd August

I took a leisurely start on a pleasant morning with one last breakfast of bacon, pancakes and maple syrup. After an early reduction due to all the coastal walking in Cornwall, Devon and Dorset, my waistline has returned to its pre-trip size and possibly more so. I haven't been on a single run during this trip, one of the many things I thought I would do but didn't. I'll have to rectify that once I get home.

My first stop of the day, after crossing into Monmouthshire, was at Peterstone Wentlooge, mostly because it had a great name. I walked from the village along a path through fields to a grassy sea wall, behind grasslands that ran up to the water's edge. In 1606 the village was flooded with six feet of water. The sea defences were put in place to ensure there was no reoccurrence.

I carried on to Newport and parked near the River Usk, then walked along a stretch of the river that had been redeveloped with various angular buildings and the Newport City Footbridge. To the north was Newport Castle. I headed to the high street for a sit down and my last coffee and cake (lemon cheesecake, delicious). Before leaving the city I felt compelled to take a look at the

Newport Transporter Bridge, having visited the Tees Transporter Bridge in Middlesbrough. The carriage was on its way across the river when I got there, very exciting. I feel that I have joined an elite group of transporter bridge spotters.

Not wishing to join the M4 too soon, I drove through the back roads to Gold Cliff, where I walked onto a sea wall to look at a muddy 'beach' in front of me. When I walked down again a man with a van said "don't suppose you found much to photograph up there". He wasn't wrong.

It was time to join the motorway, and at 1.35pm I crossed the older of the two Severn bridges, leaving Wales behind and returning to England in what I'm going to call Avon, for old times' sake. I had one last stop to make, at Severn Beach, not because it was a particularly nice place to visit, but just because it tied up the loop nicely before I headed home.

I drove into Bristol along the Portway under the Clifton Suspension Bridge, and at 2.45pm I arrived home. The road had been dug up to replace some water pipes, so there was nowhere to park near the house. Nothing changes. In fact that's very true of travelling, you may have been all over the world, seen and experienced many wondrous things, you may have even changed a little as a person, but when you get home, generally nothing has changed.

It's hard to describe what the last five months has been like. To be honest it all seems a little surreal right now, when I think of what I've done. It feels like I left home yesterday, but at the same time feels like I was gone for an eternity. I've been away for 150 days, have stopped or stayed at 1,062 places, while driving 7,440 miles through 44 counties in three countries. I have eaten more cake than was probably good for me.

But I'm glad to be home, I can see my family and friends, go to the Olympics, and then make a start on doing all the

things I didn't do while I was away.
 And maybe start to dream up my next trip.

Home Again

Physically arriving back at home wasn't really the end of the journey, there was still a bit of 'sinking in' to be done and the small matter of a campervan that had served its purpose.

Back To The Real(ish) World

It's now mid November as I write this.

I was glad to get home, five months had been a long time to be away, and I had plenty of things I wanted to get on with for the rest of my sabbatical period. So it didn't take much effort to slot back into life at home, although it was obviously easier to not have to slot straight back into life at work. I parked the van on my Mum's drive, where I could keep it until I found a buyer for it. It seemed easy at the time to walk away from the van and the life I had lived in it.

I never really used to understand what people meant when they said that something hadn't 'sunk in' yet, but I think I'm starting to get it now. Over the last few months my thoughts have often drifted back to those five months on the road. The freedom to get up in the morning, with no real worries apart from maybe where the next night's stop would be, and to head off to wherever I fancied and do whatever I pleased, was a liberating experience. I suppose there was a certain amount of enforced structure to the trip, I had set out to travel around the entire British mainland coastline, so I had loosely imposed a route upon myself. Very occasionally this made it feel like a chore, if the weather wasn't good and the scenery wasn't great, but it had also given me a goal and an achievement to aim for. I honestly don't know how many people have made the same journey, or how they fared, but I'm incredibly glad that I did it. I have great memories of many wonderful places, which I may choose to return to later in my life.

In all honesty I maybe spoilt things slightly by successfully applying for Olympics tickets. I originally thought that the whole trip would take me six to seven months, which would have taken me beyond the Olympics in August, so my intention was to leave the coast a couple of days before the first of the events that I had a ticket for, and return to wherever I had left off after the last event. For the most part I took every day as it came, spending as much or as little time as I wanted in each of the places that I passed through. I had a lot of comments from friends about how fast I seemed to be going, yet to me this wasn't the case and at times it felt as though I had been away from home forever. I guess that shows how your perception of time can change if you step away from the rat race for a while. But as I was working my way back down the west coast I made a conscious decision that I would try to get all the way home before I went to the Olympics, it seemed to me that if I left the coast and spent a week or so in London it wouldn't be the same returning to the coast again afterwards, that I would maybe re-assimilate into city life and lose some of the impetus to continue with the trip. So maybe I rushed things a little through Wales, I could maybe have stayed longer in a few places, but overall I believe that I saw what I wanted to see and did what I wanted to do. But as I say, I was ready to return home after five months, and having now been to both the Olympics and the Paralympics, I really wouldn't have missed it for the world, and it would indeed have been a little strange to return to the coast afterwards.

I guess what I'm trying to say, is that if (and it's a big 'if') I ever get the opportunity to do this kind of thing again, I'll maybe try to avoid imposing any kind of restrictions on myself, although the amount of time, or at least money available, will likely always be a factor. It would be nice to head into Europe, for example, with no planned route or itinerary, and just go from place to place, from country to country, in a random fashion. I imagine there are plenty of people living this kind of lifestyle, in their campervans and motorhomes of various sizes and layouts.

Anyhoo, my work here is very nearly done, I have spent a fair amount of time sitting in cafes since I got home, often while writing and editing this book (but have had very few tea cakes or cakes in general, I really must rectify that). Soon I'll be turning my mind to learning about photography and how to write iPhone applications (or maybe I'm still not being realistic), but there was one final chapter to finish.

The Emotional Farewell

I've never been one for giving names to my cars, or consciously assigning a gender to them, so I never named the van. But that doesn't mean I didn't become somewhat attached to it, even though I may not have realised how much. The van had been absolutely brilliant, it had got me through every narrow lane, up and down every hill and around every bend. Nothing went wrong with it, either mechanically or electrically, it did its job without complaining and never let me down, even when I occasionally reversed it into something solid or scraped it along bramble lined roads.

Over a period of several weeks, in amongst and after the Olympics and Paralympics, I spent the odd day here or there emptying out the van and giving it a good clean, both inside and out, until it was ready to show to some dealers. And that was the point, as I watched some dealers walk around the van to assess its condition, that my top lip started to tremble and I began to realise just how much I was going to miss it. It would have been great to keep hold of it, but it just wasn't practical, I would have to store, service, insure, tax and MOT it, but it was unlikely that I would make enough use of it to justify the expense. Plus I had invested a fairly large amount of money in it that I needed back to spend on other things.

When I bought the van I had taken the approach that it would hold its value pretty well and I would be able to sell it for not much less than I had bought it. I had been slightly naive, perhaps. It's certainly true that a dealer would sell it for pretty much the same as I had bought it, but I underestimated exactly how much of a profit they would seek to make out of it for themselves, so it's fair to say that I had a few offers that were, shall I say, insulting. One dealer decided to lower his offer due to the scratch marks along the side of the van, caused by the narrow lanes and branches, he figured it might cost him about £1,000 to get rid of them. I spent about £6 on some polish and pretty much got rid of the scratches myself with a little bit of elbow grease.

If I had really wanted to, I could have invested more time in trying to sell the van privately, in which case I could probably have made most if not all of my money back. But I decided that I wanted to avoid the hassle that this may have brought with it, and as it turned out I found a dealer in Bristol that would broker it for me, for a better price than I had been offered for a direct sale. They had recently sold another Timberland and were keen to get their hands on mine, as several people had shown an interest in the other one. The same dealer offered a scheme whereby they would take on your campervan or motorhome and hire it out. The beauty of this arrangement is that they would store and service it, and insure it for use by anyone that hired it, but it still belonged to you and you could arrange to use it yourself when you needed it. If I ever buy another campervan, maybe once I'm retired or I've finally won the lottery, I would certainly consider this arrangement, but my van was too old for the scheme and I needed the money for it as soon as possible, rather than a drip feed of half the hire income, which could have taken a good few years to get me my money back.

And so it was, on a grey overcast day in late September, that I drove the van for the last time and dropped it off with the dealer. We'd had some unforgettable times together, but a buyer was soon found and it belongs to someone else now. I trust they will get as much pleasure out of it as I did. Who knows, maybe they'll drive it around the coast of mainland Britain.

Hopefully they won't reverse it into anything.

Printed in Great Britain
by Amazon